ADVANCE PRAISE FOR

Inside the Upheaval of Journalism

"Accurate, independently gathered information is as necessary to our way of government as the right to vote. This book by veteran journalists is the best analysis I've seen of the precarious state of American journalism and the danger that alone poses to our democracy."

—Bob Schieffer, CBS News, author of *Overload:
Finding Truth in the Deluge of News*

"For a journalist like myself, on the road for 50 years, *Inside the Upheaval of Journalism* is a walk down memory lane, recalling, in some cases, the hard road both Blacks and women traveled to realize their dreams of becoming reporters. But the book's seasoned journalists also bring us into the present with great clarity and sometimes painful insight. They confront the challenges veterans and newcomers face as technology changes the reporting dynamic ever faster, but not always with good results. And yet, the love of the profession is constant, as is the desire to help a new generation appreciate that their job remains, as always, to faithfully record our country's journey toward a more perfect union."

—Charlayne Hunter-Gault, award-winning journalist and author

"This is an inspired examination of what's happened to American journalism over the past 50 years, artfully told by people who lived it, who helped shape the best of it, and who warn us of the perils of the present day. Moving gracefully from personal anecdote to sweeping analysis, it is a unique and valuable volume."

—David Boardman, Dean and Professor, Klein College
of Media and Communication, Temple University

"This is an inspiring collection of essays by dedicated and accomplished journalists. Together, the authors show how the core values of Columbia Journalism School shape diverse careers and strengthen our profession."

—Steve Coll, Dean, Graduate School of Journalism, Columbia University

"At a time when a president of the United States calls reporters 'the enemy of the people,' this book is a powerful reminder that journalism is a noble calling filled with honest professionals dedicated to fairly and accurately pursuing the truth and informing the public—goals essential to the functioning of American democracy. As the contributors from the Columbia Journalism School's Class of 1969 make clear, the news business has changed dramatically since they graduated a half century ago. But the core values they learned as students endure—and are as important today as ever."

—Michael Isikoff, Chief Investigative Correspondent, Yahoo News

Inside the Upheaval
of Journalism

Lee B. Becker
GENERAL EDITOR

Vol. 28

The Mass Communication and Journalism series
is part of the Peter Lang Media and Communication list.
Every volume is peer reviewed and meets
the highest quality standards for content and production.

PETER LANG
New York • Bern • Berlin
Brussels • Vienna • Oxford • Warsaw

Inside the Upheaval of Journalism

Reporters Look Back on 50 Years of Covering the News

EDITED BY
Ted Gest and Dotty Brown

PETER LANG
New York • Bern • Berlin
Brussels • Vienna • Oxford • Warsaw

Library of Congress Cataloging-in-Publication Data

Names: Gest, Ted, editor. | Brown, Dotty, editor.
Title: Inside the upheaval of journalism: reporters look back on 50 years
of covering the news / edited by Ted Gest and Dotty Brown.
Description: New York: Peter Lang, 2020.
Series: Mass communication and journalism; vol. 28 | ISSN 2153-2761
Includes bibliographical references and index.
Identifiers: LCCN 2019032815 | ISBN 978-1-4331-6777-5 (hardback: alk. paper)
ISBN 978-1-4331-6778-2 (paperback: alk. paper) | ISBN 978-1-4331-6781-2 (ebook pdf)
ISBN 978-1-4331-6782-9 (epub) | ISBN 978-1-4331-6783-6 (mobi)
Subjects: LCSH: Journalists—United States—Biography. | Journalism—United
States—History—20th century. | Journalism—United
States—History—21st century. | Journalism—Technological
Innovations—United States.
Classification: LCC PN4871 .I48 | DDC 070.92/2 [B]—dc23
LC record available at https://lccn.loc.gov/2019032815
DOI 10.3726/b16118

Bibliographic information published by **Die Deutsche Nationalbibliothek**.
Die Deutsche Nationalbibliothek lists this publication in the "Deutsche
Nationalbibliografie"; detailed bibliographic data are available
on the Internet at http://dnb.d-nb.de/.

The paper in this book meets the guidelines for permanence and durability
of the Committee on Production Guidelines for Book Longevity
of the Council of Library Resources.

© 2020 Ted Gest and Dotty Brown

Peter Lang Publishing, Inc., New York
29 Broadway, 18th floor, New York, NY 10006
www.peterlang.com

All rights reserved.
Reprint or reproduction, even partially, in all forms such as microfilm,
xerography, microfiche, microcard, and offset strictly prohibited.

Printed in the United States of America

To our Columbia University Journalism School professors who gave us the skills and moral compass that carried us through our careers, and to those who do so for all journalism students of today.

—*Columbia J-School Class of 1969 sweatshirt, with advice of Prof. John Hohenberg*

Table of Contents

List of Illustrations xi
Preface xiii
Acknowledgments xvii
Chapter Authors xix

Chapter One—Fifty Years of Journalism: A Sweep of Change 1
    Martin Gottlieb and Susan Spencer

Chapter Two—Technology: The Revolution of Our Time 17
    Kenneth Tiven

Chapter Three—Women: Forging Towards Recognition 31
    Dotty Brown

Chapter Four—Diversity: A Work in Progress 47
    Marquita Pool-Eckert

Chapter Five—Politics: Reporting in the Age of Distrust 65
    Alan Ehrenhalt

Chapter Six—International Reporting: A World of Difference 77
    Michèle Montas-Dominique

Chapter Seven—Criminal Justice: The Journey from "Give Me Rewrite!" 95
    Ted Gest

Chapter Eight— Medicine: From Gee-Whiz to Hard-Edged 109
    Richard Knox

Chapter Nine—Business: How Big Media Missed Small and Personal 127
    David E. Gumpert

Chapter Ten—Covering the God Beat in a Time of Change 141
    Tammy Tanaka

Chapter Eleven—Book Publishing: Authors on the Front Line 153
    Carla Fine

Chapter Twelve—J-Schools: In the Wake of New Media 175
    Tom Goldstein

Postscript: An Informed News Consumer's View 189
    Allan Mann

Index 193

Illustrations

Figure 0.1:	J-School Class of 1969, courtesy of the Columbia University School of Journalism	xiv
Figure 1.1:	Martin Gottlieb, courtesy of Martin Gottlieb	4
Figure 1.2:	Susan Spencer with Pope John Paul II, photo © Vatican Media	11
Figure 2.1:	Kenneth Tiven, courtesy of Kenneth Tiven	18
Figure 3.1:	Dotty Brown, courtesy of Dotty Brown	35
Figure 4.1:	Marquita Pool-Eckert, courtesy of Marquita Pool-Eckert	50
Figure 6.1:	Michèle Montas-Dominique with U.N. Secretary General Ban Ki-moon and former President Bill Clinton, UN Photo/Eskinder Debebe	79
Figure 6.2:	Terry Wolkerstorfer, courtesy of Terry Wolkerstorfer	90
Figure 7.1:	Ted Gest, courtesy of Ted Gest	97
Figure 8.1:	Richard Knox and Jerry Bishop, courtesy of the American Heart Association	111
Figure 11.1:	David Gumpert, courtesy of David Gumpert	164

Preface

WHY THE CLASS OF 1969 WROTE THIS BOOK

America was reeling as 101 graduate students, hoping to create a better world, arrived at the Columbia University School of Journalism for a one-year master's degree program in the fall of 1968. Just months before, on April 4, the Rev. Martin Luther King had been assassinated on the balcony of the Lorraine Motel in Memphis, where he had come to support the city's sanitation workers. Two months later, on June 4, U.S. Senator Bobby Kennedy, who was running for president, was murdered after a speech in Los Angeles. Urban rebellions in cities across the country the previous few years had killed more than 100 people and injured thousands. Columbia itself had not been spared: in student protests against the Vietnam War and the university's military contracts, 132 students, four faculty, and 12 police officers had been injured and 700 arrested that spring when 1,000 police officers converged on the campus to evict protestors who had occupied several buildings.

Members of the J-School Class of 1969 would forge unique bonds in these fraught times, although we chose separate paths within the school's curriculum: Some poured their energy into gumshoe reporting on New York City's streets. Some were drawn to TV news, which was gaining increasing credibility and viewership in the 1960s, as live coverage of events such as President Kennedy's assassination and its aftermath in 1963 mesmerized the country. And some would

Figure 0.1: The Class of 1969, with newly minted master's degrees, stands on the steps of Pulitzer Hall on Columbia's campus. We graduated into an era of manual typewriters and slow-processing TV film. While technology has changed, the values we learned at school stayed with us.
Source: *Courtesy of the Columbia University School of Journalism*

try their hands at the "New Journalism" of Truman Capote and Hunter Thompson and create an intense little literary magazine.

But we were all united in the belief that accurate and fair reporting, regardless of the medium, was what our country needed. We also felt we had to be good listeners, and some of us bonded more intensely at a weekend "sensitivity training," where we opened ourselves up to each other in an atmosphere of trust—an approach we hoped we could carry into our careers.

The Class of 1969 graduated into a chaotic world where both women and minorities were at a disadvantage, gay people were well-closeted, the morality of America's government was questioned, and President Richard Nixon's Watergate scandal was yet to happen. We had no idea of the ties that would keep us together over the decades.

Thanks to our late class member Gordon Thompson, internet services director for the *New York Times*, we had our own email list, the only online class discussion group independent of the J-School. There, we would lend support when one of us fell ill or lost a job. When a fearless Haitian radio journalist was assassinated in 2000, we were there for his wife, our classmate Michèle Montas-Dominique, and 40 of us signed a letter to the government of Haiti asking for justice. We rose in unison again in 2017 to urge J-School dean, Steve Coll, to condemn President Trump's vilification of the news media as "the enemy of the people."

Every five years, when the J-School held its class reunions, we would gather at a classmate's apartment in New York City to share with each other the latest iterations of our life journeys. One of these was held when one of our own classmates, Tom Goldstein, was dean of the school.

Journalistically, we have experienced the rise and fall of newspapers, an erosion in TV news viewership, the emergence of the internet and new sources of news including *Slate*, *Vox*, *BuzzFeed*, *Politico*, *HuffPost*, the *Daily Beast* and Fox News, the erosion of individual privacy, rising public cynicism, and distrust of the press. Indeed, the advent of unwarranted charges of "fake news" has shaken our cherished profession as never before.

We were also in the vanguard of a push to diversify the press, with women and minorities in our class breaking into largely all male, all white newsrooms. Such change over the decades has made the news media more attuned to an increasingly diverse country.

It was on group emails more than a year before our 50th reunion that classmate Kenneth Tiven, a veteran CNN producer, suggested that we write a book about how journalism had changed over the half-century since our graduation, from 1969 to 2019. In dozens of shared emails, we debated its structure and purpose. Then we rose to the challenge. We had witnessed unprecedented changes in the news business first-hand. We would tell the stories through our own experiences.

Once again, we pulled together, with more than a dozen writers volunteering to interview others in the class and do the contextual research and reporting that will give readers an inside view into the evolution of such issues as religion, business, medicine, diversity, politics, crime, and more over 50 years, and how journalists responded, even as they were buffeted by the economic and political upheavals of our trade.

As we remain intent on making our world a better place, we hope our book will inspire the next generations of journalists to do the same.

Acknowledgments

This book is our story, and it could not have been written without dozens of members of the Columbia University School of Journalism Class of 1969 cranking it out on deadline, as we journalists like to say. So, first we want to thank everyone in the class for rallying around this project. In particular, we owe our appreciation to those who authored or co-authored the chapters, taking "feeds" from their classmates and putting our experiences into historical context.

We also thank Columbia J-School Prof. Michael Schudson, himself an expert on how journalism has changed over the decades, for his advice on the book, as well as Robert Papper, Columbia J-School 1970, who provided material from his annual survey on the broadcast news business for the Radio Television Digital News Association.

We are grateful to Peter Lang Publishing, where series editor Lee Becker immediately embraced the idea for this book and made important suggestions to improve it, and acquisitions editor Erika Hendrix guided us through its writing and production.

Chapter Authors

Dotty Brown (Co-editor and Women) was a reporter and editor for 30 years at the *Philadelphia Inquirer* and "Journalist of the Year" for the former Knight Ridder news chain. She is the author of *Boathouse Row, Waves of Change in the Birthplace of American Rowing*.

Alan Ehrenhalt (Politics) covered politics at the *Congressional Quarterly*, *Washington Star*, and for 25 years at *Governing Magazine*, where he was executive editor for most of that time. He is the author of *The United States of Ambition*, *The Lost City* and *The Great Inversion*.

Carla Fine (Book Publishing) has written ten books, including the international best seller *No Time to Say Goodbye: Surviving the Suicide of a Loved One*. She is a featured speaker and conducts workshops on writing as a pathway to healing.

Sylvana Foa (International) covered wars in Vietnam, Cambodia and Lebanon and reported coups, earthquakes and upheaval in a dozen countries. She held the titles of UPI Asia Pacific Editor, UPI Foreign Editor and Univision VP for News. In 1996, she was named Spokesperson to the Secretary General of the United Nations, the first woman to hold the position.

Ted Gest (Co-editor and Criminal Justice) has covered crime and justice for most of his 50-year career—at the *St. Louis Post-Dispatch*, *U.S. News & World Report*, and *TheCrimeReport.org*. He has published a daily news digest on criminal justice since 2003 and heads the national non-profit group Criminal Justice Journalists.

Tom Goldstein (Journalism Education) served as dean of the graduate schools of journalism at Berkeley and Columbia universities. He is the founding dean of the Jindal School of Journalism outside New Delhi and is the author of several books on journalism ethics.

Martin Gottlieb (50 Years) held top editing posts at the *New York Times, International Herald Tribune, Newsday, Daily News,* and the *Village Voice*. As editor of *The Record* of Bergen County N.J., he oversaw prize-winning coverage of its expose of the massive, politically ordered traffic jams at the George Washington Bridge.

David Gumpert (Business) was a reporter for the *Wall Street Journal* as well as an editor with the *Harvard Business Review* and *Inc.* magazine. He also authored or co-authored ten books including, *How to Really Create a Successful Business Plan, The Raw Milk Revolution,* and *Inge: A Girl's Journey through Nazi Europe*.

Richard Knox: (Medicine) reported on medicine and health care for 47 years at the *Boston Globe* and *NPR*'s Science Desk. He is author of *Germany's Health System: One Nation, United, with Health Care for All*.

Allan Mann (Copy Editor and Postscript) finished a career in journalism, education and public relations as Vice President of Public Affairs for Kaiser Permanente. He later taught public relations and business communications at the college level and now does *pro bono* communications consulting for community non-profits.

Michèle Montas-Dominique (International) devoted her career to human rights, justice and freedom of the press and suffered the consequences of doing so. Radio Haiti, which she ran with her husband, was attacked; he was later assassinated. An award-winning journalist, she served as Spokesperson for the Secretary General of the United Nations.

Marquita Pool-Eckert (Diversity) was an Emmy-winning television news producer at CBS Evening News and a senior producer at CBS News Sunday Morning. She also taught journalism at Hunter College, CUNY and the Columbia University Journalism School.

Karen Rothmyer (International) worked for publications ranging from the *Wall Street Journal* to *The Nation* magazine, where she was managing editor. She spent 10 years in Kenya, teaching journalism and served as the country's first public editor.

Susan Spencer (50 Years) covered the environment, medicine, Congress, and the White House during more than 30 years as a correspondent for CBS News. She joined the newsmagazine "48 Hours" in 1993 and is an occasional contributor to CBS Sunday Morning.

Tammy Tanaka (Religion) has been a lifelong student of spiritual and religious issues. She spent the first part of her career as a staff writer for Religion News

Service and later was a special education teacher, working with emotionally disturbed children.

Kenneth Tiven (Technology) kept pace with rapidly changing technology as a television reporter, anchor, producer, and manager. The largest part of his career was at CNN where he held responsibility for the interface of technology and news. He helped launch 30 media channels, many abroad, and CNN.com.

Terry Wolkerstorfer (International) focused much of his professional energy on Vietnam, serving in the AP Saigon bureau during the war and later starting a humanitarian aid project there. He was a reporter and editor at the *Minneapolis Star* and taught international journalism.

Also making a significant contribution was class member Leslie Berkman, among the first women to cover hard news at the *Los Angeles Herald-Examiner* and the Orange County edition of the *Los Angeles Times*. She was also a business reporter at the *Press Enterprise* (Riverside, California). Her interviews with former colleagues helped bring to life several chapters of the book.

CHAPTER ONE

Fifty Years of Journalism: A Sweep of Change

Graduating from the Columbia University School of Journalism in the spring of 1969, Martin Gottlieb and Susan Spencer entered into a news world that would change dramatically over the course of their careers. Neither they, nor anyone else for that matter, could envision how profound those changes would be.

Back in 1969, many newspapers—the career path which Gottlieb took and reflects back on—were still on the upswing, cash cows that would flourish for another two decades before starting a relentless decline in both circulation and revenue. The changes would kill jobs and newspapers alike, leave many communities bereft of local reporting, and multiply the responsibilities of print journalists, requiring them to take photographs and videos and file repeatedly throughout the day to social media and websites while still reporting and writing stories for the next day's paper.

Television news, too, would be transformed. Spencer, a long-time CBS-TV correspondent would herself experience those changes. Video instantaneously transmitted by anyone with a smart phone from almost anywhere in the world would ultimately replace unwieldy tapes that once took days to ship and edit before being viewed by the public. Broadcast news organizations staffed by vetted journalists would lose ground to a wild west of social media where such hallowed tenets of journalism as fairness, objectivity, and accuracy were often ignored if not spurned. The notion of America trusting a single news source, as was true in the days of CBS-TV anchor Walter Cronkite, would be replaced by a cacophony of broadcasters, both professional and amateur, voicing many truths—or untruths—confounding the nation.

The assault on these two pillars of the news began almost imperceptibly on October 29, 1969 just months after Gottlieb, Spencer and 99 other young journalists set out on their careers. On that day, a student at the University of California at Los Angeles typed the letters "l" and "o" (for "log on") and sent them electronically 350 miles away to the Stanford Research Institute. That tiny accomplishment marked the birth of the internet.

Newspapers: A Storied Past, A Fragile Future

BY MARTIN GOTTLIEB

My interest in newspapers began when I was in grade school and my father took me to the composing room of the trade journal publisher on West 12th Street in New York City where he worked as a Linotype operator. There, amid the cacophony and bustle, the vats of molten lead, and the dinosaur-like Linotype machines that ate the lead and molded it into print-ready paragraphs, his co-workers set my name in Bodoni, Cheltenham, Franklin Gothic, and more type faces. Thirty-six points or better. I was hooked.

My father was still setting type when I went to journalism school, but rather than feeling undiluted pride in the generational handoff, he had doubts about whether that was where I should be. In the five years before, four of New York City's seven English-language dailies had closed. The first to go, the New York *Daily Mirror*, boasted the second largest circulation in the country at the time.

Since Walter Cronkite had nursed America through the assassination of President Kennedy in 1963, the same year the *Mirror* closed, it was clear that newspapers' primary reason for being—delivering the news—had been usurped. Television news was king. Maybe, my parents suggested, I should become a teacher or a lawyer.

I'm glad I didn't. I've made it through 50 rewarding years of newspapering, the last 20 under the shadow of a looming new technological giant that belatedly proved my father right about the future of the industry that raised us into the middle class.

There have been developments good, questionable and downright bad for newspapers over the past half-century, but none has been as existential as the one they face in 2019.

With the exception of a few quality national publications that seem to be solving the digital transition, newspapers are staggering. Many of them are already dead. With the digital revolution overwhelming the Gutenberg one of the fifteenth century, the question is not whether any newspapers will be around in 50 years; it's whether they will exist in 10.

Thanks to digital readership, any number of newspapers have a greater circulation than ever. But that most typically is through clicks on a handful of stories read for a handful of seconds rather than through the packaged, department store-like assemblage that has defined the newspaper in print and, later, through its desktop home page, as well.

As the nature of the news product has changed, the influence of legacy publications has shrunk, and the ad revenue they attract hardly floats the boat.

Figure 1.1: As editor of the raucous *Village Voice* in the 1980s, Martin Gottlieb (left, in dark jacket) at a demonstration with Dominican-Americans who were protesting the phrasing in a story. Source: *Courtesy Martin Gottlieb*

Lost in good part, at least to me, is a special reading experience, a personal one in which a newspaper took its place at the dining room table much like a visiting aunt or uncle, with a character as unmistakable as theirs. In their print editions—and to one extent or another in their digital ones—newspapers at their best have always undertaken a range of responsibilities and displayed a range of emotions on the same page: They could explain a budget, fuel a crusade, pick a fight, and deliver the comics. As they imparted the news, they revealed their vitality, character, gravitas, and quirks. They made mistakes, but for the most part got up the next day and tried harder.

In jeopardy, too, is the non-verbal language the best newspapers use to communicate with readers—the subtle presentation of articles in a way that conveys the publication's personality and what it thinks is most important and interesting. This became a consuming interest and responsibility when I served as weekend editor of the *New York Times* and, with a lot of wise staff members, looked at blank pages that would become front pages. Was a headline worth one column or two, and if two, how many lines should it take and what size? *Ital* or Roman? All caps or upper and lower? How many "reefers" to sidebars should be included before the end of the front-page run?

Each inflection played its role in helping to define for the reader how the paper saw the world, and itself. So did the mix of stories chosen for the page—the balance between hard news and soft; news analyses and narratives; our own enterprise and the stuff everyone was chasing; and the offerings of all the *Times*'s desks—foreign, national, local, business, science; sports, culture, style, and more.

Nothing's quite emerged online to match it all.

The putting-it-together part was the treasured heart of my professional life as a reporter, desk editor, and, at some places, *the* editor. The drive for the story will survive any technological innovation, and already has been enhanced immeasurably by the digital revolution. Largely diminished are those fabled reporters who could worm their way through layers of courthouse documents that few people knew existed—the veterans who even figured out how to count tax stamps on recorded deeds to figure out what properties really sold for. Today, there's a wealth of information transparent and available with a finger tap.

Diminished, too, is the raucous newsroom camaraderie that, for me, reached a peak at the New York *Daily News,* when our rather intense night city editor, Dick Blood, commanded us to P.J. Clarke's at our shift's end at 1 a.m. for three hours of drinking, often in the company of George Steinbrenner, various former New York Yankees (Mantle included), and the self-professed world's greatest police reporter, Pat Doyle. When Doyle, who spoke of himself in the third person, stuck to the facts, he was brilliant—a telephone virtuoso, with identity-stretching salutations. When he moved beyond that, he described himself as in the company of Twain and Hemingway.

Now, readers can sculpt their own news feeds amid valid concerns over what may get lost in the process—contrarian viewpoints, local news, serendipitous discoveries, water-cooler debates built on shared reading experiences.

From the standpoint of Gutenberg's children, plenty of jarring statistics underscore the severity of the situation. About 1,800 of the 9,000 daily and weekly metropolitan and community newspapers that were published in 2004 have merged or gone out of business, according to a study by the University of North Carolina's School of Media and Journalism. That leaves 2,000 of the country's 3,143 counties with no daily and 171 of them with no newspaper at all. More than three million people live in those places.[1]

Nicco Mele of Harvard's Shorenstein Center on Media, Politics and Public Policy says, "It's hard to see a future where newspapers persist." He predicts that half of the surviving newspapers will be gone by 2021.[2]

Newspaper newsroom employment fell from 71,000 in 2008 to just under 38,000 in 2018, according to the federal Bureau of Labor Statistics.[3] Those with college degrees who continue to work in newsrooms earn $8,000 less a year than the median for all college-educated workers, according to a Pew Research Center analysis of census data.[4] Because of the demands of the internet, daily beat reporters' lives have changed dramatically. Rather than having hours to dig into a story unencumbered, they have to file for the web, Twitter, Facebook, and Instagram, and many of them shoot video, too. That does a lot for spreading a story, at the cost of building one.

Meanwhile, on the economic front, print advertising revenue fell from about $49.4 billion in 2005 to $14.3 billion in 2018.[5]

While my journalism school class studied at Columbia, *Time* magazine still published an annual list of the country's 10 best newspapers, studded with terrific regional papers, often owned by local families in places like Louisville and Des Moines. That would be unthinkable today. And *Time*, like almost every other magazine, isn't what it used to be, either.

Before the deluge, any number of advances over the past half-century made newspapers more authoritative, readable, and harder hitting. The "New Journalism," which transformed non-fiction writing, emerged early on in the rejuvenated *New York Herald Tribune* through Tom Wolfe, Jimmy Breslin, and a cast that built around them. Columnists like Breslin and Pete Hamill, Mike Royko in Chicago, and counterparts in a dozen cities became the personifications of their newspapers and of those cities themselves. Newspaper reporters on the ground in Vietnam called official lies to account almost daily.

Three years after our class graduated, Bob Woodward and Carl Bernstein broke the Watergate story in the *Washington Post*. The spread of investigative journalism continues on many fronts. Even many newspapers that are contracting financially nonetheless keep their I-teams afloat because they deliver what every metric shows their readers hold dear. (Another contemporary corporate benefit of investigative efforts is that they help make many newspapers look like they're still flying the flag while executives gut staff and leave important beats, state capitals, and day-to-day local stories uncovered.)

Underlying these advances was something more profound that had been building since at least the 1940s—the continuing professionalization of the American press from its rowdy early days in the nineteenth century and the partisanship and yellow journalism of latter press barons like William Randolph Hearst and Joseph Pulitzer. "The standard today is to keep the news pages fair and maintain a strong dividing line between the editorial and news departments," said one *New York Times* editorial several years ago. "It was the signal professional triumph of American journalism in this century," and it established what the editorial described as a tradition of "hard-headed nonpartisanship."[6]

Thousands of students coming out of Columbia and other J-schools were trained this way and filled the once burgeoning ranks of newspapers.

In the years before the digital transformation, plenty else was going on that was less sanguine. My father was right about predicting a nationwide dwindling of dailies based on what he experienced in New York City.

Beginning in his day, newspapers were undergoing a huge trend of consolidation and chain newspaper ownership, leading to what was often seen as the biggest crisis in newspaper journalism pre-internet. Some chains like Gannett boasted large profit margins that they often achieved by shrinking staffs, executing what amounted to a transfer of value from readers to investors. Operating margin—profit divided by revenue before taxes—is typically used as a measure of profitability. In 1997, when manufacturing firms were averaging a margin of 7.6 percent, Gannett's was 26.6 percent.

The *Louisville Courier-Journal* and *Des Moines Register* were still credible papers after they were bought by Gannett, but many readers as well as press critics saw unmistakable slippage in these and other chain papers, as well as a bleeding of the local character that shaped the papers' personality.

The threat to the journalistic ideal defined in the *New York Times* editorial also came more directly through a development in the tabloid press, which still prospered in isolated locations. This was the purchase of the *New York Post* in 1976 by Rupert Murdoch.

The *Post*'s new salaciousness, giddy irreverence for fact, and catchy headlines caught eyes around the country. A thin layer beneath was the shameless politicization of the paper and its use of news columns to bludgeon its critics and pump its favored politicians, like former Mayor Ed Koch, even when they were polling in the low single digits. Murdoch and the *New York Post* became kingmakers, not only in New York but nationally as they shredded Teddy Kennedy, Jimmy Carter, and, most of the time, Bill and Hillary Clinton, and as they wired stories for favorites from Ronald Reagan to Rudy Giuliani to Donald Trump. Murdoch and the *Post* began to influence the country's politics, and then reaped any number of economically beneficial fruits, not only from political favorites but from those who feared them and hoped to mitigate the wrath.

In New York, local television news reporters scrambled to match *Post* exclusives, real or hyped. Later, Fox News spread its influence in the same way, except where the *Post* punched, it steamrolled.

Meanwhile, the notion of unbiased professionalism was receiving another challenge from the alternative press—weeklies mostly filled with liberal politics and voluminous arts coverage. In place of the divide between news and opinion came deeply personal reporting in which both were comingled in almost every single story. Unlike the *New York Post*, which masqueraded its biases as fact, the writers of the alternate press shared theirs proudly as expressions of their beliefs and experiences. The balance between powerful, often heartfelt journalism and self-indulgence was ever present.

This was the kind of journalism I saw out there as a young reader and that I found when I assumed the editorship of the *Village Voice* in 1986. Along with its unmatched tradition of local investigative reporting and acute arts criticism, the *Voice* at times could stop your heart with vivid, deeply personal journalism. Among the pieces I won't forget was Paul Cowan's "In the Land of the Sick," written as he was fighting his losing battle with leukemia. "I want to describe some of what I've seen during the voyage I've made, the journey from being a person who took his health for granted to one who's trying to survive a life-threatening illness," he wrote. "I want to chart some of this wilderness for others who will be here one day."[7]

From the *Boston Phoenix* to the *LA Weekly*, the *Voice* model and experience were replicated in scores of cities and towns, to the point where during the late 1960s and early 1970s, hippie-influenced alternatives to the alternative press sprouted, often in psychedelic splendor, from the *East Village Other* to the *Chicago Seed* to the *Berkeley Barb*.

Then came *le déluge*. The *Voice* died in 2018, Boston's *Phoenix* five years earlier. The *LA Weekly* has been riven by ownership changes, mass firings, and internal dissent in one form or another for years. The hippie press is long gone, as are so many other weeklies and dailies.

By 2016, the number of daily newspapers in the country had plummeted to 1,286 compared with 1,748 in 1970, by one count.[8] As of 2019, only four U.S. cities have two daily newspapers with circulations more than 100,000—New York City, Boston, Chicago, and Detroit. In 2017, total daily newspaper circulation on a weekday was 31 million, compared with more than 60 million in the 1970s.[9]

Newspapers run by and for African Americans, which historically provided lifelines of information that helped build the civil rights movement and alerted residents to many issues that would not have otherwise have gained traction, are likewise suffering. In surveying the African American focused media presence, which is growing online, Christine Schmidt, writing on *NiemanLab.org* in 2019, said, "In many African American communities, traditional legacy newspapers are either in the process of closing or have already ceased operation. In the worst cases, this leaves some communities without an operating source of local news."[10]

In the larger world of mass circulation regional newspapers, the news has the same flavor. The big profits at the Gannett chain are gone. At Denver's surviving daily newspaper, the *Post*, its new owner, hedge fund Alden Global Capital, eliminated 30 jobs from a news operation that had fewer than 100 journalists. At the Cleveland *Plain Dealer* in 2019, its unionized staff of journalists, which numbered 340 in the 1990s had dropped to 33, according to the newsroom union.

In places like New Orleans and Detroit, once-vaunted daily newspapers began to be printed only a few days a week. Then in 2019, the New Orleans

Times-Picayune, an institution in the city it had covered so well, particularly in the aftermath of Hurricane Katrina, was bought by a rival from Baton Rouge, *The Advocate,* which saw an opening and moved in. Only a modest number of *Times-Picayune* staffers was retained. The *Advocate* won a Pulitzer in 2019 for exposing systemic racial biases in jury selection, making New Orleans perhaps unique: The death of its vaunted paper at least came with a journalistic handoff that serves the city.

To look at this from 30,000 feet is to see something troubling. To look at it on the ground is to watch something heartbreaking. The *Bergen Record* in New Jersey was where I had my first real full-time reporting job, back in the early 1970s. It was already well known as a serious paper that bred journalists who developed fine careers, there and across the country. When I returned as editor in 2012, it had gotten far better. I was blessed with a newsroom staff of more than 200, down from its heights a few years before, but still far outside the norm for a paper of that size. Its editorial leadership team was exceptional, as were its star reporters and columnists. Any number could have had successful careers anywhere, including the *New York Times,* where I spent the better part of my professional life.

We broke stories left and right—in no small part because, long after fabled family newspaper dynasties like the Binghams, Bancrofts, and Chandlers had left the scene, the Borgs were still fighting the good fight in north Jersey—and living there, too. The *Record* broke the story of the politically contrived traffic jams at the George Washington Bridge, and we followed it with two years of big scoops that fed the scandal and deeply damaged Governor Chris Christie politically. The big first scoop came because our publisher, Stephen Borg, had a neighbor who had a more than usually miserable time getting into New York City for two days. It was easy to hand off that tip to a staff that never let go.

The Borgs, who owned the paper for nearly a century, held on for as long as they could, hoping for a turnaround after the recovery from the economic collapse of the mid-aughts. They expanded online, introduced a list of glossy, money-making magazines, and consolidated operations, but recovery was not to be. Retrenchments had to come and they did through a sale to Gannett, as they would have, even if there had been no purchase. In 2019, there were still quality *Record* staffers in the house, including the editor, Dan Sforza. And the *Record* continues to produce award-winning coverage and projects that it can be proud of. Just not as much. And in less visible ways, the coverage is not what it was. How could it be? It's a loss to readers whether they come online or to the printed page. To someone who benefited from the newsroom talent that had been built over decades and is now dispersed—and in many cases gone from journalism—the loss is grievous.

Is there hope for a new landscape that holds a place for newspapers? For the quality national dailies, the experience of the last five years says yes. At the

New York Times, the *Wall Street Journal* and the *Washington Post*, readers have lined up by the millions to pay for digital, and even print, subscriptions. At the *Times*, circulation revenue outstrips print advertising revenue for the first time.

The three major national newspapers are profitable and all are hiring. For the *Times* and the *Post*, there is some question of how much of their success is tied to readers' revulsion with President Trump and desire to see investigative reporting undo him, but odds are that they have built a lasting economic model.

How well this translates to once mighty regional giants and small newspapers still is to be determined, as these newspaper-based organizations strive for the same kind of subscription success.

Many of them have been helped by the efforts of outsiders, in a way that reminds me of the work of the Peace Corps where some of my classmates did tours before heading to J-School. The Knight Foundation has invested $300 million in trying to revive the local press. *ProPublica*, the investigative news organization, has paid for the placement of investigative journalists at several local outlets. Report for America, a project of a non-profit group called The Ground Truth Project, has positioned scores of journalists in local news organizations across the country—from struggling local papers to emerging non-profit online sites.

Even at legacy newspapers, the input often has focused on how to make a transition to a world their founders could never have imagined.

And with a fond nod back to those stacks of papers that piled high at newsstands for much of my life, I have to say, with a twinge of sadness, that's the way it should be.

Television News: When the Big Three Ruled

By Susan Spencer

I first walked through the door of CBS' Washington bureau on July 7, 1977. I distinctly remember pausing to take in the three huge brass letters by the door: C.B.S . . . and then thinking, Uh oh . . . Here goes!

It was nicknamed the Tiffany Network then, and it was almost entirely lily-white and male. Certainly, no sign of today's parade of attractive young women in bright sleeveless dresses. Staid Walter Cronkite held forth every night and everyone trusted what Uncle Walter said. The compact with the viewer was simple: go about your business, then watch us and we'll keep you informed on what happened today and on the big stuff that matters.

As Walter put it, "That's the way it is."

And it was. I had a wonderful career at CBS; I went places and saw things I never would have imagined. I was hired amid a push to get more women on the air. I had come from WCCO, the respected CBS affiliate in Minneapolis. There I was treated like everyone else, even though I was the only "girl reporter." Granted, when I first showed up there in 1972 I'd been handed the last "girl reporter's" file —on witchcraft—but things improved dramatically after that. I joined CBS at the age of 30, determined to take full advantage of my good luck.

The Big Three networks still dominated the news then, with CNN the upstart newcomer in 1980. It was soon clear where the Tiffany Network got its nickname. Money seemed no object. Early on, I do not recall ever hearing the word "budget." Nor can I remember anyone jettisoning a story because coverage cost too much.

Figure 1.2: During the 1988 filming of an episode of "48 Hours," which took viewers inside the Vatican, CBS correspondent Susan Spencer is granted an audience with Pope John Paul II. "I think it was about 20 seconds," she recalls. Source: *Photo © Vatican Media*

You did what you had to do. If you needed a helicopter, don't worry. As it happened, CBS had its own, complete with pilot.

Of course, a lot has changed since those heady days—some for the better, some not so much: women and minorities are no longer on-air rarities; viewership is still high at the major networks, though increasingly fragmented among competing cable stations and news websites; technological advances means live coverage from anywhere in the world, sometimes so fast it can't be vetted; and public trust has eroded as some cable stations adopt a political bias.

"The web has closed in on television as a source for news," the Pew Research Center reported in 2018, with 43 percent of adults reporting that their main source of news is either news websites or social media, compared with 49 percent for television. Radio news accounted for 26 percent of consumers' prime news sources and print newspapers lagged way behind as a main news source at 16 percent.[11]

The glorious political campaigns of the 1980s may have been the height of CBS' astonishing, and no doubt wasteful, largesse. I covered Senator Edward Kennedy's 1980 quest for the Democratic presidential nomination for almost an entire year. (This was a quaint time when campaigns didn't start the day after the previous election.) CBS' full-time entourage included two cameramen, two sound men, two producers, and another correspondent. This was partly because of assassination fears, given the Kennedy family's tragic history. Manpower wasn't very different on other campaigns—a sharp contrast to today's reliance on resourceful "embeds," who report, shoot and feed video all by themselves.

It seems amazing now, but until the campaigns got their own press planes, we hired Lear jets to hopscotch from event to event. It was not uncommon for two or three Lears to land in sequence, ferrying the networks and a hitchhiking newspaper reporter or two. Upon deplaning, we'd frequently be met by driver and limo to race to the feed point. Granted, we were working non-stop, but for months nobody would notice: After Americans were taken hostage in Iran in January 1980, the CBS Evening News had little interest in what Senator Kennedy was doing at some cow pen in frigid Iowa. Days passed without my getting on the air. Never mind. The Kennedy campaign was deemed historic. It HAD to be covered. Not because he was young and good looking, but because it was a responsibility.

Over the years, covering Congress, the environment, medicine, and the White House, I always felt that implied responsibility. I stayed on the hard news side of things until 1993, when I left for the newsmagazine "48 Hours."

My timing may have been inspired. A few years before I left daily coverage, something seemed to happen to the "responsibility" thing. Economics reared its ugly head and network news underwent a subtle but fundamental change. We stopped asking, "What does Joe NEED to know?" and instead asked "What does Joe WANT to see?" What stories will produce the most "eyeballs?" The phase conjures up a cringe-worthy mental image, but reporters began to realize that "eyeballs" now were a big concern of the front office.

Flying around in those Lears, we hadn't thought much about the front office ... or eyeballs. I remember thinking we shouldn't do so now, that what people "wanted to see" should not be our first concern. The idea had been that we were spending time and resources so the audience didn't themselves have to delve into issues vital for citizens in a democracy to know and understand—about government, medicine, the law, etc. And that we were doing so in the most objective way possible.

But competition was increasing, profits were on the line, and Uncle Walter was not around to be the Voice of God. Ratings soon were considered the measure of a broadcast's quality.

The new assumption was that to get those ratings, news needed more pizzazz. That meant more consumer features, more pop culture, more crime, more conflict. Faster-paced shows. Shorter pieces. The use of the present tense to imply immediacy, which today has morphed into the very odd reliance on "-ing" verbs, as in "the President announcing a new program ..." or "prosecutors today revealing indictments." Apparently, at some point, any form of the verb "to be" became a time-waster, or should I say, "becoming" a time-waster. Clearly this makes me crazy.

Shifting economics brought on sad rounds of layoffs and bureau closings. In 1986, CBS had 16 overseas and nine domestic bureaus. The numbers wax and wane, but by 2019, only seven foreign bureaus (including two manned only by a producer) and six domestic bureaus remained. Goodbye Boston, Denver, Seattle, Seoul, Bangkok and, believe it or not, East Beirut.

Of course, technology made this possible. And while it didn't mean you couldn't do a very good job, there were obvious tradeoffs. It meant more reliance on freelancers and stringers, which can make it difficult to verify information. It meant, of necessity, correspondents voicing pieces they hadn't reported from places they hadn't been, a practice that today is accepted as standard operating procedure.

And then, somewhere along the way, the idea took hold that correspondents were themselves fascinating creatures who needed to be a part of the story. Years before, in the early 1970s, my Minneapolis station WCCO hired a consultant to help drag the broadcast out of the Dark Ages. The consultant's main recommendation was for "more reporter involvement!" For weeks, we dutifully marched around the newsroom, repeating the mantra, "Reporter Involvement!" It seemed so silly; we laughed at it. It also made us uneasy, having thought that getting involved was the last thing a responsible reporter was supposed to do, lest it get in the way of the story itself. And yet, one day I found myself doing a story at a school, sitting on the floor at a tiny table surrounded by bewildered kindergarteners. I was, in effect, on a set—a phony set, but a set.

Today, technology makes it possible to broadcast stand ups like that live from anywhere and, since we can, we do ... putting the reporter at the center of the action if possible. It may also put a reporter as far away from his sources as possible, but in a breaking news situation, it does convey a sense of place and urgency.

It implies, too, that the reporter has an understanding of what's going on. After all, he or she is there! You don't cover a wildfire or plane crash from the studio. Still, my heart always goes out to the poor bedraggled correspondent when "live at the scene" means standing in freezing rain outside an obviously locked building where something happened yesterday, or where a decision may be made tomorrow. It creates faux drama, but usually doesn't add much to the story.

Sometimes, it isn't possible to add to the story, because there really isn't a story. But there IS video! And that frequently seems the only thing that matters. Local stories that would not have had a chance of coverage even 10 years ago now get on the evening news because there is video, no matter how shaky or meaningless. So what if that tornado didn't actually touch down, we've got it on a cellphone! Or the four-car pile-up in New Mexico—it's on Dash Cam! Or that argument over a parking place in Sioux Falls—someone had his iPad out!

To be fair, cellphone video today is a vital reporting tool and has added context and content to countless important stories. What seems sometimes forgotten is that having video of something doesn't in itself make it important.

That and many of the concerns I've cited—meaningless stand ups, reporter involvement, obsession with ratings, etc.—are more about style than substance and certainly not news to journalists today. I am grateful to have been with CBS in the heyday of the Big Three Networks, but if I could get in a time machine, I don't think I would return to the "Good Old Days" for two reasons.

First, technologically. It's a challenging and exciting time, with so many new toys—small backpack LiveU units capable of both shooting and transmitting broadcast quality video; interactive in-studio graphics unimaginable a few years ago; fantastic editing software; programs to retrieve archival video and information instantly. Reporters' expanded roles now include jobs done only by producers in the past, and vice versa. There are hundreds of outlets, with a smorgasbord of styles, approaches, and new voices. There is room for serious long form investigative work, sometimes, as with John Oliver's *Last Week Tonight*, presented in a highly entertaining—albeit often scatological—form.

All of which leads to the second, more important reason. I am encouraged at what I hope is a return to an appreciation of what's at stake. The political right's "Fake News" campaign may have damaged our credibility, but it also has been a wakeup call, reminding us that while styles and hardware come and go, the fundamental reason we exist hasn't changed at all: there really are important things citizens need to know for a democracy to work. Yes, ratings count. And no, we can't put on substantive stories too boring to watch. But we are starting to ask the right question again . . . What does Joe NEED to know?

Fifty years later, we are back where we started. Gather the information, write the story clearly, use the technology to sex it up without getting in the way and all will be well. Uncle Walter can rest easy. I do miss the Lears, though . . .

NOTES

1. Penelope Muse Abernathy, "The Expanding News Desert," UNC School of Media and Journalism, 2018, 11, accessed May 20, 2019, https://www.cislm.org/wp-content/uploads/2018/10/The-Expanding-News-Desert-10_14-Web.pdf
2. Keach Hagey et al., "In News Industry, a Stark Divide Between Haves and Have Nots," *The Wall Street Journal*, last modified May 4, 2019, https://www.wsj.com/graphics/local-newspapers-stark-divide/
3. "Newspapers Fact Sheet," Pew Research Center, Journalism and Media, last modified July 9, 2019, https://www.journalism.org/fact-sheet/newspapers/
4. Elizabeth Grieco, "Newsroom Employees are Less Diverse than U.S. Workers Overall," FactTank, last modified Nov. 2, 2018, http://www.pewresearch.org/fact-tank/2018/11/02/newsroom-employees-are-less-diverse-than-u-s-workers-overall/
5. "Newspapers Fact Sheet," 2019.
6. "Teaching Mr. Murdoch," *The New York Times*, last modified March 31, 1993, https://www.nytimes.com/1993/03/31/opinion/teaching-mr-murdoch.html
7. Paul Cowan in "103: Scenes from a Transplant," This American Life, accessed May 21, 2019, https://www.thisamericanlife.org/103/transcript
8. "Number of Daily Newspapers in the U.S. from 1970–2016," *Statista*, accessed May 10, 2019, https://www.statista.com/statistics/183408/number-of-us-daily-newspapers-since-1975/
9. "Newspapers Fact Sheet."
10. Christine Schmidt, "Here's the State of African-American Media Today," NiemanLab, last modified March 1, 2019, https://www.niemanlab.org/2019/03/heres-the-state-of-african-american-media-today-and-steps-it-can-take-going-forward/
11. Elisa Shearer, "Social Media Outpaces Print Newspapers in the U.S. as a News Source," *Fact Tank*, Pew Research Center, last modified Dec. 10, 2018, https://www.pewresearch.org/fact-tank/2018/12/10/social-media-outpaces-print-newspapers-in-the-u-s-as-a-news-source/

CHAPTER TWO

Technology: The Revolution of Our Time

KENNETH TIVEN

When we emerged from Columbia University Journalism School in the spring of 1969, I knew what lay ahead, having joined the *Hartford Courant* as a reporter in 1963. When shown to my desk at the *Courant*, I was stunned to find myself facing the city editor. It turned out to be a stroke of luck.

Sitting three feet from City Editor Charles Towne provided a master class in media management. When the presses rolled at 8:30 p.m. for the first edition, the vibration upstairs in the newsroom reinforced the sense of power and responsibility that came with journalism. Responsibility was reinforced that summer covering the Civil Rights March in Washington, D.C., with all-access credentials.

The previous occupant of my desk had left me a book: *The Fading American Newspaper*[1] with its prediction that improved facsimile technology could deliver news directly to the home, killing printed newspapers. Did a reporter give up on a media career after reading it? I have never forgotten its message: technology is the basis for dramatic change in journalism. Even if that Connecticut newsroom did not comprehend print media change in November 1963, the emerging role of television news was obvious from the coverage of President Kennedy's assassination in Dallas, Texas. Five decades later, the internet had rearranged media in ways beyond what most journalists had ever imagined.

We members of the Columbia J-School Class of 1969 are the journalists with a solid grounding in both eras.

The year 1963 was a magical one in news. It never occurred to me to make a living any other way. After college, I was a journalist in the U.S. Army for two years, also working nights for newspapers as a reporter. I was discharged from the Army on a Friday and arrived at Columbia University on a Monday in 1968. In one decade I had finished high school, college, graduate school, and the Army, finding my career in all of that.

HOW MY STORY STARTED

I became one of many news executives who actively created the transition from "yesterday's news today" to "today's news as it happens." Some days I like the credit, other times I am disappointed that it has led to a cacophonous communications environment often with scant distinction between fact and fiction. Now, it seems, thoughtful analysis and fact checking have fallen victim to a footrace, accelerated on social media and websites. Every minute is a deadline for one output platform or another. Bonds and trust between audience and news purveyors become difficult to create.

Figure 2.1: Kenneth Tiven, early in his long career as an advocate of new media technology, explains videotape at KYW-TV in Philadelphia in 1975. Source: *Courtesy of Kenneth Tiven*

This analysis of 50 years in print and broadcasting was influenced by exposure to some of the greats in American media. At Columbia, legendary CBS News producer and president Fred Friendly was in his exuberant second year teaching at the J-school, inspiring us to do more than recite facts, reminding us that small pictures (individuals) tell big stories that reveal American life.

As an editor on the *Washington Post* foreign desk after graduation, I absorbed Executive Editor Ben Bradlee's philosophy. I had a clear view of Bradlee's office, where he often stood in the doorway, voice booming, to inform the newsroom about some journalism point or decision. Like Friendly, he demonstrated winning editorial leadership with the Pentagon Papers and Watergate coverage.

Later, as CNN vice president for television systems, I worked directly for Burt Reinhardt, then vice chairman, observing how his deliberate approach saved money. Burt was tenacious, but his manner was never nasty on a personal level. His leadership guided CNN through perilous early years to expand into a global phenomenon. Ted Turner provided imagination about what "could be," while Reinhardt made it happen at a cost Turner could afford.

In my time at KYW Television in Philadelphia and later in creating the Orange County Newschannel in California, my insight into the business of media expanded while working with Alan Bell, a rare intellect in media management. He combined advertising sales, station management, and program production, conducting business with the skill he admired in classical music maestros. He was an early enthusiast for the way technology could improve television content.

Media motivations differ: reporters covet stories; media editorial leaders desire a memorable brand to attract viewers and readers. Corporate owners, especially, worry about advertising revenue. Audience size is critical to advertising revenue, so the brand's appeal is important. For most of the twentieth century, media executives believed they "controlled" the best way for business and merchants to reach an audience to encourage consumption of goods and services.

In the 1990s, a hundred years after technology allowed for mass media, confidence in older media forms began to collapse. Television, radio and print had learned to co-exist and were often co-owned by a parent company. The internet, however, was pernicious because it changed the relationship between consumer and publisher. In a 1999 BBC interview, the late singer David Bowie forcefully described it as an alien life force, set to change the world.

> "I don't think we've even seen the tip of the iceberg. I think the potential of what the internet is going to do to society, both good and bad, is unimaginable. I think we're actually on the cusp of something exhilarating and terrifying."[2]

In a stroke, distribution barriers dissolved, allowing collaboration between senders and receivers, with few editorial quality control points. All manner of electronic devices could use it. Images and sound had a fidelity beyond people's expectations. The computer revolution was seemingly in full flower.

The internet's impact on the media oligopolies of the twentieth century was comparable to the trebuchet 600 years earlier. Medieval castles enjoyed security until this new type of catapult used gravity and a seesaw effect to easily breach castle walls. The internet challenged the fortresses mentality of media owners, complacent because of competitive protection including licensing and regulatory favoritism, legal decisions, technology limitations as well as capital costs that inhibited competition. Media prospered as do most businesses operating in a near monopoly. This lack of awareness—living in a "bubble"—was compounded by American business attitudes. Expensive consulting firms substituting MBA-jargon for experience did not help in most instances. While internet start-ups charged ahead playing offense, mainstream media owners played defense. As smartphones and computers grew into a standard element of young people's lives, those playing offense won. Bewildered parents had trouble comprehending the allure of cinema quality video games played on the internet.

THE HISTORIC POWER OF NETWORKS

Networks have a revolutionary impact on society. In the late nineteenth century, electricity, rail, roads, and telephones all changed the course of life on earth. It took all of these networks to create and sustain modern mass media. Business power grew for media owners. The telephone and the typewriter remained the mainstays of content creation for decades.

In the late 1950s and early 1960s, high school and college editorships provided a grounding for new journalists in hot metal printing, an industry standard first used in the late nineteenth century. Linotype machines set lead type upside down and backwards (negatively) so the ink on the page would be correct (positive). At several big-city newspapers—the *Toledo Blade*, the *Hartford Courant*, *Trentonian* (NJ), the *Washington Post*—we used then traditional reporting tools—typewriters, pencils, and glue pots—to put a story together for the editor to review. Typewritten pages of a story were edited in pencil, pasted together, rolled up, and sent by pneumatic tube to the composing department where printers retyped it on Linotype machines as part of the complex process that made curved plates for cylindrical, rotating printing presses.

At the weekly *Princeton* (NJ) *Packet* in 1968, I saw for the first time photocomposition of type pasted into page templates for offset printing presses. Years later we learned that eliminating metal type had significant health benefits compared to breathing lead fumes. The common wisdom of the day was that photo composition/offset printing was fine for small press runs but would not work for big-city newspaper circulation. Later, desktop printing made typesetting easier and cheaper. Computerized layout for page design further transferred work to the editorial department formerly done by printers.

In retrospect, ownership and editorial layers of metropolitan newspapers generally disdained the printers and pressmen. These craftsmen were considered necessary evils in the middle between writers and readers. Union rules ranged from reasonable to absurd, adding to the antagonism. That their pay scales were often higher than the editorial wages amplified the feelings.

Columbia J-School Class of 1969 classmate Lewis Fisher, who spent 21 years as a suburban newspaper group publisher and owner, notes:

> "Financial savings from the latest technology—offset composition and printing—spurred the growth of major news-oriented suburban groups by the early 1960s. Metropolitan dailies were still wrestling with unions trying to preserve the greater number of jobs required by hot type plants, even though hot type's inferior reproduction put metro dailies at a competitive disadvantage with the more nimble, offset-produced suburban dailies and weeklies."[3]

By the time of Fisher's presidency of Suburban Newspapers of America in 1988–89, the nature of its membership was changing as entrepreneurial types were being replaced by publishers answerable to a corporate headquarters. When technology came back to bite suburban papers in the form of the internet and Craigslist, which decimated classified revenue, the wheels began coming off parent media companies' wagons as well. Their suburban papers, too, went into a sharp decline. In 2012, Suburban Newspapers of America changed its name to Local Media Association to reflect the growing membership of those working through blogs and websites rather than newspapers to provide information to suburbia.

Animosity and economic necessity put the focus for faster production and cost reduction on the technical crafts. In the early 1970s, *U.S. News & World Report*, a weekly news magazine battling contract printers and costs, tried a new concept: computerized type setting. A start-up company called Atex linked keyboards to a mainframe computer. Editorial content streamed directly to printing technology. This weekly magazine gave Atex time to work out bugs and obtain real time feedback from a small group of users. Had a larger daily newspaper tried it first it probably would have failed. By today's computing capabilities it was Donkey Kong, but back then before laptops, servers, gigabit Wi-Fi, and Ethernet were an everyday occurrence, it was spectacular. By the late 1980s almost all daily newspapers had computerized the writing and editing functions. As pagination improved, so did computer-generated graphics and design, leading to more attractive print products.

For many newspapers, these technology changes initially meant hiring more journalists with money not spent on printers. Editions got larger, geographical coverage enlarged, but inevitably a newspaper would be limited by its need to be printed and then delivered. Television did modest amounts of news, limited in geographical reach on the basis of locally licensed channels. A CNN 24/7 product delivered by satellite to cable systems was still a decade away. Network TV news remained quite limited in content diversity: politics, crime, weather, and sports being the staples.

IT STARTED WITH RADIO

Radio and television broadcasters in the twentieth century enjoyed believing they supplied the greatest free mass media in the world. For America, struggling with the Great Depression, the invention of radio was a tonic. What had been strictly an entertainment medium enlarged its role during World War II as news became crucial to informing the nation of progress against the Axis powers. Ed Murrow's CBS radio news team became legends for fearless reporting from the battlefields. Broadcasters did news because it was a licensing condition to obtain free use of limited electronic spectrum space controlled by government. The same rules governed commercial TV when it arrived in 1948. Initially hampered by technical problems and limited distribution, TV was clearly a big deal. By the mid-1950s color images, more channels, and national coverage caused its popularity to surge. Advertising poured in as a post-war economy boomed. Owners joked that the Federal Communications Commission had given them a license to print money. Absorbing the cost of news programming was less onerous than a license fee.

Evening TV news viewing and the birth of all-news radio reduced the value and circulation of afternoon papers, yet overall print circulation grew. Perhaps it was the contents of the paper, or population growth and economic prosperity or all of these reasons. By 1970, nearly seven million copies sold each weekday. Print media optimism, barely tempered by concerns about the encroaching TV news viewing, led to better presses and more colorful newspapers. Yet most aspects of the production process were constrained by old technology and expensive, craft-oriented workflow.

The decade of the civil rights struggle and Vietnam War coverage forced media to adapt to changes in tempo and subject matter for news events in America. This accelerated the transition from film, with its time constraints, to videotape and live events on television and ultimately digital media for both motion and still photography.

A great deal of industrial thinking mitigates against change. Research and development are usually focused on products to sell, not ways to improve a company's functionality. Capital outlays for change are seen as harming current operations; a new product line could cannibalize present lines. Attention devoted to change distracts from making current assigned financial targets.

But when technological change positively impacts both operating costs and speed, it gains adherents. Early adopters and revolutionary thinkers are most often newcomers, not the people currently in power.

Today it is hard to realize that computing grew up from office desktops to laptops long before the internet provided access to instant information from search engines. To learn the exact distance between Utica, New York, and New York City's LaGuardia airport for an airplane crash story required a road map, a ruler, and some calculations. Today just ask Google. (Answer: 238.5 miles.)

The expectation today is that journalists will have more specific information when it helps tell a story. We expect that journalists will search through social media to better understand who is involved in a story. This has pluses and minuses.

Computing initially was perceived as a solution to typewriters and a way to eliminate expensive printing staff. The impact is far deeper. Few journalists thought about the ultimate consequences for American media. Futurists and businesses do not share the same timeline for change. Media companies were making money and that was what counted most. American business leadership learned over time that predictions of change are slow to arrive but faster once here. The marketplace behavior with network chat apps demonstrates the trend. The wait-and-see attitude is exemplified by advice we have all heard at one time or another: "If it ain't broke, don't fix it."

Regardless of time and change, lessons imparted in the J-School by Fred Friendly are as relevant today as back then. He inspired us to tell stories that had meaning for readers and viewers.

PUSHING FOR CHANGE

After a useful stint as a foreign editor at the *Washington Post*, I managed to shift to WTOP TV channel 9, a CBS affiliate, which the paper owned. On January 5, 1970, I walked into the WTOP TV fifth floor newsroom for the first time. The new TV chief, Jim Snyder, hired me to solve serious problems with news film editing. I had learned and loved 16mm film cameras and editing at graduate school with John Schultz, Friendly's CBS editor. At WTOP TV I could not touch the equipment, just advise a union cameraman or editor. My desk in the news film area gave me a close-up view of how smoothly things did or didn't work. Within a few weeks it was clear that the entire newsroom was only minimally organized to meet its nightly deadlines. Then new executive producer John Baker was doing his best to meet Snyder's quality objectives. Surprisingly, several of the oldest staff members barely knew critical details of their assigned tasks. That was shocking at a station in the nation's capital. I lacked the experience to know this was common to television operations.

Eventually it became clear that in haphazard increments TV news had transitioned from radio-style scripts illustrated with silent film to reporters interviewing people and writing stories that integrated the sound clips with visuals. In television's second decade, academic training was scarce and on-the-job training haphazard at best. Workflow imported from radio, with unionized wrinkles, had not improved to meet expanding news programs and schedules.

The impact and virtue of live television news became clear in April 1971 while I was producing coverage of an anti-Vietnam War demonstration on the mall between the Lincoln Memorial and the Washington Monument. Live television news outside the studio in the 1970s was severely limited by the cost of technical constraints—cameras required plug-in electrical power and we had no easy way to get the signal back to the channel headquarters. While combat cameramen risked bullets filming the horrors of war in Vietnam, domestic news cameramen were tear-gassed filming the anti-war protests spreading across America.

Film is the operative phrase meaning yesterday. LIVE means today. In Washington, Channel 9 did live coverage of that large anti-war demonstration using an old-fashioned outside broadcast truck connected to Broadcast House by video lines leased from the phone company. It was expensive and tedious to set up. But it was challenging and exciting, an inkling of what television news could be if the tools were flexible and easy to deploy.

The 1968 Democratic Party nominating convention had been raucous. It wasn't clear how 1972 would turn out. Both presidential political nominating conventions were in Miami, and CBS News was prepared for limited live outside coverage, using a Phillips Norelco TV camera repackaged for "portability." It was much heavier and bulkier than a film camera but could produce live pictures. The core limitation of film was processing time. Film stock was expensive to purchase, took time and money to process, and was archived or tossed. This initial effort at an electronic news camera was hindered by the significant cable connection to back-end electronic systems and power. The Holy Grail was a shoulder mounted, self-contained electronic camera with live broadcast capability. Videotape of the proper quality and portability was still two years away.

WSB-TV was the first TV channel launched in Atlanta in 1948. Cox Broadcasting also owned radio station WSB as well as two newspapers. It was a dominant force in Georgia media and intended to remain so. Despite mediocre and often badly produced news programs, it was still watched by nearly 50 percent of the news audience. I arrived in 1974 from WPLG television in Miami to become executive producer. Protecting this reputation became my wedge to push WSB-TV to adopt live coverage when I took charge as news director later that year.

Ironically, Japan's electronic companies rebounded from defeat in World War II by licensing USA transistor patents to develop miniaturization and enter the largest consumer market in the world—the USA. By 1974, Sony had shifted beyond TV receivers to building television cameras and videotape recorders suitable for broadcast. The tape cassette could be erased and reused several times. The 32-minute tape cassette was nearly three times greater in recording time than the 11.5-minute duration of a 400-foot-long magazine of film, useable but once.

Nashville's WLAC-TV got there first, marrying a then unknown Ikegami HL33 color camera with a new Sony videotape recorder and a miniaturized transmitter from Cincinnati Microwave. A startling transition was unfolding because this new gear fit into a small Ford van. It was a sports car compared to an outside broadcast tractor-trailer. Then new microwave transmitters solved the "getting it back to the channel" issue. I spent a day there asking questions and making sketches.

My boss, General Manager Don Heald, agreed with me that live daily coverage would cement WSB-TV leadership. Heald asked the chief engineer, who had never seen an Ikegami camera, for an opinion. He said, "cheap Japanese junk. I'll buy it when RCA makes it." His arrogance reflected the TV industry perception of Japanese equipment. Estimated cost for the project was $250,000 for everything. Instead of being parked in wait of breaking news, it would be used two shifts every day. I teased Heald that if he were still the WSB weatherman I'd have him outside live in the first thunderstorm.

With no complex return-on-investment calculations or committee discussions, he said, "Tell Miss Alice in Purchasing I gave you $250,000." WSB's news brand was "Action News" so we called it the "Live Action Camera."

Its deployment every day changed local news in Atlanta, establishing the pattern that would be adopted nationally. Coverage of a tornado that took the roof off the governor's mansion, Governor Jimmy Carter's LIVE announcement to seek the American presidency, nighttime meetings and events to ordinary feature stories were all brought into Georgia's living rooms.

Thirty minutes of blank videotape cost a small fraction of equivalent film stock, even before calculating the value of reusing it about four times. While the cameras and editing machines were significantly more expensive than film gear, in a year's operation the change made economic sense as well as solving speed to broadcast. Channels had to convert to compete. From 1974 through 1994, many technological aspects of broadcasting changed. Electronic cameras made the reality television series practical. National and local TV news became the fountain from which most Americans drank their information. The newspaper industry saw its circulation and advertising revenue slip, but only in the mid-1990s did it become obvious that internet-supplied alternative sources threatened all mainstream media formats.

America was in flux. Civil rights legislation and post-Vietnam attitudes pushed television to rethink gender and race. I urged Heald to find a woman to pair with John Pruitt, their best talent, as a main anchor duo. Jane Pauley, then an unknown on TV in Indianapolis auditioned with Pruitt. We loved the pairing. But the owner of the Indiana station, Corinthian Broadcasting, warned, "steal my reporter and I will cancel business contracts with Cox Broadcasting's advertising rep company." Heald told me to forget her, but that audition tape quietly went to NBC Chicago, which hired her.

Next, we tried to hire, from Nashville, a woman named Oprah Winfrey. She declined as well, but she paved the way for WSB in 1975 to hire Monica Kaufman, the first black woman to regularly anchor the main newscasts in Atlanta. An inspired choice, she retired after 37 years in the job.

NEW TECHNOLOGY UPENDS TV

A year later, Alan Bell poached me to shake up things at KYW-TV in Philadelphia. As general manager, he was an early supporter of a rapid transition, recognizing it would change television news and programming. Reporters had to adjust to talking live rather than having time to reflect and write scripts and record stories. The changing standards opened the field to people who were smarter if less photogenic and weeded out many barely passable journalists who couldn't hack the pressure of live reporting.

Philadelphia's daily newspaper circulation and advertising took a beating because the three main TV channels competed using live coverage in a news war as if the fate of the city depended on it. If Atlanta was the match that lit the explosion in TV News, Philadelphia was the blaze that portended how bad it would get for the print industry in the decade ahead.

The big advance in television news in the 1980s was the creation of the newsroom computer system specifically for television production, loosely derived from the Atex system that was changing the newspaper industry. It was necessary because Atex and computing had allowed news agencies to eliminate teletype circuits. More news was arriving in newsrooms faster than ever before.

ABC News hired me as the bureau chief and senior producer for the Chicago bureau, managing Max Robinson, an anchorman for World News Tonight. Producing that national program was an exciting but awkward effort, as it had three anchors—Robinson in Chicago for domestic news, Frank Reynolds in Washington for political news, and Peter Jennings in London for international news. ABC was third in the ratings and needed something different.

We had to squeeze all the news and three anchormen into 22 minutes. We used typewriters, then faxed our scripts to a central executive desk in New York, which made editorial changes—as much to prove authority as to improve clarity—then faxed them back to us, asking that we re-fax our final prompter script to them. In my third month on the job I asked Roone Arledge, ABC news president, for permission to propose a newsroom computing solution for ABC News. "Take a week or two, write it up," he told me.

Working with a team at Control Data Corporation, then a mainframe and supercomputer firm in Minneapolis, the demo in New York was scheduled for Monday, November 5, 1979. Unfortunately, on November 4, 1979, Iranian students took 52 Americans hostage at the U.S. Embassy in Tehran, which meant all ABC news execs were unavailable. Subsequently, in June 1980, CNN launched and got its newsroom system to work. It would be several years before ABC had a serious newsroom system.

After another term as a local news director, I took six months off to rethink my career. It was 1984. I was 40 years old. With a borrowed Commodore "home" computer, I wrote my manifesto on television management and the coming impact of electronic news gathering, 24 hours of CNN, mobile phones, and computers. Three subsequent excursions into media positions tested the theories I had developed.

It was clear to me why media companies fail to adapt to changing market conditions: Owners think of their product in terms of a "delivery" format, a natural response to the words "newspaper, television, and radio." Actually, the brand is the "information" product but most misunderstand this. In today's digital environment, a multi-platform approach seems logical because the product IS information. It is more than semantics. It is attitude.

A modest staff properly organized with a smart workflow can accomplish a great deal. I called it "modular production"—the idea of finishing a section of work, including the anchor introductions, and then combining it not just in editing but eventually in real time transmission. Since typically the news content was gathered, written, and edited before the broadcast, it made no difference if the anchors—connective tissue to the stories—were recorded to videotape on a just-in-time basis. It sounds simple enough. You report live from a studio only when there is a reason. Smarter production techniques, in my opinion, could improve quantity and quality of news.

The reverse has happened for both print and broadcast reporters in the last few years with the pressure to use social media like Twitter and Instagram along with live reporting. The time for gathering and sifting information seems to disappear on some stories.

CNN TAKES ON THE WORLD

In 1992, after building two innovative television companies, I joined CNN just before the internet browsers arrived. Intentionally, the internet was open to anyone. Initially, many media entities did not take the internet seriously, CNN television executives included. Like many journalists who believed in their own media's permanence, media leaders did not consider it a long-term change agent. Because there was so little experience with computers and mobile phones, hardly ubiquitous at the time, this is perhaps understandable.

However, early on three of us took it on ourselves to visit Ted Turner unannounced to provide a 45-minute explanation of why NOW was the time for internet at CNN. We hoped Turner, who had an innate sense of audience, would listen. Our fervor was not lost on him. It was his company and he gave us $5 million in start-up funding. That first move gave CNN a position on the internet that it has never lost.

In July 1995, the first digital professional still cameras debuted and opened the floodgates for more colorful still images for both print and for websites. This gave photographers the ability to produce transmission-ready images straight out of the camera. Today, the capability of smartphone cameras has many news organizations asking reporters to also take pictures.

At the time I think most journalists underestimated the changes these technological shifts would bring to advertising, the lifeblood supporting most media companies. Print and television advertising works on the shotgun principle—all adverts will hit something. Digital advertising is much closer to a sniper rifle with an added benefit: the recipient of a message is known by URL and email address to the sender. This is a bit of oversimplification, but the extraordinary expansion of internet use for all sorts of devices has dramatically altered behavior in a number of key economic and lifestyle areas.

The internet has enabled thousands of individual commentators to communicate directly with others through blogs or instant message services. The impact on American politics was starkly clear in 2016. Projects like Wikipedia have contributed to the reordering of the media landscape, with users no longer restricted to established organizations for information.

It didn't appear that way at the start. Search engines aggregate information in a logical way and were viewed initially as a benefit to media companies, funneling them potential print readers. However, too many papers treated web publishing merely as a way to repurpose the content and thinking of a newspaper, not a medium with specialized potential. Later, realizing the search engines took advertising dollars as well as readers and didn't pay for the content "borrowed" from websites, many publications started subscription schemes for access. Revenue from newspapers' proprietary web sites was a small fraction of the sums generated by the previous print advertising revenue streams.

Faced with declining revenue, the print industry reacted defensively by cutting staff and coverage to save money. This did not help compete with internet-delivered content that now mixes print, video, audio, and all manner of content and advertising. Display advertising revenue in print is valued at about a third of what it was at peak. Financial losses came in many shapes and sizes. Reporters and editors lost their jobs, but owners also lost as the value of print entities collapsed, wiping out the money the owners expected for retirement or their heirs.

Is this inevitable as technology changes? Few cried for the pager companies that disappeared because of mobile telephones. Millions of messengers lost work when telephones displaced telegraph systems. Medieval scribes took a beating with the invention of the printing press. Progress always leaves victims.

If media entities did not understand new competition and concepts, maybe it was because the vast majority of managers in most companies had risen through the ranks of a single organization—often barely understanding how or why they did what they did. Learning and managing by rote provided little awareness of alternative solutions. Resistance to workplace change is as old as work. In often highly unionized media companies, the blame is placed on union resistance to change. My experience suggests resistance was stronger among middle management than at the union level. Managers claimed to be ready for change "except in my area, which is operating better than ever." People who believe this also agree that dinosaurs and humans roamed the earth together. In the 1980s the widespread adoption of mobile phones, laptop computers, and email began to have a discernible impact on media companies.

The internet is one of the greatest change agents the world has ever experienced, not all of it good. It has altered communication and business in ways never experienced with the telephone, which changed the twentieth century. Browser software and search engines like Google in the 2000s became the vehicle of choice to explore the internet. Search engines have no obvious fees but bandwidth access costs. The revenue, which has made these search engines among the largest and most profitable global businesses, comes from advertising and, not generally discussed, from selling data acquired about the users' behavior to advertisers and basically anyone who will pay for it. Data privacy issues became a serious concern after the 2016 U.S. presidential election. It will remain a serious issue for the next few decades.

The implications for democracy, political involvement, and the nature of the societies in which we live have rarely been as challenged. We did not see it coming because few could imagine that selling personal data being gathered would become more valuable than selling advertising based on broad numerical estimates of audience size.

I believe that advertisers, large and small, understood the internet much more quickly than did media owners. It was more than just a cheaper way of reaching an audience. Counting clicks seemed more accurate compared to the estimated measurement of television audiences and newspaper readership, especially as audited circulation shrank. Advertising revenue that had sustained mainstream media began to flow instead to Google, Facebook, and others, altering entertainment and politics. The internet both creates and obliterates. Amazon comes, Sears Roebuck goes away.

As high-speed digital networks have spread, we have seen new information and entertainment models spring up, mostly from upstart companies backed by wealthy investors and from technology companies. By 2016, social media sites were overtaking television as a source for news for young people and today news organizations are increasingly reliant on social media platforms for generating traffic. This shift is accelerating because the smartphone and internet destroy older information instincts and habits.

This is not a new phenomenon. It has been going on since the start of time. All of the journalism skills required for print and broadcast are embodied in these new delivery mechanisms. Over time, old brand names will adjust as new brands and offerings establish credibility.

NOTES

1. Carl E. Lindstrom, *The Fading American Press* (Garden City, NY: Doubleday, 1960).
2. David Bowie, interview with Jeremy Paxman, *BBC*, 1999, accessed on May 13, 2019, https://twitter.com/bbcnewsnight/status/818669202374467584?lang=en.
3. Lewis Fisher, email to author, March 6, 2019.

CHAPTER THREE

Women: Forging Towards Recognition

DOTTY BROWN

As the 38 women of Columbia University's School of Journalism went job hunting in the spring of 1969, we were upbeat about our prospects. Newspapers were thriving, with circulation on the rise. That year, news companies sold nearly 50 million papers every Sunday, raking in $5.7 billion in advertising revenue. Over the next 35 years, revenue for these "cash cows," as newspapers were called, would continue climbing.[1]

Young reporters with journalism degrees were in high demand as a veteran generation of newspaper staffers was retiring. Almost all of them were men, more notable for their ability to write than their academic credentials. With the women's movement gathering strength (the National Organization for Women was three years old), newsrooms seemed poised to finally crack open their doors for women.

Nonetheless, my J-School classmate Amy Stone, who was seeking a job in TV broadcasting, believes gender bias thwarted her first efforts to find work after graduation. Besides her prestigious new Columbia University Master's Degree in journalism, she had worked as a reporter already, something that many of the 101 students in the J-School Class of 1969 had not done. Yet the manager of an educational TV station in Scranton, Pennsylvania instead hired her classmate, David Platt, a college history major with no journalism experience.[2]

Stone also futilely sought work on the West Coast with King Broadcasting in Seattle. "I was interviewed for a newsroom job by the news director," she said. "Seeing my resume—Peace Corps Thailand, first non-Thai reporter for the *Bangkok Post*—he told me, 'You'd make a bitching good reporter, but you'll just go get married.'

"I never forgot that," she says. "In fact, when I didn't get married until the age of 59, I figured, I sure proved him wrong. . . . Not that it made any difference."

Other women of the Class of 1969 would encounter resistance as they tried to break into the male media universe. But over the decades they would persevere, disproving stereotypes and overcoming biases to eventually climb to some of the highest ranks of their profession. During their careers, they would also experience first-hand the upheaval of the news industry, which, among other challenges, was struggling to retain and recruit women readers so crucial to their survival.

Knowing that being married was a liability, my classmate Karen Rothmyer was careful to say during her 1969 interview for a wire desk job at the Associated Press that she "had no plans to get married or have children. I knew that it was important to state that clearly if I wanted that job, or, as far as I knew, any job." It is a moment she looks back on now "with incredulity and a little embarrassment, but not anger. It was a different time then."

Another classmate, Leslie Berkman, was 23 in 1969 when she strode into the *Los Angeles Times* newsroom in skirt and heels, clutching a briefcase stuffed with writing samples. She remembers that day clearly:

> "I hoped against hope to have a chance to do what I loved. I recall that the editor I approached did not take his feet off the desk to interview me and was not impressed by my Master's Degree. 'But can you write?' was his gruff reaction. Neither would he even glance at the many stories I had written on the race for mayor of Los Angeles that year between incumbent Sam Yorty and Tom Bradley—coverage that had won positive reviews from my J-School professor. He advised me to start at some smaller paper and get back to him later.
>
> "I thought nothing of my gender as I headed toward the elevator to leave the building. I just felt very green and unaccomplished. Then I heard footsteps coming up the rows of desks behind me. It was a reporter I had seen on the campaign trail who I had helped catch up with speeches he missed when he had to find a phone booth to call in his stories. He told me not to take the rejection personally. He said, 'Look around and what do you see? All suits and ties.' Only one intrepid female journalist, Dorothy Townsend, had forged her way onto the *Times* metro staff at that time."

When Mary Bralove applied to the *Wall Street Journal* in 1969, it had only two female reporters. Even so, when editors came to the J-School to interview applicants, Bralove joined the line of hopefuls. At her turn, she said, "I could tell in the interview that [the editor] just wasn't interested. So I said, 'My major paper [at the J-School] was on Women's Liberation.'" When he looked startled, she followed with, "'I scared you, didn't I?' That really shocked him and caught his attention."

As a sign of the times, Bralove said, the day she started at the *WSJ* it ran a light-hearted story on its front page about a woman so big breasted that crowds of men followed her to work.[3]

Susan Anderson had waged a battle just to get into the J-School. Graduating from the College of Wooster, she had been waitlisted for the Class of 1968 while two male classmates with whom she had worked on the school paper were accepted. (Neither ultimately attended.)

Determined to win admission the next year, Anderson got a job writing about weddings for the Passaic, New Jersey *Herald-News*. And she began pestering Christopher Trump, the admissions dean. When she asked why her Wooster classmates were admitted and she wasn't, Trump, she recalls, told her that they had a quota of women for the class, "since women can't get jobs anyway."

"Whether there really was a quota that year, I don't know," she says. "I visited each member of the admissions committee . . . and finally was accepted for the Class of 1969. I believe it was [Professor] Penn Kimball who told me, 'Well at least you're persistent, and that's what it takes to be a reporter.'"

According to James Boylan, a former professor at the J-School and author of its history, *Pulitzer's School,* women were only admitted "in the single digits" until the 1960s. That policy had been instituted by Carl Ackerman, who served as dean from 1931 to 1956. "Women of superior ability will be admitted to the School in numbers proportionate to the opportunities which shall develop for them in the future in professional work," Ackerman had said. "Since few women held journalism jobs, few were admitted."[4]

By the Class of 1969, of the 101 members, 38 were women. Still, at least one member of the admissions committee for the Class of 1970 "clearly displayed a bias against women," according to Michael Brourman, a 1969 classmate who served on the committee. (In the wake of the 1968 Columbia student protests against Vietnam and racism, the J-School had placed students on the admissions committee.)

"He spoke more than once about not wasting valuable space on someone who was likely to get married, have children and leave the profession within a few years," Brourman recalled. But, he added, "my sense was that his concern was not shared by the other voting members. Or, if they did share it, they did a good job of disguising it."

Shortly before graduation from the J-School in 1969, Edee Holleman became concerned about stories she was hearing that women starting out at both *Time* and *Newsweek* "would be hired as researchers instead of reporters, as the young men were, and never got promoted," she said.

So while still at the J-School, she wrote to Katherine Graham, owner of the *Washington Post* and *Newsweek*, and informed her that the bias was common knowledge at the J-School. "I then asked her why she wasn't doing more for women," said Holleman. "No answer." A few weeks later, Holleman, getting a phone call from the office of the J-School dean, was hopeful it was about a job. Instead, the dean, apparently having been contacted by Graham, pressed Holleman to reveal who had told her about discrimination at *Newsweek*, she said.

"All I told [the dean] in that uncomfortable phone call was that it was common knowledge," Holleman said. "I lost all respect for Katherine Graham. Attempts in movies like *The Post* . . . to burnish her reputation as a female role-breaker, always remind me of that phone call."

Hired by *Newsweek* that summer, J-School classmate Laurence Leamer, who later became a prolific biographer of American politicians and personalities, saw first-hand what Holleman had heard. "Like all the writers, I had an office outside of which sat a researcher," he said. "The writers were men. The researchers were women. When I wrote a story and didn't know a fact, I wrote 'tk' [to come] or '00.' The researcher was responsible for filling it in and fact checking the story. Any errors were her fault."

In 1970, 46 women at *Newsweek* filed a historic complaint with the federal Equal Employment Opportunity Commission, claiming discrimination in hiring and promotion under Title VII of the Civil Rights Act. When little resulted, they filed again in 1972, after which women finally began to be hired as reporters.

ABANDONING "WOMEN'S NEWS"

Even as the women of the Class of 1969 struggled to find reporting jobs, the feminist movement was challenging news outlets to rethink "women's news." Pioneering women editors, though few in number, were pushing brides off the covers of their women's sections to give better play to such significant issues as contraception, childcare, and equal opportunity.

At the *Dallas Times Herald*, the women's pages "got away with murder because the dumb male editors never bothered to read it," remarked Molly Ivins, a 1967 J-School graduate who early on forged an important career in journalism. "They were writing about birth control. Abortion. But it wasn't considered 'real news.'"[5]

Going further, these editors—as well as non-journalists in America fighting for women's equality—argued that stories about women's issues were "news" and should run in the front section of the newspaper, not siloed in the back.

Among those pioneering journalists was Marj Paxson, who was Women's Editor at the *Philadelphia Evening Bulletin* when I was hired as a food writer in 1971 at age 25. But it was only in researching this chapter and learning about her personal papers at the University of Missouri that I became aware of her frustrating behind-the-scenes efforts for better play for women's news.

In a 1974 memo to the *Bulletin*'s executive editor, George R. Packard, she wrote, "Mr. Packard: Today's paper upsets me as women's news editor. It is completely male-oriented. In fact, looking through the pages of the B-section,

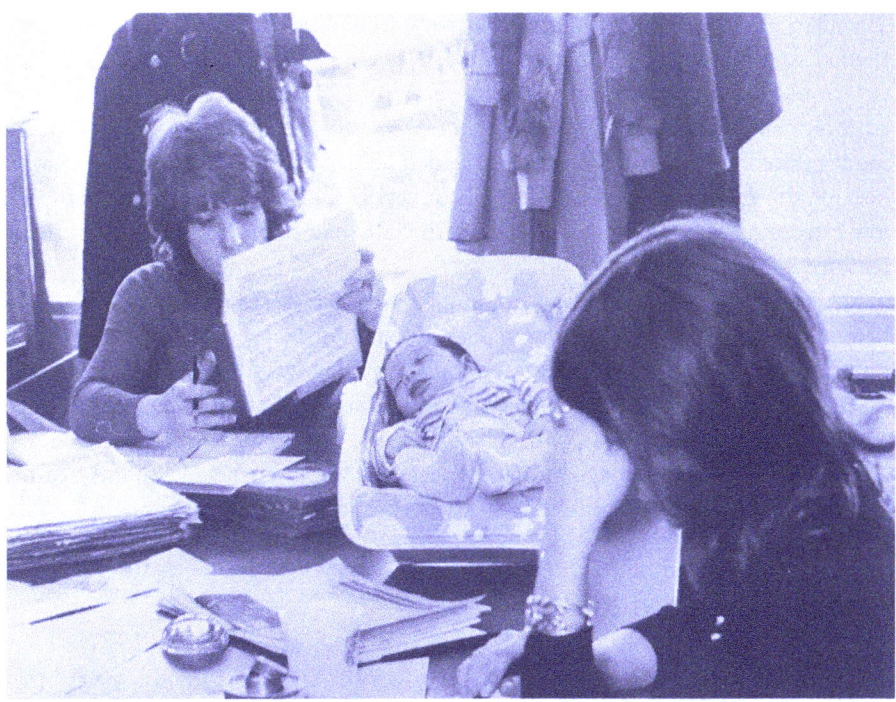

Figure 3.1: Three weeks after giving birth, Dotty Brown brings her infant daughter to work at the *Philadelphia Bulletin* in 1974. She was the first woman in the newspaper's history to have a baby and return to work. Source: *Courtesy of Dotty Brown*

I wonder if women do anything but sing for the president and produce babies. This male dominance of the paper is happening so regularly that I am concerned. It's a mistake, a big mistake."[6]

In the early 1970s, *Roe v. Wade* was making its way to the Supreme Court, Gloria Steinem was demanding equal pay for equal work, and the Equal Rights Amendment had passed both houses of Congress and garnered President Nixon's signature. (It would later fail, several states short.) Yet instead of bringing such stories into their news sections, news executives initially responded by renaming their women's pages, aiming for a coed audience. The *Washington Post* was the first large paper to do so. In 1969 it replaced its "For and About Women" with "Style." Eighteen months later, the *Los Angeles Times* started "View" "to provide wider feature coverage of a city and region that were emerging as trendsetters."[7] Soon, women's sections were being remodeled across the country with names such as "Living," "Accent" and "Lifestyle."

Others were assigning topics to their daily feature sections, hoping to appeal to both men and women. The *St. Petersburg Times* had "Day," as in MonDAY,

TuesDay. As the decade of the 1970s continued, some newspapers launched themed sections such as Family, Home & Design, Food, and Health.

Ironically, the demise of women's sections cost some female reporters and editors their positions. If the new sections were to also appeal to men, management's thinking went, then men were needed to bring that about. Jean Taylor, who became the *Los Angeles Times'* View editor in 1971, explained, "Women had such low esteem of what women did, so we artificially had to put esteem into women's sections by bringing men in."[8]

Among the women to lose their jobs was the *Bulletin's* Paxson, who was demoted when her section became "Focus." No matter that several of the 15 women on her team whom she had mentored, including me, would soon win a statewide journalism prize for exposing dangerous conditions in nursing homes. When a man took over, Paxson was relegated to a position in the *Bulletin's* Sunday Magazine that largely involved reading page proofs, she said. "It was the worst 14 months of my life," said Paxson, who later became a publisher in the Gannett news chain.[9]

CRACKING CEILINGS

Through the decade of the 1970s, the women of the Class of 1969 discovered that getting hired was only their first hurdle into the male world of journalism. Now they had to over-achieve to prove themselves equal to the task.

Edee Holleman, the first woman on the city hall/police beat at a small-town Texas paper, recalled having to prove "I was tough enough and good enough to do the job." She said her male editor "would periodically test my mettle by sending me to observe an autopsy or assigning me to write a story on skydiving which included my participating in the sport. At night, especially on weekends, I hung out at the police station and went on calls . . . . I passed those tests, but did not get the same pay as the male reporters did because, I was told, they had families to support. But this job and the professional respect of this editor set me on my life's career journey."

Leslie Berkman, rebuffed in her initial job interviews, quickly succeeded in becoming the second woman covering hard news at the *Los Angeles Herald-Examiner*. Thrilled with her position, she decided not to fight the sexism in the office, including a copy editor "who had been embarrassing me by smacking my behind when I walked by the rim to answer editing questions." She was grateful, though, that her editor reprimanded him. "I also learned," she said, "to be blind to the pinup girls adorning the dark room when a photographer led me in to admire the art he was developing to illustrate my story. The photographers—all men at the time—were always very respectful and businesslike so I figured the girlie pictures went with the territory."

Outside the office, she says she was "floored" when she was barred from covering a political event being held at a men-only business club favored by the city's power class. "As the only woman among the press, I was stopped from entering the elevator taking us to the candidate. I sat fuming in the lobby." It was only because the candidate stopped on his way out to apologize and answer her questions that she was able to cobble together a story, she said.

Afterwards, she wrote "about the longtime practice of the most elite downtown clubs in Los Angeles to exclude women and how that old boys concept was harmful to women who wanted to advance in business."

When Tracy Wood of UPI's Sacramento bureau was similarly barred from a "public" meeting, Wood wrote about her experience of being unable to report. That piece, she said, prompted the California state legislature to amend its open meeting law.

Among the first to break out of the corral of women in the *Bulletin's* features department was my *Bulletin* colleague DD Eisenberg, the home and design writer. Out of the blue one day in 1974, executive editor George Packard called her into his office. The suave Princeton graduate, then in his early 40s, had been inviting his young staffers to his house for touch football parties and had noticed that Eisenberg could catch a ball.

"What do you think of the idea of a woman in the sports department?" Packard asked her.

"Great idea," she replied.

"Would you like the job?" Eisenberg recalls him saying. "You play a mean game of touch football. If you don't like it, you can always go back to features."

So Eisenberg became the first woman to cover sports in Philadelphia and among "a few token women around the country," she said. She kept a "discrimination file," notes for a possible book that included questions people asked her: "Why are you taking the place of a man?" and "Why would you want to be in a locker room?" And, "Why do you want this job?—your husband is a doctor."

Barred from the locker room where male reporters were getting their interviews, she would have to wait outside until 2 or 3 a.m. for the athletes to emerge. Most, she said, were rushing to get home but "a few were on my side and would give me quotes."

Later, after Eisenberg won locker room access, the athletes would sometimes drop their towels in front of her, she said. Once, she faced the live-TV indignity of being asked by former Eagles defensive back-turned-sportscaster, Tom Brookshier, "Are you an athletic supporter?"

"He saw me as raw meat." she said.[10]

Marquita Pool-Eckert, one of nine African Americans in the J-School Class of 1969, took a different kind of risk to advance her career. She gave up a well-paid union job as a publicist for "Day Time Dramas" at ABC-TV for a per diem position that paid less money at *Like It Is*, a news and community affairs show on WABC-TV in New York City that targeted the black community.

"It was important to me to do work that mattered," said Pool-Eckert. It also helped, she said, that she was not married and had no obligations at the time. "So there was no reason not to 'go for it.'" The move paid off in many ways, she said, as she rose to become producer for CBS Evening News and Senior Producer for CBS Sunday Morning.

WE WERE THE FIRST SUPERMOMS

If making one's way as a woman was hard, doing so as a new mother proved ridiculously difficult. By 1974, I had been promoted from food writer to Food Editor of the *Bulletin* and was determined to hold on to my rung on the career ladder. If I ever stepped off, I feared I would never regain my footing. With maternity leave (let alone paternity leave) barely in the nation's vocabulary, I worked straight through my pregnancy, never missing a day of work until I went into labor. Three weeks later, I was back at my desk, the first woman journalist in the history of the *Bulletin* newsroom to have a baby and not quit. A week after I gave birth, Arlene Morgan, deputy features editor at the rival *Philadelphia Inquirer*, also had a baby and became its first female news staffer to return to work. "There was a bet on about whether I would come back or not," Morgan said.[11]

Besides proving to male bosses their commitment to their jobs, the new mothers had financial considerations. I remember getting $30 a week in "sick pay" for the three weeks I was out, a small fraction of my salary, which was about $200 a week. It was only in 1978 after Congress passed the Pregnancy Discrimination Act that companies were required to cover maternity-related disabilities like other medical conditions.

To prove herself equal to the otherwise all-male *Bulletin* sports staff, Eisenberg hid her pregnancy into her fifth month as she lugged around heavy equipment and worked nights and weekends. It was only when she was caught vomiting by a tennis tournament official that she finally told her editor. Later, she would wonder if pushing herself had been a factor in her son's premature birth. She only took a few weeks off, leaving her newborn in the care of a baby nurse.

"At that time, you didn't stay home. You had to show everyone you could come back," she said.

Having hidden pregnancies, mothers felt they also had to hide the demands of childcare if they were ever to get ahead. There was truth to that worry. I actually lost out on a promotion in 1984 after the executive editor told me I had "too many family responsibilities."

Classmate Mary Bralove at the *Wall Street Journal* believes she failed herself and other women by not standing up as a journalist-mother after her daughter was born in 1979. Packing up one day to get home, her boss suddenly announced a meeting in his office. "I'll be there in just a minute," she said, and in a panic called her husband to drop everything and relieve the sitter.

> "I've thought about that a lot. . . . [Women] turn their lives inside out to fit a corporate culture of a man being the sole breadwinner."[12]

On the other hand, Karen Rothmyer, who by the early 1990s had risen to become an editor of New York's *Newsday* while raising two boys, felt it important that women keep proving that they could handle the time demands of journalism as her generation had. She was sometimes annoyed that women on her staff, 10–15 years younger than herself, would tell her "they had to leave early, or couldn't cover something because of childcare concerns. I kept wanting to ask whether the kid didn't have a father, too. It seemed to me that these women were regressing to attitudes of the 1950s, rather than fighting to increase the gains my generation had made. It seemed to me that they were very different than women my age who had had to learn to not ask for any favors if they wanted to get ahead. I know it's more complicated than that but that's how I felt, and feel."

WRITING STORIES THAT SPEAK TO WOMEN

As women journalists fought their way out of features, not only did they make their mark covering hard news, but they also helped to broaden its definition.

In 1975, Bralove wrote a *Wall Street Journal* Page One story on the stress of working couples. The headline read, "For Married Couples, Two Careers Can Be an Exercise in Frustration." Its subtitle: "Many Find Tight Schedules, Fatigue, Care of Children Bring Unexpected Strains." While that may sound obvious today, in the 1970s, when the first huge generation of women was pursuing their career dreams, the job-parenting juggle was a wrenching new social phenomenon.

The next year, she wrote one of the first major stories of any news publication on sexual harassment in the workplace. The piece, again on Page One, was headlined, "A Cold Shoulder: Career Women Decry Sexual Harassment By Bosses and Clients." Dozens of women called her afterwards with stories of unwanted advances, endured to keep jobs.

"We thought if we surfaced the issue, people would talk about it and deal with it," Bralove said. But it would be 40 years before the #MeToo tsunami would roil the nation and force powerful perpetrators from their jobs. That it's taken so long and appears so widespread is "incredibly disheartening," said Bralove.

The decade of the 1970s was a pivotal time for women and the news. In 1973, Title IX of the Educational Amendments demanded that high schools and colleges support men and women equally. In 1974, First Lady Betty Ford revealed details of her mastectomy, bringing the unmentionable "women's disease" to the front pages of major newspapers.

Two years later, Barbara Walters, at ABC, became the first woman to co-anchor an evening news show and Pauline Frederick became the first woman to moderate a presidential debate (Gerald Ford vs. Jimmy Carter). At the *Wall Street Journal*, Bralove was named assistant New York bureau chief, the first woman at the *WSJ* to be promoted to newsroom management.

Despite such achievements, female reporters at media organizations including the *New York Times*, *Washington Post*, *Reader's Digest*, and *San Francisco Chronicle* began charging their employers with sex discrimination, particularly unequal pay.

No longer a food writer, I was an investigative reporter on the *Bulletin's* city desk, where only one woman had worked in 1971 when I was hired. By 1979, of the 60 metro reporters, 11 were women. I had won two major state prizes, one of which was also a Pulitzer finalist: an expose of a secret file of hospital medical malpractice deaths.

But in January 1982, the *Bulletin* failed, part of the first huge contraction of the newspaper industry that left many cities as one-newspaper towns. Afternoon papers were vanishing along with America's blue-collar workforce, who had bought those papers on their way home from factories. Technology was also at play: the evening TV news was a compelling alternative.

I was among the "boat people," saved from the *Bulletin's* sinking by the rival *Philadelphia Inquirer*. But the signs were obvious to me. I said to myself, "Newspapers will last my career but not much longer."

The *Inquirer*, enjoying an advertising revenue bonanza with the *Bulletin's* demise, executed a major expansion. In the early 1980s, as part of the Knight Ridder chain and under the leadership of Executive Editor Gene Roberts, it blossomed into a national newspaper, with its own national and foreign bureaus and a talented staff that would win the paper 17 Pulitzer Prizes between 1975 and 1990.

At the same time, it expanded locally, going head-to-head with suburban newspapers through a half dozen "Neighbors" sections, each with its own staff of reporters, editors, and local offices. But the *Inquirer*, hopeful of winning readers of the defunct *Bulletin*, saw only a small boost to its Sunday circulation and barely any daily. Those readers had simply vanished. Over the decades more and more would.

The loss of women readers was particularly worrisome. A 1994 study conducted for the *Inquirer* noted that the gender gap was growing. "The *Inquirer* needs to implement a program for attracting more women to the newspaper," the consultant recommended, pointing to a nine-point gender gap on Sundays and a 13-point gap on weekdays. "It is particularly important for the Sunday newspaper to be made more attractive to female readers, since Sunday readership losses in the past two years seem to be almost exclusively among women readers."[13]

PROTESTING FOR PROMOTIONS AND PAY

As newspaper publishers struggled with circulation challenges, the growing numbers of women staffers at publications around the country were becoming increasingly angered by issues of lower pay and fewer promotions. They resorted to protests and in some cases lawsuits.

The issue of blatant salary discrimination had emerged at the *Bulletin* in the early 1970s when the women cloistered in the features department, myself included, learned that the city editor was quietly allowing his staff—virtually all men—to routinely pad their expenses by about $70 a week without providing receipts. When the women appealed to the features editor, he refused to allow the same, which is one reason the women supported unionization in 1976.

Promotions were another big issue. At the *Philadelphia Inquirer*, women, including me, formed a caucus in 1984 to protest management's failure to elevate more women to editing positions and to coveted national and foreign assignments. Roberts responded with what seemed like a dare. He offered City Hall Bureau Chief Jane Eisner, the mother of a one-year-old, the London bureau, a post requiring constant travel. Disproving all assumptions that mothers could not handle such a job, Eisner (J-School Class of 1978), with her husband's backing, leapt at the offer:

> "It wasn't so much a decision as a thrilling opportunity I couldn't help but accept. I had never thought of myself as a foreign correspondent, but as soon as the position was offered, it was all I wanted to do. I made the decision for myself and on behalf of my family, not necessarily as part of a greater cause.... What was revolutionary, and frankly also quite frightening, was that I was the first mother that the *Inquirer* sent overseas, and one of only two mothers in the American press corps in London. There was no roadmap. We had to forge our own path. And I will be forever grateful to [editors] Gene Roberts and Jim Naughton for giving me the chance to accept and then for supporting me while I was there."[14]

Eisner opened opportunities for other women, who soon were named to other foreign bureaus and editing positions. Eisner later was named the *Inquirer*'s editorial page editor and then editor of the *Forward* in New York City before being named Director of Academic Affairs at the Columbia University J-School.

Landmark promotions of women were happening at some other big newspapers: Janet Chusmir in 1987 became executive editor of the *Miami Herald*. She was the fourth woman to be named editor of any paper in the country with circulation of over 100,000 and "the first woman in the history of American journalism to be in charge of the newsroom at a major metropolitan daily newspaper," according to Tom Rosenstiel, executive director of the American Press Institute.[15]

The proliferation of newsroom positions during the 1980s also opened opportunities for women reporters at the *Los Angeles Times,* some of whom moved downtown from the zones and to national and foreign bureaus.

Nonetheless, around the time of Anita Hill's testimony during Senate hearings for Supreme Court nominee Clarence Thomas in 1991, the *Times'* women "were seeing evidence of the 'glass ceiling' in who got which choice assignments and beats, and were hearing pretty solid rumors about salary differentials," said Patt Morrison, a colleague of Berkman. After the women presented their findings and demands to management, "I recall that some opportunities opened up, although changes were still slow to come," said Morrison, now a columnist for the *Times* with a share in two Pulitzer prizes.[16]

Across the country, the salary gap between male and female newsroom staff has closed at a glacial pace and is still not at parity. Despite the Newspaper Guild minimums (the union-negotiated salary baseline set for new employees, regardless of gender), salaries for most women haven't kept pace with the bonus raises that men were more likely to get, whether because of "old boy" relationships between male editors and reporters or women's inferior bargaining skills. Whatever the reason, the bonuses compounded by regular Guild-negotiated raises over the years amplified gender pay disparities.

Studies show that the problem continues to today. In 2016, the Washington-Baltimore Newspaper Guild reported that male reporters at the *Washington Post* earned $7,000 more than women reporters.[17]

An April 2018, Los Angeles Times Guild study of staff salaries revealed gender gaps across all age groups, with women of color most affected. Among the most experienced reporters—those ages 61 and over—men on average made about 15 percent more than women. Among the youngest—those 21-to-30—the gap was 4 percent.[18]

Bettina Boxall, a veteran environmental writer, supported the 2018 vote to unionize at the *Los Angeles Times,* the first in its 136-year history. Boxall in 2009 had won the Pulitzer Prize in explanatory reporting with Julie Cart for a series on escalating wildfires in the West. Neither woman received a raise or bonus for their accomplishment, Boxall said.

IN PURSUIT OF WOMEN READERS

Even as newsrooms were shortchanging female staffers, they were lamenting the loss of women readers, especially after Sunday circulation began its relentless descent after peaking nationally in 1993 at 62.6 million copies. Women made up more than half of the population, but men accounted for the majority of regular readers.

My J-School classmate Susan Miller was among the first news executives to focus on this problem. In 1989, as vice-president/editorial for E.W. Scripps Newspapers (formerly Scripps Howard), she wrote a special report, "Women's Lifestyles," which was published in the magazine of the American Society for Newspaper Editors (ASNE). It spelled out why fewer women were reading newspapers. The vocal women of the 1970s who once decried the notion of "women's sections," were now "time squeezed," she said, pursuing careers, having babies, doing household chores. They were still readers but more often, the stories that spoke to their interests were not in newspapers but in women's magazines. Miller called on news executives to offer "a different balance of topics," and provide the information in easy-to-read ways. "Give us 15 minutes and we'll save you 15 minutes," was the idea.

"It required the men in top management to accept that their interests [namely hard news and sports] were not shared with 51 percent of the people in their market," she said. "I recommended that they look at how they allocated budget and staff—for instance, the space, staff and budget devoted to sports—and prioritize instead based on the interests in their market."

"It was not rocket science," she said, but news executives did not heed her call.

In her 1993 follow-up report, she concluded, "On reflection, the abolition of the women's section was probably a mistake. While making it a ghetto for all news about women was wrong, its mainstay topics were a strength that newspapers have lost."[19]

The Newspaper Association of America did a massive media survey in 1998 entitled, "So Many Choices, So Little Time," a title referring to the explosion of media outlets paired with the time pressures on readers. In 1961, 80 percent of adults in the country had read a newspaper the day before. By 1998, that number was down to 59 percent. The report largely dismissed the internet as a threat, since only nine percent of those surveyed then used it as a source of daily news. Instead it focused on the urgency of re-tuning the print product.

"As much as we editors and publishers think we've changed our newspaper," the report said, "we haven't changed them sufficiently. As improved as we may find our journalism, it isn't credible enough or relevant enough to many of our readers ... So it's time—it's way past time—to shore up our weaknesses and play to our strengths."

Women, the report said, would increasingly dominate the market as the population ages. "Daily newspapers have a problem ... attracting and keeping female readers. Women read newspapers less often than men, they are interested in somewhat different news content, and generally, they have greater interest in advertising."

What was the solution it recommended nearly three decades after the women's pages were disbanded? Like something out of *Back to the Future*, it prescribed specific sections on topics of greater interest to women, especially clothes and fashion, health and fitness, local community/neighborhood news, faith, and religion. Those sections, it said, would also attract the ads that most appealed to women—food and grocery ads, clothing ads, health and beauty ads.[20]

Whatever news organizations have done since then to attract readers hasn't been enough. Instead of 59 percent of Americans reading a newspaper the day before (the figure lamented in 1998), by 2012, only 29 percent were doing so, either in print or online.[21]

Meanwhile women in news organizations remain a minority. A Women in Media Center report showed that in 2019, men continued to dominate news reporting, whether in print, TV, news wires or the internet, producing about 63 percent of news reports.[22]

The number of women in newsrooms of all types, including digital, has more or less stagnated for nearly two decades, inching from 37.5 to 39.1 percent between 2001 and 2017. Women of color have trailed, with black women making up just 2.6 percent of the journalism workforce, Hispanic women, 2.47 percent and Asian women, 2.39 percent, based on 2016 data.[23]

And with shrinking news budgets and persistent layoffs, women's overall numbers have declined along with the men. In January 2019, 1,000 journalists lost their jobs, the majority from digital media. On the other hand, nearly two-thirds of news organizations reported in 2015 having at least one woman among their top three editors.[24]

Many women of the Class of 1969 who went into journalism as opposed to public relations or other writing-related careers earned the recognition of their peers and over the decades won awards and climbed to leadership positions. Some examples:

Susan Anderson, who had such trouble getting into the J-School, studied film editing and easily landed jobs at several San Francisco TV stations. Her 1977 documentary filmed in Cuba, "Yankee Come Back!" won her Northern California Emmys in writing and producing. Later, she ran a paper, the *Casper* (Wyoming) *Journal*.

Valerie Coleman Morris, who started out as a researcher for a TV station, launched the financial arm of CNN.

Connie Bruck, who once struggled as a freelance writer, became a regular contributor to the *New Yorker Magazine*.

Sylvana Foa, after exposing American bombing of Cambodia for *Newsweek* in the 1970s, became foreign editor of United Press International, the first woman to hold such a post for a major international news network.

Karen Rothmyer became managing editor of *The Nation*.

Susan Spencer became an anchor for *CBS News*.

Michèle Montas-Dominique, a Haitian class member whose journalist husband Jean Dominique was assassinated in 2000, took over their independent

Haitian radio station. After receiving death threats and the murder of her driver, she moved to New York where she became the spokesperson for U.N. Secretary General Ban Ki-Moon.

Susan Miller, who had urged newspapers to revamp their coverage in order to attract women, did that very thing as editor and publisher of the *Monterey County Herald*. "We saw circulation go up for five years," she said.

Marquita Pool-Eckert became a senior producer at CBS News where she won numerous Emmy awards.

Leslie Berkman, who in 1973 was the only woman on the metro staff of the Orange County Edition of the *Los Angeles Times*, became an award-winning business reporter, working at the *Times* for 22 years.

And I eventually became Medical, Science and Education Editor of the *Inquirer*, overseeing two editors and 15 reporters, edited a series that won the 1997 Pulitzer Prize in Explanatory Journalism, and was named Knight Ridder Journalist of the Year.

In 2011, as Projects Editor for Print and Multi-Media, I took one of numerous buyouts at the shrinking *Inquirer*. In 1989, it had bustled with 721 newsroom staffers. By 2018, a merged *Philadelphia Daily News-Inquirer* staff was down to 250. And in an experiment to save the news organization, its last owner, H.F. "Gerry" Lenfest, donated his investment to turn it into a non-profit.

My 1982 prediction that newspapers would only last my career was proving fairly accurate.

NOTES

1. "Newspapers Fact Sheet, State of the News Media," Pew Research Center, last modified June 13, 2018, http://www.journalism.org/fact-sheet/newspapers/0.
2. Unless otherwise noted, any information or quotations from members of the Columbia University School of Journalism, Class of 1969, were obtained through emails or interviews between September 2018 and February 2019.
3. Mary Bralove, interview by her daughter, Steph, "I scared you, didn't I?" Small Answers, last modified June 9, 2014, http://smallanswers.us/i-scare-you-dont-i/.
4. James Boylan, *Pulitzer's School: Columbia University's School of Journalism, 1903–2003* (New York: Columbia University Press, 2003), 79.
5. Sarah Jaffe, "From Women's Page to Style Section," *Archives: Behind the News, Columbia Journalism Review,* last modified February 19, 2013, https://archives.cjr.org/behind_the_news/womens_page_to_style_section.php.
6. Kimberly Voss and Lance Speere, "Marj Paxson: From Women's Editor to Publisher." *Media History Monographs*, 2008, 8, accessed February 20, 2019, https://www.academia.edu/245907/_Marjorie_Paxson_From_Womens_Editor_to_Publisher_().
7. Kay Mills, *A Place in the News* (New York: Columbia University Press, 1990), 116.
8. Mills, 122.

9. Voss and Speere, 8.
10. DD Eisenberg, phone interview with author, September 28, 2018. Subsequent quotes from Eisenberg from interview.
11. Arlene Morgan, email to author, October 19, 2018.
12. Mary Bralove, "I scared you, didn't I?"
13. Clark, Martire & Bartolomeo, Inc.: "Study of Reader Satisfaction," September–November 1994, conducted for the *Philadelphia Inquirer*, Spring, 1995, 48.
14. Jane Eisner, email to author, October 21, 2018.
15. Thomas B. Rosenstiel, "Journalism History Made: A Woman Lands the Top Newsroom Job at a Major Daily," *Los Angeles Times,* last modified June 12, 1987, http://articles.latimes.com/1987-06-12/business/fi-3907_1_city-editors.
16. Patt Morrison, email to Leslie Berkman, September 26, 2018.
17. "The *Washington Post*'s Union Says Women Make on Average 86 Percent of What Men Make," *American Press Institute*, last modified, May 24, 2016, https://www.americanpressinstitute.org/need-to-know/up-for-debate/washington-posts-union-says-women-make-average-86-percent-men-make/.
18. "Los Angeles Times Pay Study," L.A. Times Guild, last modified April 2018. https://drive.google.com/file/d/1CFPE3wS3xESTAXYqbeIiN3kOCMC2dKnA/view
19. Susan Miller, "Opportunity Squandered: Newspapers and Women's News," *Media Studies Journal* (Winter/Spring 1993), 167–82.
20. "So Many Choices, So Little Time, Media Usage Study," Newspaper Association of America, 1998, 1–10.
21. Russell Heimlich. "Number of Americans Who Read Print Newspapers Continues to Decline," *FactTank*, last modified, October 11, 2012, http://www.pewresearch.org/fact-tank/2012/10/11/number-of-americans-who-read-print-newspapers-continues-decline/.
22. "Divided 2019: The Media Gender Gap," Women's Media Center, last modified January 31, 2019, http://www.womensmediacenter.com/reports/divided-2019-the-media-gender-gap.
23. "The Status of Women of Color in the U.S. News Media 2018," Women's Media Center, 2018, http://www.womensmediacenter.com/assets/site/reports/the-status-of-women-of-color-in-the-u-s-media-2018-full-report/Status-_Women_of_Color_Report_2018.pdf.
24. Catherine York, "Women Dominate Journalism Schools but Newsrooms Are a Different Story," Poynter, last modified September 18, 2017, https://www.poynter.org/news/women-dominate-journalism-schools-newsrooms-are-still-different-story.

CHAPTER FOUR

Diversity: A Work in Progress

MARQUITA POOL-ECKERT

In 1968, six months before I entered the Columbia University School of Journalism, President Lyndon Johnson ordered the publication of the Kerner Commission Report. The report took particular aim at the nation's mainstream press for failing in its responsibility to report on the oppressive conditions in poor communities, which had contributed to the urban rebellions of the late 1960s. More than 200 people had died in those uprisings and more than 10,000 were wounded.[1]

"The press has too long basked in a white world looking out of it, if at all, with white men's eyes and white perspective," said the Report of the National Advisory Commission on Civil Disorders, as it was officially called.

Diversity in newsrooms was virtually non-existent back then. "Fewer than 5 percent of the people employed by the news business in editorial jobs in the United States today are Negroes," the report said, using the racial terminology of the time. "Fewer than 1 percent of editors and supervisors are Negroes, and most of them work for Negro-owned organizations."

"Our nation is moving toward two separate societies," the report concluded, "one black, one white—separate and unequal."[2]

This is the journalism world I entered as an African American. The news—especially the way it was presented so viscerally on TV—had long fascinated me. My father was involved in Chicago politics during Mayor Richard J. Daley's administration, and as a young girl I would eavesdrop on his conversations with friends. I even remember listening to political conventions on my grandfather's Zenith radio. In high school during the height of the civil rights movement, I was stunned by the brutality of the demonstrations and captivated by the images of the brave young activists televised on the nightly news.

In my dorm at Boston University, a TV was parked in the corner of the lounge and I was parked in front of it most nights before dinner, watching the civil rights story unfold. Rev. Martin Luther King had received a PhD from Boston University, so I felt a special connection. When President John F. Kennedy was assassinated in 1963, I sat transfixed with my dorm mates, watching the flickering black-and-white images of those unthinkable events late into the night. The Dallas motorcade. Vice President Johnson's swearing-in with Jackie by his side wearing her blood-spattered suit. Jack Ruby shooting Lee Harvey Oswald point-blank on camera. The president's funeral procession. The Kennedy assassination became the seminal moment when television took over the news as events were broadcast in real time. Television became the most powerful form of mass communication and it expanded my view of the world.

After college, I got a job as a photo researcher at Time Inc., where it quickly became obvious to me that women's opportunities for advancement in journalism were limited. In the editorial departments, women were employed as administrators and researchers; men were reporters, photographers, and writers. Among the very few minorities was the dashing and brilliant Gordon Parks, who was a member of the legendary core of *Time-Life* photographers.

So I applied to the J-School, believing a master's degree would help expand my career possibilities. At Columbia, the J-School was going through its own transition. Originally conceived as a professional school for white men, it eventually began to admit more women and minority students.[3] Of the 101 students in my Class of 1969, nine, including myself, were African Americans, one was Asian and another seven were international students of color, by my count.

A milestone hire in 1968, just before I arrived, was that of Luther P. Jackson, the school's first black professor. A 1951 J-School graduate, Jackson had been among a handful of minority reporters at the *Washington Post* in the early 1960s. That same year, Professor Fred W. Friendly, the acclaimed documentary producer and former *CBS News* president, had been so shaken by the Kerner Report that he started the Summer Program for Broadcast and Print Journalism for Members of Minority Groups at the J-School.

The program (later renamed the Michelle Clark Fellowship Program)[4] was funded by the Ford Foundation, CBS, and NBC, and would train more than 200 journalists of color over the next seven years, pay their expenses, and guarantee them jobs.

One enrollee was a college student and part-time employee of WBLT-TV in Jackson Mississippi, named Randall Pinkston, who later became a White House correspondent for *CBS News*. "I recall Fred Friendly's lectures and the card he gave us about the role of a journalist," Pinkston told me. "I carried that card with me for years. The Summer Program was my only formal training in journalism."[5]

Broadcasters likely underwrote Friendly's program in part because of a pivotal case which would wind its way through the federal courts for 16 years. In the early 1960s, the Rev. Martin Luther King Jr., Andrew Young, and others had been appalled by Jackson, Mississippi, station WLBT-TV's biased coverage of civil rights demonstrations and school segregation. Besides having no African American on-air reporters in a city that was 40 percent black, the station had done such things as flash "Sorry, Cable Trouble," on screens when the national network was featuring prominent blacks such as Thurgood Marshall, then chief counsel for the National Association for the Advancement of Colored People.[6]

United Church of Christ vs. WLBT-TV was filed after the FCC granted the station a license renewal despite its biased news coverage and lack of black employees. WLBT later lost its license. Other broadcasters viewed the suit as a signal to hire minorities or confront license challenges of their own.

Meanwhile, Time Inc. had begun offering an annual company-sponsored scholarship to train one minority journalist. The scholarship was not widely publicized to its few black employees and I found out about it only after I was already accepted at the J-School. The scholarship had been granted to another student in our class, Jacob Simms, who was not an employee of Time Inc.

When I told my boss about my plan to attend Columbia, she arranged for me keep my job by working part time with flexible hours while attending the J-School. The school discouraged full-time students from working, but I was able to do both.

Originally, I gravitated to the print concentration, but when I chose the four-week option to learn about television in a program directed by Friendly, I knew I had found what I was looking for. What had seemed so out of reach suddenly became possible.

After graduation, I returned to Time Inc. full time and began my search for a job in television. I also introduced myself to the director of Time's scholarship program, a former president of the United Negro College Fund, to let him know that I had earned a journalism degree without the aid of the company scholarship. Needless to say, he was surprised. He commended me and then asked what a young woman like me planned to do with an advanced journalism degree—and when I planned to get married. I don't think that would have happened today but back then it happened all the time.

When black women got jobs, they saw themselves as a "triple minority—black, female, young," said Valerie Dickerson Coleman Morris, a J-School classmate who after graduation was hired by KRON-TV in San Francisco's Bay Area as a researcher.

With women competing against minorities for jobs, there was a "fear factor," she said. "What if there is room for only one of us? ... There was a bifurcation in the women's movement. White women saw a way via the glass ceiling. Women of color were left with a concrete ceiling."[7]

Figure 4.1: Marquita Pool-Eckert stands before a TV storyboard for CBS Sunday Morning News, where she worked for 16 years, earning 11 Emmy awards. Some African American women worried that they counted as a two-fer, both minority and female. Source: *Courtesy of Marquita Pool-Eckert*

PROVING THEMSELVES AMONG THE BEST

The mandate of the Kerner Commission—along with watchdog civil rights groups and the organizing efforts of minority trailblazers in the 1960s and early 1970s—built a foundation for the next generation of minority journalists.

In 1961, J-School graduate Dorothy Gilliam became the first African American woman reporter to be hired by the *Washington Post*, joining only two other African Americans, both men, in the newsroom. On one assignment, Gilliam impressed First Lady Jacqueline Kennedy with her sharp questions about poor conditions at a city orphanage for black children, and shortly thereafter it was closed.[8]

In her memoir, *Trailblazer: A Pioneering Journalist's Fight to Make the Media Look More Like America,* Gilliam recounts how she became assistant editor of the *Washington Post* Style Section and recruited other talented writers to the paper:

> "I knew the vast and complex black cultural world, which was unknown to white readers, was largely missing from the section, and I longed to help unveil what some called a secret world and make the marvelous culture of black America better known and understood by all races. [Ben] Bradlee finally asked if I would be interested in becoming one of the new assistant editors."[9]

Melba Tolliver titles her forthcoming memoir the *Accidental Anchorwoman*. Tolliver got her break in 1967 during a broadcasters' union strike when ABC News correspondent Marlene Sanders, honoring the picket line, refused to anchor her five-minute network show called *News with a Woman's Touch*.

"ABC Network President Elmer Lower asked if any of the other execs knew a woman who could sub for Marlene," said Tolliver. "I was a secretary, but I had taken acting lessons and won 'Miss New York' in a Summer Festival, so my boss [WABC-TV news director Al Primo] suggested me. He never mentioned that I was black and we never had a discussion about race." That's how Tolliver became the first black person to anchor a network show.

Tolliver was not the kind of person to back down. In 1971, she claimed another "first" when she dared to be the first African American woman reporter to wear her hair in an afro style on a news show—to report Tricia Nixon's White House wedding, no less. WABC-TV's executives "didn't want me to be seen on-camera reporting the story," Tolliver recalled. "They didn't allow me to appear on the set to talk about my story. They even thought I should wear a scarf." Tolliver refused to change her hairstyle or wear a scarf. While her trademark afro hairstyle was eventually accepted, it was not widely copied on air by other reporters.[10]

(Nearly 50 years later, the appropriateness of African American hairstyles is still debatable at some stations. A.J. Walker, a television anchor for the Sinclair Station, Channel 12 News in West Palm Beach, Florida, in 2019 was permitted to wear her braided hair on air for the first time in her career.)[11]

Other African Americans were proving themselves equal to the best. In 1969, Les Payne, who during his Army service had written speeches for General William C. Westmoreland, began making waves at *Newsday*. In 1974, he was part of a team that won a Pulitzer Prize for *The Heroin Trail*, a 33-part series that tracked the narcotics trail from poppy fields in Turkey to the streets of Long Island, New York.

At the *Philadelphia Inquirer*, Acel Moore—who for six years had worked as an editorial clerk before being promoted to staff reporter in 1968—quickly began winning prizes, including the 1977 Pulitzer for local investigative reporting for a series on inmate abuse at a state mental hospital.

The launch of black-owned *Essence Magazine* in 1970, a self-described "lifestyle magazine directed at upscale African American women," also opened doors for black journalists. Marcia Ann Gillespie, a colleague and researcher at *Time*, became managing editor, then editor-in-chief from 1971 to 1980. By 1992, she would be editor-in-chief of *Ms. Magazine*, the first African American woman to hold such a position for a mainstream publication in the United States.

Still, progress was uneven and opportunities for minority reporters did not come easily. In 1972, a group of young black reporters at the *Washington Post*, a white family-owned newspaper in the predominantly black city of Washington D.C., filed a complaint with the U.S. Equal Opportunity Commission (EEOC). "The Metro Seven," as they came to be known, alleged discrimination in hiring and assignments—an action that was the first of its kind and which eventually helped prompt the *Post*, under executive editor Ben Bradlee, to accelerate minority hiring.

African American journalists thought that more progress could be made by pulling together, networking, training, and holding job fairs to promote hiring. In 1975, a group of 44 formed the National Association of Black Journalists (NABJ). Some of the early members recall being told by their employers that they could lose their jobs if they joined, but they were determined. Some, like Les Payne, were less concerned about organizational structure than about progress. "Bylaws? We need to kick some behinds," Payne remembered saying.[12]

HOW I AIRED ANGELA DAVIS' STORY

With some dedicated networking, I landed a position with *Like It Is*, a WABC-TV news and public affairs show that targeted New York's black community. The staff—all African American—was small and the production budget tight, but it provided me with great opportunities to refine my skills and do meaningful work. We were edgy and provocative, and our integrity was tested and proven repeatedly. Sometimes management disagreed with our choice of stories, but nothing we produced was kept off the air. We were a trusted voice for the city's black community.

My first big chance to prove myself came less than a year after I arrived at *Like It Is*. One night during the 1970 Christmas holidays, I was alone in the office, finishing arrangements for the show we were planning to tape the next day. Joe Walker, long-time editor of *Muhammad Speaks* newspaper, came hurrying through the newsroom into our office. He was brandishing the audiotape of an interview that Angela Davis had just conducted with her lawyer, Margaret Burnham, from her jail cell in the New York Women's House of Detention in Greenwich Village.

Davis, a member of the Black Panther organization, who had purchased guns used in a courtroom murder of four people, had been the most wanted fugitive in America, and no one had heard her speak since her arrest two months earlier. Walker knew it was important to disseminate the interview of Davis telling her story to the black community in her own voice as soon as possible. *Like It Is* had to agree to broadcast the entire 20-minute interview, unedited, crediting Walker and *Muhammad Speaks* as our source. I listened to the tape and as de facto producer of the show, I agreed, even though it meant scrapping the show we were set to tape and producing a new show from scratch.

That night my J-School training served me well. As luck would have it, our regular film editor was on vacation. The substitute editor was unhappy about having to stay late to edit an audio interview with the notorious black communist that had no pictures. He protested that it couldn't be done. But thanks to my experience editing our class documentary project, I knew it could be done.

I ordered film from the archives and we went to work. Even though I could not actually touch the editing equipment or the film because of union regulations, I could tell the reluctant editor exactly which frame to cut to sync the A and B rolls of audio and video. He was surprised that I knew how to edit. The atmosphere was tense, and when I walked from our production office to the editing room, little paper American flags mysteriously appeared tacked to the doorways, presumably a patriotic protest against giving Davis unfettered airtime. I ignored them. The interview aired, and our little show made big news. By the time I left in 1974, I had been named producer of the show.

The Angela Davis story was just one of many events at *Like It Is* that demonstrated the value of having a staff committed to presenting stories with accuracy, fairness, and sensitivity to the concerns of the community they covered.

In 1971, *Like It Is* producer Richard Watkins won an Emmy and a DuPont Columbia Award for a documentary about the Attica Prison uprising in which 2,200 prisoners rebelled against poor conditions, taking 42 staff hostages and leaving 43 people dead. The prisoners knew the show was a pipeline to the community they wanted to reach, so during the siege they talked exclusively on an open phone line to Watkins, who was stationed with a camera crew outside the prison.

KERNER: 10 YEARS LATER

In 1977, a "Kerner Plus 10: Conference on Minorities and the Media," organized by Melba Tolliver, was held at the University of Michigan. In his keynote speech, Robert C. Maynard, co-founder of the Institute for Journalism Education, expressed concern about the relatively insignificant progress made by the news media in meeting the minority hiring goals set forth by the Kerner Report a decade earlier. Maynard warned:

> "As much as I might be concerned about the effects of segregation and bigotry in the news on blacks, I am even more concerned about its effects on the whole of our society. This schism to which Kerner referred is indeed a serious matter .... A task force of the Justice Department came out the other day with a new report on Civil Disorders and Terrorism. It said simply that it could find no evidence that the conditions that brought on the rebellions of the 1960s had changed substantially and that we should be ready for another round of the same .... It urged society to consider what measures it would employ in dealing with such rebellions if they should recur, and it surmised that we might want to consider suspending a civil liberty or two during the emergency. It didn't mention the Bill of Rights specifically, but that, I suppose, is the thought on which we should ponder for a moment..."[13]

Martin Gottlieb, a 1969 J-School classmate and award-winning journalist and editor-in-chief who has overseen hiring at a time of increasing pressure for greater newsroom diversity, explained why he thinks newsroom change is difficult:

> "People are protective of their roles. They have succeeded there. They've carved out their spot and want to keep things like they are. I always found that if you came there and were not part of the culture that had been established, it became a very tough place to be. Some people can make it because they have sharp elbows and are willing to ruffle feathers. Sometimes the culture is too much to overcome ... [News staff] contractions leave newcomers very vulnerable, but unions gave protection to those who had seniority, just like colleges use tenure."[14]

By 1975, I had advanced from local TV news to network broadcasting at *CBS Morning News*. Then in 1977, *CBS Evening News* brought me on board as associate producer. It was a thrilling accomplishment to be working for the most highly rated evening news show under Walter Cronkite. The show's producers were hard-driving, competitive, and in the beginning, distant and skeptical of my ability to deliver. At first I was confused and uncomfortable, since they had recruited me from *Morning News*. Also, while I made good friends, I didn't have a mentor.

One day, after I had been at the *Evening News* for about six months, I heard a rumor that my job was on the chopping block. A veteran *CBS News* producer who I didn't know had become executive producer, charged with upgrading the *Evening News* show and its staff.

CBS News had a reputation for leaking stories about impending staff changes before they actually became official. A correspondent I had worked with wished me luck as we passed in the hallway. Another, whose story I was producing for the show that night, said he was sorry to see me go. I was blindsided. I didn't know where this was coming from because no one had spoken directly to me. I didn't have an agent to negotiate for me at that time, so rather than wait for bad news to come to me I approached the executive producer directly. I had nothing to lose. He seemed surprised at my approach and acknowledged he had floated the rumors. In his opinion, I "just didn't belong" there. He thought I wasn't experienced enough to work on the top news show in the country. It turns out he didn't know anything about me. I pushed back, knowing this was my only shot at making my case. I laid out my news experience, how *Evening News* had recruited me, and impressed with my forthrightness, he agreed to "give me a chance" to prove myself. It was a career challenge that never really ended during the 31 years I spent at *CBS News*.

Before every show, around 4:30 p.m., producers who were not assigned a story that day would gather in the Fishbowl (the glass enclosure where the executive producer and senior producers worked) to await the last minute assignment to edit the inevitable late arriving videotape. The first months, I sat on the sidelines, waiting in vain to be tapped for this urgent task. Every other producer got chosen but me. Eventually, one night there was nobody else. Again, I got a break, another chance to show that I could be one of the most skilled producers in videotape.

When Walter Cronkite retired from *Evening News* in 1981 and Dan Rather took over the anchor chair, a new management team arrived. Howard Stringer became Rather's new executive producer. Stringer was popular, accessible, and open to new ideas. I started getting better assignments.

Whenever I could, I produced black-themed stories that gave a more complete perspective and countered the one-dimensional negative narrative that still defined the image of the black community. I won my first Emmy Award for a three-part series I conceived and produced in 1983, *The Vanishing Family: Crisis in Black America*.[15]

Ever ambitious, I really wanted a foreign assignment. I let Stringer know of my interest and a few weeks later he asked if I would like to go to Beirut, Lebanon. Not really. But I knew that legendary correspondents like CBS *60 Minutes'* Ed Bradley and Morley Safer had made their reputations reporting from war zones and they were the role models. If I declined, I thought I might not get another opportunity.

I arrived in Beirut in November 1983, just weeks after a truck drove explosives into the U.S. Marine barracks, killing 241 American service personnel. My colleagues said I was the first woman producer that the *Evening News* had sent to an active war zone. I don't know if that was true, but at the time I did not know of any other women who had preceded me in that position. Martha Teichner was a London-based correspondent assigned to work with my team. As women, we learned to be cautious and courageous at the same time.

Lebanon was a tense, dangerous, place. Car bombs went off at all hours and the camera crews that I managed scrambled toward the sound. Yasir Arafat and his Palestine Liberation Organization (PLO) had sought refuge there in the midst of the Lebanese Civil War. Teichner and I followed Arafat and his entourage as he gave press conferences or visited his wounded soldiers in hospitals. A target for assassination, Arafat moved around at night under cover of darkness. We also traversed the territories of the different Lebanese factions—Druze, Phalangists, Shiite Muslims, and feuding families—names that still dominate the political landscape today. In the Middle East. I learned just how much antipathy there could be between different ethnic groups for generations. Until then I had only experienced the American brand of racial hostilities.

TRAINING, ORGANIZING, PRESSURING

By the 1980s, other efforts were underway to get more minorities into newsrooms around the country. Sometimes it was because watchdog groups exposed inequities, sometimes because of lawsuits. Increasingly, news organizations were realizing that it was in their interest to expand market share by appealing to a wider audience. Training programs and minority news organizations were emerging to better prepare minorities, run job fairs, and help young journalists to network.

One of the oldest minority training programs—the Robert C. Maynard Institute for Journalism Education—was founded in 1977 at the University of California at Berkeley by a group of instructors who had been part of Columbia J-School's Summer Program for Minority Journalists. The program was renamed for Maynard—who bought the *Oakland Tribune* in 1983, becoming the first African American to own a major city newspaper. The institute's commitment to presenting more complete and accurate coverage of communities of color continues by training thousands of journalists, media managers, content creators, and diverse voices.

In 1979, Acel Moore of the *Philadelphia Inquirer* established the Art Peters Fellowship Program, a copy editor internship that launched the careers of over 50 minority journalists. Then in 1984, he created what is now called the Acel Moore Journalism Workshop that trains hundreds of Philadelphia high school students.

Six years after African Americans launched the National Association of Black Journalists, the National Association of Asian Journalists created its own group in 1981, followed by the National Association of Hispanic Journalists in 1982, and the Native American Journalists Association in 1984. The four Associations, later joined by the National Lesbian and Gay Journalists Association, collaborated in 1990 to form Unity: Journalists of Color.

"Many supporters credit the coalition with taking a leading role in diversity efforts at a time when interest was waning," said Paul Delaney, a founding member of NABJ and former reporter at the *New York Times*. "Members of AAJA, NABJ, and NAHJ spoke of ending discrimination, pressuring white media managers to promote their members, ending community stereotypes, and making their employers more cognizant of and sensitive to non-white issues, among other goals."[16] The coalition disbanded in 2018 because of competing visions and lack of funds.

At the *Philadelphia Inquirer*, starting about 1990, Arlene Notoro Morgan, led a minority task force whose goal was that 50 percent of all new hires be minorities. She also cajoled the Knight Ridder newspaper chain, then among the largest in the country, to improve diversity at its other properties, including the *Miami Herald* and the San Jose, California, *Mercury News*.

"At the time," said Morgan, "about 10 percent of *Inquirer* newsroom employees were minority and it was worse on the business side of the company." Within about 15 years, that number had risen to 20 percent of the *Inquirer* newsroom. "It was hard slogging because everyone else was out there recruiting. We were competing with the *New York Times*, the *Washington Post*, the *Mercury News* and others."

"It was about improving journalism," said Morgan, author of *The Authentic Voice: Best Reporting on Race and Ethnicity* and assistant dean at Temple University's Klein College of Media and Communication. "If you want to reflect who lives in your community, it's helpful to have a culture in the newsroom to help you do this, otherwise you're covering people in your own image and likeness," said Morgan whose parents were Italian immigrants. "Hopefully those diverse voices show up in news meetings and can look at a story in its totality. It's about being sensitive to who's in your community."[17]

In 1992, the William Monroe Trotter Group was started by 20 black newspaper columnists headed by DeWayne Wickham, Les Payne, and Derrick Jackson who met to discuss the common challenges writers face when developing their authentic voices. The group, supported by the John S. Knight Fellowships Program and the Nieman Foundation at Harvard, was named for Trotter, an outspoken graduate of Harvard University and civil rights activist who in 1901 founded an independent African American newspaper, the *Boston Guardian*. As Les Payne said at the first Trotter Group meeting, the members are committed to using their work as "instruments for change."[18]

COVERING JESSE JACKSON

In 1984, I was uniquely positioned to cover Rev. Jesse Jackson's first presidential campaign, seen by some as the next phase of the civil rights movement. Coming from Chicago, I was familiar with Jackson and the players in Chicago politics.

As a black person, I wanted to witness and report on the historic campaign and I thought I had the insights to do that well.

While many of the themes of his campaign—including universal medical care, the Equal Rights Amendment, and a wealth tax—are echoed by Democratic and progressive candidates today, Jackson's main issue in 1984 was voter registration: "Hands that once picked cotton will now pick presidents," was a mantra he recited in his stump speech. His campaign spearheaded a drive by civil rights organizations and churches to register more than two million black people to the voter rolls, establishing the importance of black voters to the Democratic Party.[19] Jackson finished third in the Democratic primaries after Walter Mondale and Gary Hart.

Political campaigns were opportunities for journalists. A reporter who covered a winning presidential candidate would often get assigned to the White House press corps. Jackson's press corps included a large contingent of black reporters who were covering a political campaign for the first time. They faced significant challenges. Jackson's prominence created safety concerns and his unexpectedly high vote tallies invited extra scrutiny. But most controversial were two questions that emerged in 1984 and recurred in Jackson's 1988 campaign: Can black reporters who follow a black politician be "objective" about his candidacy? Can they be fair and honest reporters? I don't recall that question being asked of white reporters who followed white candidates.

In addition, some editors were asking a question of Jackson, a black man running a stronger campaign than they had ever imagined and successfully registering growing numbers of black voters, "What does Jesse Want?" "Protest candidate or power broker?"[20]

PROGRESS—BUT NOT ENOUGH

Speaking at the NABJ national convention in 2011, Acel Moore, who helped found the group in 1975, reflected back to that time when "there were fewer than 100 black journalists at the 1,800 daily newspapers in this nation. That 2,500 people are attending this convention is surely a sign of progress."[21] Still, minority hiring in newsrooms did not match the communities they covered, though many reporters of my era had found success.

Nonetheless, a number of minority members of our class had noteworthy careers following graduation.

Valerie Dickerson Coleman Morris, who believes she was the first pregnant anchor in the Bay Area, by 1994 was a financial correspondent with CNN.[22]

Joyce Young Shelby, also a member of our class of 1969, became an award-winning reporter for the *New York Daily News*, where she worked in the paper's

Brooklyn bureau for 22 years until her death in 2009. She was a font of knowledge about the mosaic of Brooklyn neighborhoods and cultures and a generous resource and mentor for young reporters. Shelby shared her reporting expertise by teaching at the J-School for a dozen years.[23]

After a stint at *Time* magazine, classmate Jacob Simms taught journalism at the college level.

L. Priscilla Hall spent a year at the *New York Times* before deciding her personality was better suited to the law. She ultimately became a judge, serving on the Appellate Division of the New York State Supreme Court.

Tammy Tanaka, an Asian American, became a reporter for Religion News Service, an independent non-profit news service subscribed to by news organizations around the country.

I culminated my 31-year career at CBS News as a senior producer at *Sunday Morning*. During that time I received 11 Emmy awards, (six for stories I produced or was part of a winning team and five for *Sunday Morning* stories that I supervised as the senior producer).[24]

Several minorities and women now hold key positions at *CBS News*. Susan Zirinsky, who became its president in 2019, has appointed an ethnically diverse senior management team.

Yet, a controversy over the team of journalists that CBS initially assigned to cover the 2020 Presidential campaign shows there is still room for improvement. Thirty-five years after I was assigned to the Jackson campaign in 1984, CBS in January 2019 announced "the formation of our political embed unit—our boots on the ground for the 2019–2020 election cycle."[25] The line up of eight embedded digital producers and four associate producers did not include a single African American despite the growing number of African American candidates and the growing significance of the African American electorate.

This did not necessarily mean that *CBS News*' political reporting would not be fair and balanced, but the omission did raise questions: Was it no longer considered a priority to include black producers in the diversity mix to help provide a more insightful perspective and interpretation of events? Sometimes, such understanding is a matter of a reporter's experience; sometimes, it comes with a reporter's ability to empathize with the people in the story or have access to principal figures in the story.

Concerned about the diversity issue at CBS, the Congressional Black Caucus met with company executives and issued this statement:

> "As Members of the Congressional Black Caucus, we wanted to express our deep concern about the lack of diversity within the CBS 2020 Presidential Campaign team, which we feel undervalues the increasingly prominent role African Americans continue to play among the national electorate."[26]

The National Association of Black Journalists and other prominent journalists issued similar statements of concern.

After the first announcement of its campaign team, CBS subsequently added two African American producers. *CBS News* Vice President and Washington Bureau Chief Christopher Isham later offered this response: "As we said at the time, the initial list of campaign reporters that surfaced in January was simply the first round of hiring for the digital embeds ... *CBS News* has a deep commitment to diversity which is reflected in the composition of the political unit." As of August 2019, he said, there were 11 embedded digital campaign producers, "a majority of whom are diverse, including two African Americans. Our commitment to diversity extends beyond the political unit with diverse leaders in key editorial and management roles, such as EVP [executive vice president] of News; EVP of Strategic Professional Development; VP of News Operations; VP, National Editor; and the Managing Editor in Washington."[27]

After 50 years, efforts to reach the goals set forth by the Kerner Commission to mirror the general population have still proved challenging. But there has been progress. When the 1968 report mandated that news organizations fulfill their duty to U.S. citizens by broadening their coverage, fewer than five percent of people in editorial jobs were non-white, and of the one percent who held supervisory jobs, most worked for black news organizations.

In 2018, the numbers nationally were much improved. People of color made up 22 percent of print newsroom staff, 24 percent of online news staff, and 25 percent of television newsroom staffs.[28]

The *New York Times* 2018 diversity website indicates that people of color made up 25 percent of its news and opinion staffs, while management in those areas was 20 percent minority, including its executive editor, Dean Baquet.[29]

That contrasted with the U.S. population of about 39 percent of people of color, including whites who identify as Hispanic or Latino.[30]

A Pew Research Center study echoes the data, finding that newsroom staff are still "more likely to be white and male than U.S. workers overall," with 77 percent of newsroom employees in newspaper, broadcasting or internet identifying as non-Hispanic whites. But it also found that younger hires are more diverse, indicating that over time there may be better minority representation in newsrooms.[31]

On the other hand, with the decimation of print newspapers—with thousands of newsroom employees laid off in recent years and the shuttering of nearly 1,800 local newspapers between 2004 and 2018—hiring has been stymied, even as the nation itself becomes increasingly diverse.

U.S. Census projections show that by 2045, the United States will no longer be majority white, and even sooner, by 2027, the minority population under age 29 will become the majority for that age group.[32]

Right now, the millennials' trust in the news media is at an all-time low. However, a plethora of new websites, blogs, and podcasts have been created that would not have been possible 50 years ago, focusing on news for people of virtually any ethnicity. Here, as elsewhere in this brave new digital world, the onus is on the consumer to determine credibility.

The website BlackNews.com lists more than four dozen news websites of particular interest to African Americans; NBC, *HuffPost* and others have their own Hispanic news channels; and AsAmnews.com, among others, is devoted to the Asian American community.

Richard Prince, one of the *Washington Post* "Metro Seven," is now editor of "Richard Prince's Journal-isms," the widely read online media column he started in 1991 for the Maynard Institute for Journalism Education's website. Prince publishes "Journal-isms" independently, tracking the professional movements of African American, Hispanic, and Asian journalists. "I had no idea that what we started back then would evolve into what it is now. It does manage to place in one package all the jobs I've had—reporter, copy editor, diversity advocate, op-ed editor, editorial writer," Prince said.[33]

Also, new opportunities for investigative journalism and collaborations are emerging. The Ida B. Wells Society was founded in 2016. The group's mission is to train and mentor more investigative reporters of color. It honors Wells, a former slave who became a pioneering investigative journalist when she set out to document the rampant lynching of black men in the United States in the 1890s.

New York Times investigative reporters Nikole Hannah-Jones and Ron Nixon, *ProPublica* reporter Topher Jones, and Corey Johnson of the *Tampa Bay Times* are the founders of the society. In an interview, Hannah-Jones, who won a prestigious MacArthur fellowship in 2017, said:

> "There were large swaths of my career where I was warned against writing about racial inequality, where I was warned against focusing so much on the black experience, where I was told I was going to pigeonhole myself, where I was told I was too biased, that I wasn't going to be able to rise up through the ranks .... So the fact that I was able to tell these stories, and also get some modicum of success, is kind of astounding and also feels a bit like revenge to all those folks who told me I couldn't do it."[34]

Where there are challenges, there are also opportunities.

NOTES

1. Virginia Postrell, "The Consequences of the 1960's Race Riots Come into View," *New York Times*, last modified December 30, 2004, https://www.nytimes.com/2004/12/30/business/the-consequences-of-the-1960s-race-riots-come-into-view.html.

2. "The News Media and the Disorders," in *The Report of the National Advisory Commission on Civil Disorders (Kerner Commission Report)*, 1968.
3. James Boylan, *Pulitzer's School: Columbia University's School of Journalism, 1903–2003* (New York: Columbia University Press, 2003).
4. Michelle Clark, a 1972 graduate of the Columbia minority program, was one of the first black reporters to work with CBS. Clark, who was rumored to be working on a Watergate exposé, died in a mysterious plane crash December 8, 1972, when she was traveling with the wife of Watergate conspirator E. Howard Hunt.
5. Randall Pinkston, email to author, March 22, 2019.
6. Sidney A. Shapiro, "United Church of Christ vs. FCC: Private Attorneys General and the Rule of Law," *Researchgate*, last modified June 2006, https://www.researchgate.net/publication/228136875_United_Church_of_Christ_v_FCC_Private_Attorneys_General_and_the_Rule_of_Law.
7. Valerie Dickerson Morris, email to author, January 30, 2019.
8. John Gregory, "Pioneering Journalist Dorothy Gilliam," Kentucky Educational Television, last modified October 31, 2015, https://www.ket.org/public-affairs/pioneering-journalist-dorothy-gilliam/.
9. Dorothy Butler Gilliam, *Trailblazer: A Pioneering Journalist's Fight to Make the Media Look More Like America* (New York: Hachette, 2019), 163.
10. Melba Tolliver, interview with author, January 26, 2019.
11. Richard Prince, Journal-isms, last modified March 8, 2019, http://journal-isms.com/2019/03/taking-seriously-both-black-and-journalist/#Short%20Takes.
12. "The Beginning—NABJ Founders," *YouTube*, last modified August 11, 2015, https://www.youtube.com/watch?v=d5J_3s0P3MU.
13. Robert Maynard, "This Far by Fear," *Nieman Reports*, Winter/Spring 1978, 32, https://niemanreports.org/wp-content/uploads/2014/04/Winter-Spring-1978_150.pdf.
14. Martin Gottlieb, interview with author, April 15, 2019.
15. "The Vanishing Family: Crisis in Black America," *CBS News*, accessed May 10, 2019, https://vimeo.com/73244403.
16. Paul Delaney, "The Death of Unity, Why a Collaboration between Journalists Collapsed," *Columbia Journalism Review*, last modified, March 29, 2019, https://www.cjr.org/first_person/unity-organization-journalists-color-diversity.php.
17. Arlene Notoro Morgan, interview with Dotty Brown, member of Class of 1969, May 3, 2019.
18. Richard Prince, "The Trotter Group, Opening Statement," *journal-isms*, last modified May 28, 2018, http://journal-isms.com/2018/05/william-monroe-trotter-perhaps-the-most-rude-african-american-journalist-this-nation-has-produced/.
19. Arnold Sawislak, "Democrats Spending Big on Voter Registration," UPI Archives, Aug. 29, 1984, https://www.upi.com/Archives/1984/08/29/Democrats-spending-big-on-voter-registration/5624462600000/.
20. Andrew Rosenthal, "As Jackson Rises, Reporters Search for Proper Balance," *New York Times*, last modified April 8, 1988, https://www.nytimes.com/1988/04/08/us/as-jackson-rises-reporters-search-for-proper-balance.html.
21. Cassie Owens, "Acel Moore and the Future of Minority Journalists in Philadelphia," Billy Penn, last modified March 4, 2016, https://billypenn.com/2016/03/04/acel-moore-and-the-future-of-minority-journalists-in-philly/.
22. Valerie Dickerson Morris, email to author, Jan. 30, 2019.

23. Clem Richardson, "Longtime Daily News Brooklyn Reporter, Joyce Shelby, Dead at 62," *New York Daily News*, last modified March 21, 2009, https://www.nydailynews.com/new-york/brooklyn/longtime-daily-news-brooklyn-reporter-joyce-shelby-dead-62-article-1.367768.
24. "Marquita Pool-Eckert," *The History Makers*, accessed on May 10, 2019 https://www.thehistorymakers.org/biography/marquita-pool-eckert-41.
25. "CBS News Announces 2020 Presidential Campaign Digital Journalists," *CBS News*, January 11, 2019, https://www.cbsnews.com/news/cbs-news-announces-2020-presidential-campaign-digital-journalists/.
26. "CBC Meets with CBS News," Congressional Black Caucus, last modified January 23, 2019, https://cbc.house.gov/news/documentsingle.aspx?DocumentID=989.
27. Chris Isham, email to author, August 9, 2019.
28. TV data is from Bob Papper in "2018 Research, Women and People of Color in Local TV and Radio News," Radio Television Digital News Association, last modified June 27, 2018, https://rtdna.org/article/2018_research_women_and_people_of_color_in_local_tv_and_radio_news.
29. "2018 Diversity and Inclusion Report," New York Times Co., accessed on May 18, 2019, https://www.nytco.com/company/diversity-and-inclusion/2018-diversity-inclusion-report/.
30. "Quick Facts United States," U.S. Census Bureau, accessed May 10, 2018, https://www.census.gov/quickfacts/fact/table/US/RHI125217
31. Elizabeth Grieco, "Newsroom Employees are Less Diverse than U.S. Workers Overall," FactTank, last modified November 2, 2018, http://www.pewresearch.org/fact-tank/2018/11/02/newsroom-employees-are-less-diverse-than-u-s-workers-overall/.
32. William H. Frey, "The U.S. Will Become 'Minority White' in 2045, Census Projects," Brookings, last modified March 14, 2018, https://www.brookings.edu/blog/the-avenue/2018/03/14/the-us-will-become-minority-white-in-2045-census-projects/.
33. Prince email to author, March 17, 2019.
34. Taryn Finley, "We Built This: Nikole Hannah-Jones has Raised the Bar for Investigative Journalism," *HuffPost*, last modified February 19, 2019. https://www.huffpost.com/entry/bhm-nikole-hannah-jones_n_5c69adc0e4b01757c36c969e.

CHAPTER FIVE

Politics: Reporting in the Age of Distrust

ALAN EHRENHALT

On February 27, 1968, a few months before the Columbia University School of Journalism's Class of 1969 entered school, Walter Cronkite looked straight at his CBS Evening News audience and delivered an opinion that defined him as a maker of change in American government.

What Cronkite did was declare the Vietnam War unwinnable for his country. "It seems now more certain than ever," he said on the air, "that the bloody experience of Vietnam is to end in a stalemate. The only rational way out will be to negotiate."[1] President Lyndon Johnson, watching the broadcast, is said to have remarked to one of his aides, "If I've lost Cronkite, I've lost middle America."[2]

It's not entirely clear that Johnson actually uttered those words. But the fact that they have been accepted as historical truth tells us a great deal about America in the 1960s—and about the role journalists played in American society. The story attributes to Cronkite, to his network, and to his entire profession a stature and authority utterly incomprehensible half a century later.

The decline in respect for authority over the last generation is familiar to most Americans in one way or another; it has affected once-trusted institutions—from law enforcement and the judiciary to public schools and the Catholic Church. But it has hit political journalism as hard as or harder than most of the other victims. The giants that dominated the journalistic world in 1968 mostly still exist, but not in the way they did then. The *New York Times* and *Washington Post* are seen by most of the politically aware public, whether positively or negatively, as protagonists of liberal public values rather than purveyors of established truths about public questions.

The major television networks reach a small fraction of the audience they did when Cronkite concluded his nightly broadcasts by saying, "That's the way it is." In the years since 1980, evening news viewership on the three major networks has declined from a Nielsen rating of 42 to a rating of 18.[3] *Time* and *Newsweek*, packagers of weekly news and managers of public opinion throughout the second half of the twentieth century, have dwindled to insignificance.

Americans still consume a reasonable amount of political news, but the most intensely interested among them are getting it from sources that reinforce their deeply ingrained values: blogs such as the *Daily Beast* and *Huffington Post* and the cable network MSNBC on the left, Fox News and a multitude of talk radio outlets on the right.

The answer to the riddle of why Americans disagree so angrily about politics may not be that they are interpreting the facts differently, but that they are absorbing rival sets of facts from ideologically entrenched and antagonistic sources. In 2016, millions of Americans who supported Hillary Clinton for president were at a loss to understand how anyone could believe she should go to prison for misfiling her email accounts. But it was perfectly understandable to those who ventured into the precincts of conservative talk radio. Her underlying criminality was a "fact" that right-wing talk radio performers hammered away at every day of the campaign.

The current climate of intense antagonism is one in which the proliferation of diligent fact-checking operations at newspapers and independent websites does relatively little good. These operations do not persuade many of those who have come to distrust mainstream journalism and its efforts to convey factual information. In today's splintered world, it should not be a great surprise that many American voters are more inclined to trust Donald Trump's description of journalism as "an enemy of the people."

A BARGAIN BROKEN

For those covering government and politics, the decline in journalistic authority has been accompanied by another important decline: in meaningful access to the people making news. On Capitol Hill, in the old days, a quiet bargain existed between members of Congress and the reporters representing the major newspapers: The bargain was that the members talked freely to the press in the secure belief that nothing negative about them would appear in print.

On an ordinary news day, it was common to see the congressional correspondent of the *Washington Post* walking arm-in-arm in the Speaker's Lobby with the chairman of the House Ways and Means Committee, or to hear his counterpart on the *New York Times* regale colleagues with tales of golf outings with the Speaker of the House. Less entitled members of the congressional press corps wondered what juicy story the *Post* or *Times* was about to break. The answer, most of the time, was nothing juicy at all. The most prestigious reporters in the press gallery achieved intimate personal access at the cost of maintaining discretion. That was how the system worked. I knew a congressional reporter for the *New York Times* who used to spend much of his day schmoozing with congressional power brokers, then sidle up to me in the press gallery at 5 o'clock and ask if I had anything good for the next day's paper.

The hundreds of congressional reporters who lacked credentials from a top news outlet didn't stroll down the corridor with the Ways and Means chairman or play golf with the Speaker. But they benefited from the age of access in other ways. Until shortly before his death in 1969, Senate Republican leader Everett Dirksen used to saunter into the press gallery, put his feet up on a chair, light a cigarette, and talk frankly about whatever any of the reporters wanted to discuss. It was all "off the record;" rarely did a morsel of Dirksen's wisdom make its way into print.

This age of access is commonly believed to have ended with Watergate, but in the case of Congress, at least, that isn't entirely accurate. Up through the 1970s and into the 1980s, the Speaker's Lobby just outside the House chamber was a goldmine of journalistic access and a remarkable opportunity for political education. The mere presentation of a newspaper business card was sufficient to lure into that lobby the most interesting and best-informed members of the institution. They talked, and they enjoyed talking. The only cost to the reporter was adherence to the rules of "background" or "off the record" disclosures.

Covering the House of Representatives in the 1970s and 1980s with *Congressional Quarterly* and the *Washington Star* was a good way to study not only politics, but human nature. One year, at the start of the congressional session, I obtained an interview with House majority leader Tip O'Neill on the Democratic agenda for the coming months. One by one, the majority leader ticked off a list of issues he wanted the party to pursue. Then he came to one that puzzled me. "There's prison reform," O'Neill said. "When I think of those poor guys rotting away year after year in their prison cells, I know we have to do something about that." I was puzzled because I had never heard about prison reform as a significant congressional topic—it had always been essentially a state issue. But I took the information down. After the interview ended and I was walking down the Capitol corridor to leave, I was accosted by O'Neill's press secretary. "Forget that stuff about prison reform," he told me. "The card said pension reform."

For a long time after that odd episode, well into his ensuing speakership, I underrated Tip O'Neill, considering him an inarticulate party hack with precious little knowledge of the details of legislation or public policy. It took me most of a decade to realize that O'Neill was in fact an effective political leader, one who may have skipped over some of the details but who grasped his members' needs, wishes, and foibles, and understood how to win close votes in sticky situations. I had made a mistake similar to the one that scores of White House reporters were making about Ronald Reagan, a mistake that virtually all of them came eventually to admit.

Spending long afternoons on the Speaker's Lobby sofas during endless and tedious House floor debates, I formed equally firm judgments about some of the other House characters who walked past me and often stopped to talk.

One of the more intriguing new members at the end of the 1970s was a greying but boyish young Republican from Georgia, Newt Gingrich. Gingrich loved to invite reporters to his cramped House office where he spun tales of how he was going to raise the House GOP from its existing status deep in the minority to control of the House and of Congress. He had the whole scenario plotted out on his office blackboard, a detailed presentation of what seemed to me wishful thinking and post-adolescent dreams.

As most of us now know, Gingrich wasn't dreaming. He made those wishes come true. He converted his House Republican conference into a newly aggressive challenger to Democratic hegemony, picking arguments with O'Neill and the other Democratic leaders on the floor, beaming them back on C-SPAN to an enthusiastic conservative audience and laying the groundwork for an intensive effort to recruit a new breed of ambitious Republican candidates. In 1994, they took over the House majority and Gingrich himself became Speaker.[4] I had written Gingrich off as a stimulating charlatan. He turned out to be much more than that.

In 1978, the same year that Gingrich won his first term, Wyoming sent to Congress Dick Cheney, the former White House chief of staff whom many had expected to aim for higher office. Cheney's intellect was unquestioned; what also seemed genuine were his modesty, decency, and friendliness. He would spend time chatting with me in his office about his personal life as well as his political life, his health problems, and our shared delight at being new fathers. This self-effacing man bore no resemblance to the vicious political infighter that he became in his later years as vice president under George W. Bush. Ever since, I have wondered whether Cheney's character and personality had changed over the years, possibly as a result of his several heart attacks and the intensive drug treatments he had to undergo, or whether the intemperate zealotry that marked his White House period had been lurking under the surface even in the early years, waiting for the right situation to emerge.

But of all the members of Congress I came to know in those press gallery years, the one whose memory I find hardest to dismiss is Phil Burton, the endlessly scheming House Democrat from San Francisco. Profane, alcoholic, abusive to practically anyone he didn't like, Burton was also unyielding in his commitments to the environment and social justice. He was a master of the legislative process, perfectly willing to make a deal with enemies he had insulted if that would help him gain what he wanted. If you go back over the roster of Republicans who served on Burton's Interior Committee in the 1970s, you will find that nearly each one has a national park or preserve or lake named after them. Burton had dangled those prizes to win the votes he needed on legislation he desperately wanted.

Burton was also, in his way, accommodating to reporters. When I asked him a question, he would take it seriously and do his best to enlighten me. But first he would issue a warning. "I'll answer your fucking question," he would say, "but I don't want to see it in your goddamned story."

For most of the reporters of that period, discretion of that sort was a small price to pay. Absorbing secrets from the nation's political leadership and agreeing not to divulge them was more than a way for reporters to educate themselves. It lent the entire congressional enterprise an aura of importance and gravitas that it has lost in this current age of aggressive inquiry. In fact, that aura began to disappear not too long after Watergate in the early 1970s. It's true that the investigative reporting of Bob Woodward and Carl Bernstein made the two reporters into national heroes and inspired many in our Baby Boom cohort to launch journalistic careers, but even as that happened the general public's confidence in journalism as an enterprise was starting to decline, along with confidence in other major societal institutions.

Members of Congress still allow themselves to be interviewed, of course, and the number of reporters on Capitol Hill is much larger than it was a generation ago, due in part to the emergence of specialized single-issue publications, most of them digital rather than printed.

But the nature of congressional reporting has changed dramatically. Members of Congress answer questions with what appear to be scripted responses; they are wary of reporters, seem to be on guard against them, worried that anything they say may be spread all over the country in an outbreak of viral spontaneity. Members used to be comfortable speaking with reporters alone, whether in the Speaker's Lobby, in the Senate reception room, or in their offices; today, they nearly always have a press secretary at their side to discourage excessive candor.

If members seem impatient when they emerge to give interviews, it is often for a reason they do not wish to talk about: Even a small amount of time spent with a reporter is time that can't be used for soliciting campaign contributions on the telephone. While at *Congressional Quarterly*, I remember one afternoon in the Senate reception room when I wanted 15 minutes with Senator Alan Cranston of California, the majority whip, who was once among the most accessible of legislators. After a considerable wait, Cranston's administrative assistant came out. "Do you realize," he asked me, "how much money he can raise in 15 minutes?"

Coverage of state government and politics has evolved in a different but in some ways a parallel manner. In the 1970s, nearly every big-city newspaper had a squad of veterans at the state capital with two or three decades of experience on the politics beat. These men ate, drank, and gossiped with the most important political figures in their state, acquired inside information about what was going to happen—and then kept most of it out of the paper. Like their contemporaries in Washington, they valued their relationships with senior political players more than they valued the free flow of sensitive information. Most of them were not under any serious competitive pressure; many were operating in monopoly newspaper markets.

One day in 1974, assigned at *Congressional Quarterly* (CQ) to write about the election prospects of Nevada's governor, "Big Mike" O'Callaghan, I called up the best-connected political reporter in the state, Don Lynch of the *Nevada State Journal*, and asked what he thought. He told me that he had just had dinner with the governor and that O'Callaghan was a shoo-in. That's what I wrote in my article. A few days later I saw a story in Lynch's paper with the headline "Big Mike Safe, CQ says." He was attributing to me information that he himself had provided, hyper-cautiously, on background.

In this century, mainstream media reporting in any state capital has evolved almost beyond recognition. For one thing, there is much less of it. The Pew Research Center found several years ago that the number of reporters covering state capitals had declined by 35 percent in the previous decade; the number has been reduced further since then.[5] Media outlets that cover state legislatures today nearly all do so by sending in a reporter just for the period in which the legislature is meeting. Most of the time, the person sent is a green reporter with limited knowledge of how a legislature actually works. "Many cycle through their states fairly quickly," says one long-time state government analyst. "There isn't a deep command of state political culture."

The 24/7 nature of today's internet news cycle also hinders in-depth political reporting. The reporters who do get to cover a legislature must be adept at multi-tasking—using mobile devices to dispatch a never-ending stream of instant news stories and updates to newspaper websites as legislative issues unfold. They must send along photos and videos from their smartphones, too. Then, in many cases, they must write a longer piece for the next day's print paper. There's little time to engage in old-fashioned research or digging into diverse angles of a story.

Major newspapers have reduced the amount of space devoted to state issues by an amount proportional to the decline in staffing. It's true that more total information may be available than ever, ranging from live broadcasts of floor debates to the multitude of web-based political blogs that are now ubiquitous in every capital. But the audience is the small cohort of politically sophisticated readers who have the time or inclination to follow a legislature closely; these people know more about state politics than they could possibly have known in pre-internet days. The ordinary voters who depended on a mainstream newspaper to tell them about state politics and routine legislative action are mostly out of luck. We have gone from a time in which most people knew a modest amount about state government to one in which a small number of aficionados know a great deal and the rest of the American public knows scarcely anything.

COVERING THE PRESIDENTIAL SWEEPSTAKES GETS PERSONAL

The twin phenomena of declining authority and declining access apply as well to the one political event that still draws saturation media coverage: the campaign for the presidency. Candidates used to possess virtual immunity from disclosure of their personal weaknesses, whether these were weaknesses for women, alcohol, or financial misconduct. Reporters on the campaign trail with John F. Kennedy in 1960 were aware that he was a serial adulterer, but none of them considered disclosing it to the public. Not only were reporters fearful of alienating a presidential candidate, but most of them felt that Kennedy's sexual adventures were a personal matter and ought not to be publicized. Serious presidential candidates possessed a gravitas that the press wanted the public to appreciate. Unmasking personal foibles would not only have been a form of professional misconduct, it would have been an assault on the respect for American democracy that reporters wanted the public to hold, even if they themselves tended toward private cynicism. Discretion on the campaign trail was a gesture of respect for public authority and the democratic process.

It is not difficult to pinpoint the moment when this elaborate system began to fall apart. It was the moment in 1987 when the *Miami Herald* reported that Democratic presidential aspirant Gary Hart, who was married and had two children, was sleeping with Donna Rice, a beauty pageant winner from South Carolina. Hart had insisted he was doing no such thing, but the paper sent reporters and photographers to his townhouse and printed a story about the affair.[6]

The *Herald's* story not only ended Hart's political career, it served notice on all future candidates that nothing in their private lives was off the record. The cloak of respectability that the press had draped over presidential candidates for most of the twentieth century was gone, and it would never return. The fact that Donald Trump was able to win the presidency in 2016 despite a taped confession of sexual harassment did not represent any change in the rules. A better symbol of the nakedness of the modern-day politician is the number of elected officials who have been brought down by disclosures of sexual misconduct in the years since then.

Journalistic revelations of sexual dalliance and inappropriate race-tinged gestures in the last couple of years have brought down several prominent politicians who clearly deserved to be unmasked; they have also ended the careers of others whose transgressions were minor at best. Minnesota Senator Al Franken was forced to resign from Congress in 2018 following disclosure of what appeared to be little more than innocent flirting.[7] Virginia Governor Ralph Northam was urged by dozens of fellow Democrats to resign his office early in 2019 following disclosure of a 35-year-old photograph that appeared to show him in blackface, a photograph for which he apologized.[8] The merits of those episodes are debatable; what is not debatable is the slippery path on which all significant officeholders must now travel in dealing with a polarized and unforgiving political press. They have lost the veneer of protection that the presumption of authority afforded them.

In the old days, authority in presidential campaigns was not only a quality that journalists ascribed to candidates; it existed within the subculture of reporters on the press circuit as well.

Traveling around the country with presidential candidates sounded glamorous, but reporters functioned mostly as glorified stenographers, taking down the candidate's remarks at each conference or rally and reporting them verbatim for their newspaper or TV story. The only difficult job was deciding which remarks in a long day of speeches were the most important ones. But they didn't have to work hard on that decision, either. Reporters could turn to the more senior newsmen on the bus or the plane, find out what they were emphasizing, and file a similar story, knowing in full confidence that nobody would question them.

In 1972, Timothy Crouse wrote in *The Boys on the Bus*, his classic book about election-year journalism, that the most important question for most of the reporters at the end of each campaign day was "What is Walter Going With?"[9] They trusted Walter Mears, the senior political writer for the Associated Press, and whatever Mears led with, most of them led with as well. In many respects, they resembled sheep: They knew it and sometimes resented it, but they accepted the hierarchy and operated within it.

Three years out of journalism school, I learned some valuable lessons in that 1972 campaign year about what well-informed fledgling journalists should and shouldn't do. In the week preceding the Democratic National Convention in Miami, I attended an open meeting of the Arkansas convention delegation. The agenda item was a discussion of whether the delegate selection process in Illinois had been open and fair. One of the Arkansas delegates proceeded to offer an explanation that was inaccurate in almost every respect. I couldn't resist raising my hand. "Wait a minute," I said. "I think I can explain this," and I did. The audience seemed to get it. Then Governor Dale Bumpers stepped in. "Who are you?" he asked. I identified myself as a reporter for *Congressional Quarterly*. "I'm sorry," he told me. "I don't think we can allow you to participate." He was right, of course.

For the most prestigious journalists aboard a presidential plane, there were some much more consequential ways to participate in the process. Every so often, without much warning, a top-level strategist or the candidate himself would walk to the back of the plane, settle into one of the seats, and talk to the assembled newsmen off the record. The contents of the conversation didn't make it into print, but it was a perk that a select group of reporters working for prestigious news outlets considered a form of validation.

This custom essentially disappeared in the 1980s, thanks mostly to Ronald Reagan and his advisers. Reagan did his share of "informal" briefings when he was running for president in 1980, but these were scripted and predictable moments. Since the days of Reagan, few candidates have talked freely to traveling reporters in the fashion of earlier days.

There have been exceptions. Arizona Senator John McCain, running for the Republican presidential nomination in 2000, seemed to enjoy the company of reporters and talked openly to them. He named his traveling entourage "The Straight Talk Express." Eight years later, when he won the Republican presidential nomination, McCain had moved closer to the scripted approach, but journalistic memories of his once free-wheeling access to reporters were responsible in part for the flattering media treatment the senator received for the remainder of his life.

The one candidate of recent years who dared to try the older style was Connecticut Senator Christopher Dodd, who spent a good deal of campaign time in early 2008 hanging out with reporters in the bars of New Hampshire and Iowa. Dodd's openness not only seemed like an anachronism, it proved to be one. He finished seventh in the Iowa caucuses and immediately withdrew from presidential competition.

When it comes to scripting, the presidential nominating conventions are by far the best exhibit. Over the past half-century, they have lost all the meaning they once carried as decision-making political events and exist today as entertainment spectacles, carefully programmed by the candidates and their media consultants. There's little of significance for reporters to report.

This has not prevented the journalistic establishment from taking them seriously, however. In one sense, relatively little has changed. Reporters file stories documenting a week's worth of staged non-events with almost as much intensity as they used to expend on meaningful political maneuvering.

Attendance at the conventions still constitutes a form of validation for reporters whose job it is to cover politics. Not to be invited is, to many of them, an emblem of irrelevance. Long after the conventions became theatrical affairs, news organizations continued to compete ferociously for favorable seating and floor passes that allowed their reporters to roam about the convention floor in search of something to write about. As late as the 1980s, reporters campaigned assiduously for otherwise useless places on the executive committees of the congressional press galleries because those committees doled out convention floor passes and seats. That bizarre competition eventually faded away, but the fact remains that conventions continue to suck up huge quantities of journalistic time, money, and effort almost the way they did when conventions actually produced real political news.

One aspect of convention journalism has changed, however. In the old days, these extravaganzas were notable for the competition they generated among the major television networks. This part of the event has faded with time. Live TV coverage of the sessions used to take up long hours of network time every night during convention week. Now the networks televise only a few speeches that they deem important, leaving C-SPAN to report the rest of the scripted show for the relatively small audience that wants to watch it.

Something similar has happened with television coverage of election night. The major networks still treat the electoral vote count as the genuinely important national event that it is, but the amount of money they spend on the election night telecast is proportionately much less than it was in the 1980s. In those days, broadcast executives believed that the network winning the most critical praise of election night coverage and gaining the largest number of viewers for it would receive a boost in the ratings of its nightly news program that persisted for months after the election itself was over. Thus, they spent lavishly on consultants to monitor obscure congressional contests all through the night. Those days are over. Election nights are still exciting, but they are not the competitive extravaganza they once were.

DIMINISHING IMPACT OF TV POLITICAL REPORTING

It feels quaint these days, and more than a little dispiriting, to recall the stature that television network news possessed back when Walter Cronkite delivered his famous Vietnam rebuke. In the Class of 1969 at the J-School, more students chose courses in broadcasting than opted for the available instruction in either of the two major print categories, newspapers and magazines. The sense that TV news was first among equals prevailed in print newsrooms as well as in journalism education. Every evening at 6:30, editors at the *Washington Star*, where I worked in 1979 and 1980, gathered in front of television sets and learned what the networks were covering, so they could decide which stories their reporters should be pursuing the next morning. The network news, for many in those newspaper newsrooms, marked the end of the day.

Now, of course, there is no end of the day. With the ascension of cable TV, the internet and social media, news has become a never-ending commodity. No significant journalistic operation can afford to go to sleep, ever. At most newspapers, 20-something junior reporters set their alarm clocks for 4 a.m. so they can monitor what the president has been tweeting in the middle of the night. Journalism has lost the daily rhythms that the regularities of the clock once gave it.

And journalists, including those managing the best-known media institutions, have lost the gatekeeper function that they possessed for much of the twentieth century and still possessed when we were in journalism school. Politicians have learned to use social media to communicate directly with voters, bypassing the reporters and editors who used to function as intermediaries, assessing what the general public needed to hear and what was superfluous. In the last couple of years, many of them have learned that Donald Trump is not the only officeholder who can manipulate social media to his or her benefit. Their judgment is that Twitter is a more efficient way to get a message across than spreading it around via newspapers or television networks. Members of Congress who used to meet regularly with the editorial boards of major newspapers are increasingly reluctant to do it—they don't see it as helping them. When these meetings do occur, one veteran reporter says, they try hard not to say anything significant. "Everything is talking points," he notes. "They are totally cautious. They see the media as something to be afraid of."

It would be misleading to close this chapter without recognizing the excellent work still being done by major newspapers such as the *Washington Post* and *New York Times*, and on occasion by the major television networks and cable TV. Over the past two years, they have made the truth about the national scene available to people who care about it and are willing to believe it. Dogged and sometimes heroic reporting is still being done.

But none of that cancels out the fundamental changes that separate the political journalism of 2019 from the product that was produced in 1969. The profession has lost the authority it possessed in the days of Walter Cronkite, and it has lost the routine access to political leaders that it used to take for granted. The result is a disconnect between the press and the public, one of the many troubling disconnects that mark American society in the first quarter of the twenty-first century.

NOTES

1. "Final Words: Cronkite's Vietnam Commentary," NPR, last modified July 18, 2009, https://www.npr.org/templates/story/story.php?storyId=106775685.
2. Joel Achenbach, "Did the News Media Lose the War in Vietnam," *Washington Post*, last modified May 25, 2018, https://www.washingtonpost.com/national/did-the-news-media-led-by-walter-cronkite-lose-the-war-in-vietnam/2018/05/25/a5b3e098-495e-11e8-827e-190efaf1f1ee_story.html
3. Jennifer Maas and Tony Maglio, "NBC Nightly News Suffers Lowest Rated Year Ever," *The Wrap*, last modified September 25, 2018, https://www.thewrap.com/nbc-nightly-news-lowest-rated-year-ever-lester-holt/.

4. Adam Clymer, "The 1984 Elections; Congress the Overview; GOP Celebrates its Sweep to Power," *New York Times,* last modified November 10, 1994, https://www.nytimes.com/1994/11/10/us/1994-elections-congress-overview.
5. "News Just a Few Can Use," *Governing Magazine,* December 2018, 12.
6. Jim McGee et al., "The Gary Hart Story: How it Happened," *Miami Herald,* last modified May 10, 1987, https://www.miamiherald.com/latest-news/article2154781.html.
7. Elana Schor and Seung Min Kim, "Franken Resigns," *Politico,* last modified December 7, 2017, https://www.politico.com/story/2017/12/07/franken-resigns-285957.
8. Caroline Kelly, "Virginia Governor Apologizes for Racist and Offensive Costume," last modified February 7, 2019, https://www.cnn.com/2019/02/01/politics/northam-blackface-photo/index.html.
9. Timothy Crouse, *The Boys on the Bus,* paperback edition (New York: Random House, 2003).

CHAPTER SIX

International Reporting: A World of Difference

MICHÈLE MONTAS-DOMINIQUE

Michèle Montas-Dominique, a Haitian journalist and 1969 graduate of the Columbia University School of Journalism, recounts here her views on 50 years of change in the coverage of international news. She also asked four other members of her class who reported from abroad to share their reflections. Their experiences follow her story.

On November 19, 2018 and during several months in 2019, the *New York Times* ran an ad in response to President Donald Trump's accusation that the press was the "enemy of the people." The ad, part of a "truth matters" campaign, said, "Securing one more interview . . . . Braving intimidation. Reporting from multiple angles . . . Understanding the world. The truth is worth it."

But how we get to that truth in trying to understand the wider world is a difficult undertaking. News bureaus abroad are shrinking. Covering international stories has become increasingly dangerous. The immediacy of digital news has pushed investigative journalism further to the sidelines. An interactive world of bloggers, social media sites, and citizen journalists is now for many people, especially the young, the main provider of news.

Has our understanding of the world been enriched, become more accurate? Has the journalism profession—as we defined it 50 years ago when people watched a daily 30-minute capsule of the news on one of three major networks, read one or two of the major newspapers, and felt they understood the world—changed for the better?

Countless studies from professional organizations highlight the financial restraints that have forced most of the traditional media to restrict their coverage of international news; endless analyses show the changes that the internet revolution brought to our profession.

My experience as an independent radio journalist trying to report in Haiti at a time of repression is a window into the difficulty—indeed, the danger—that reporters face in their efforts to reveal what is truly happening. That work over the years has become even more challenging as news organizations cut back or eliminate overseas staff and the resources needed to support them.

MY TAKE: CRISIS REPORTING FROM HAITI

It was July 17, 1979. Anastasio Somoza DeBayle, the Nicaraguan dictator and last member of a dynasty that had ruled the country since 1936, was overthrown in a popular revolt led by the Sandinista National Liberation Front. I was a broadcast journalist in Port-au-Prince, Haiti, where I returned after graduation from the Columbia University School of Journalism.

Reporting for Radio Haiti, an independent station under the Duvalier dictatorship, my husband and I and our staff knew that any openly critical or simply fact-based coverage of the Haitian regime was risky business.

But when Jean Claude Duvalier succeeded his father after 15 years of complete censorship, we tried to expand the limitations on local and national reporting, using international news as a cover of sorts. For our newsroom, such coverage opened indirect forays into political reporting of our own national situation and became, as such, incredibly popular with our audience. Reporting on the reasons for the fall of Anastasio Somoza became "proxy reports" on our own political situation. The daily dispatches from our correspondent in Managua at the time were front-page news as Somoza was forced to flee Nicaragua.

We also were reporting extensively on the demands of the Carter administration in the United States that human rights be respected in Nicaragua as elsewhere in Latin America. We could not touch on similar pressures from Washington for the liberation of political prisoners in Port-au-Prince. But that would soon catch up with us.

On November 4, 1980, after our station held a four-hour special newscast on the U.S. elections, we announced the defeat of incumbent Jimmy Carter and the landslide victory of Ronald Reagan to the presidency of the United States. Ten minutes later, armed gunmen came to the street below our studios, celebrating loudly with gunshots volleyed into the air, shouting in creole, "Human rights are over, cowboys are back in power."

The larger impact would come less than a month later when all our reporters were arrested, Radio Haiti's studios destroyed, and my husband, journalist Jean Dominique, and I were sent into exile in the United States. I feel strongly that

Figure 6.1: After the assassination of her husband, with whom she ran Radio Haiti, Michèle Montas-Dominique (right) became spokesperson for U.N. Secretary General Ban Ki-moon (center). In 2009, they are joined by former President Bill Clinton in a visit with school children in Cité Soleil, Haiti. Source: *UN Photo/Eskinder Debebe*

the coverage of our ordeal in the U.S. media got us out of jail and saved many lives. The burgeoning Haitian news media fell silent until the Duvalier regime was overthrown in 1986, and then bloomed again until the following military coup in 1991.

In 2000, my husband Jean Dominique was assassinated. After an attempt on my own life in 2003—when my bodyguard was killed protecting me—I closed the station and fled for the United States. It was my third exile. For the next 16 years, I worked in public information at the United Nations in New York City.

Our struggle in Haiti for a free press is in no way unique. The dark clouds over freedom of the press have, in fact, accumulated with the rise of authoritarian regimes world-wide. Not only is it increasingly difficult to learn the truth of what is happening abroad, but some rulers today often use President Trump's rhetorical attacks on "fake news" to justify the arrest of foreign reporters or the crackdown on local media.

SHRINKING INTERNATIONAL COVERAGE IN THE U.S. MEDIA

The U.S. mainstream media once shed an intense light not only on wars the country was fighting, but also on many events and issues outside its borders. That was essential to the way an informed public perceived the world, and it also considerably impacted public policy. How has that changed?

Today, as an intense consumer of news, I read three major American mainstream dailies; I follow cable news and the major networks' evening news broadcasts; I am bombarded on my smartphone with news alerts and "breaking news." Paradoxically, however, I find myself and people around me less informed than 30 or 40 years ago about an increasingly connected world.

The costs of keeping American correspondents across the globe and the diversion of advertising dollars to digital sites have forced many media to reduce their footprint abroad drastically.

Essentially, because there is notably less coverage of the world with the exception of a handful of newspapers and broadcast media, most news comes in small capsules from wire services; some regions are completely ignored. To get to "the truth" and "understand the world" often takes considerable work and time, digging into digital editions of foreign media or into an array of blogs and multiple sources on the borderless net.

While the U.S. was involved in seven wars[1] in 2019, we know amazingly little of the context of so many events that seem to pop up with no warnings. It took the killing of four American soldiers in Niger in 2018 for the public in the U.S. to learn of the deployment of 800 U.S. soldiers in that country.

At the end of February 2019, India and Pakistan, two nuclear powers, were on the brink of war and President Trump was heading to another meeting with North Korea over its nuclear arsenal, yet an array of pundits were on CNN discussing President Trump's mood in his latest Twitter posts, which had nothing to do with nuclear threats.

According to *American Journalism Review*, at least 20 U.S. newspapers and other media outlets shut down their foreign bureaus between 1998 and 2011.[2] The majority of U.S. newspapers, radio, and television stations now rely on international wire services like the Associated Press, which still has 250 locations in 100 countries.[3]

Another change has been the increased concentration of newspaper ownership in the hands of large conglomerates where profit is the focus. Their assumption is often that the public's appetite for serious foreign news is limited: A terrorist attack in Afghanistan or Nigeria would not sustain the reader's interest for long, nor would it sustain the commitment of publishers and editors to cover the cost of more extensive reporting.

Digital journalism has also to a great extent changed the way the news is relayed by the mainstream media itself, with the increasing use of blogs and social sites like Facebook or Twitter. This has created additional pressures on correspondents, forced to be constantly updating content.

As a majority of millennials now get their news through the internet, digital natives like *GlobalPost*, *Huffington Post*, *Vice* or *BuzzFeed* have expanded their international footprints.

The shrinking number of correspondents on the ground has meant an increased reliance on local journalists, a change that my classmates who worked as foreign correspondents find positive. As foreign bureaus have been shrinking, these local voices—reporters or "citizen journalists"—are too often the only ones with the immediacy of on-site smartphone videos on hand during an uprising and in far corners of wars. The videos and posts of citizen journalists were the only news coming out of Syria during the vicious crackdown on pro-democracy protests by the Assad regime in 2018.

Every year, the Maria Moors Cabot Prizes at Columbia University are awarded to four journalists from the Americas for exceptional and courageous reporting. During the nine years I served on the prize board, I witnessed important changes—first in the decrease in the number of journalists covering Latin America for U.S. newspapers, but also the evolution from an emphasis primarily on print to the increased importance of digital media.

June Carolyn Erlick is board chair of the Cabot Prizes and editor-in-chief of the news magazine *ReVista: Harvard Review of Latin America*. We asked her about the changes she has seen since she was bureau chief for *Time* magazine in Managua in the 1980s, which also was the period when the news in Nicaragua was the top headline in our broadcasts at Radio Haiti. Erlick said:

"There's another reason beyond the budget crisis, and that's technology. A reporter (or editor) can talk to a dozen sources about a breaking news story through Twitter; a reporter can conduct a lengthy interview over Skype, or get some questions answered over e-mail. One can read today's newspapers from a foreign country on the internet or check out what people are saying on Facebook.

"I remember waiting for hours in Managua to get a call through to neighboring Costa Rica. When I was in Colombia, I had no way to track what was going on in Nicaragua except through long-distance calls, telex, and letters . . . Nothing beats being on the ground in real time to report a story, but before blaming the dearth of foreign bureaus on very real budget cuts, we also have to look at the role of the revolution in technology. . . . Good journalism is still being done, but there's not the penetration and knowledge that newspapers could provide us with 20 years ago.

"Fortunately—and again technology plays a role—anyone interested in a particular country gets provided with multiple sources through the internet. I can read *Confidencial* and *El Faro* online, and I can read what many U.S. and European newspapers have to say about Nicaragua, for instance."

A shift has occurred from the seasoned correspondent, knowledgeable about the social and political context of the country he or she covers, to correspondents based in a few major capitals.

Today, you are more likely to read a story on the recent presidential elections in Congo, for instance, with a Paris or London dateline. As bloody crisis points have multiplied around the world, the coverage of international news seems to have gotten increasingly lopsided. The deaths of thousands of civilians killed in Yemen or hundreds kidnapped in Nigeria or Colombia are barely mentioned in the media while a terrorist act in Europe will still get intensive coverage.

This is not always for lack of good reporting. A former correspondent for the *New York Times*, who covered in 1997 the civil war in Zaire (today's Democratic Republic of the Congo), expressed his frustrations to me. So many stories written on the ground never see the light of day once back at headquarters, where the main priorities are most often entertainment, sports, and local politics, he said.

Most of the Third World remains in the dark or is covered with the same old biases, as Karen Rothmyer describes so vividly below. Her concerns echo my own. Reading the rare stories in the U.S. media about my home country, Haiti, I never can escape the one liner —"the poorest country in the Western Hemisphere"—no matter what the subject is, reducing a difficult struggle for democracy and economic justice to that simple, hopeless tag.

KAREN ROTHMYER: ON STEREOTYPING AFRICA

When our two adult sons came to visit Kenya a few months after I went there on a fellowship in 2005, I took them for a walk around the center of Nairobi. I showed them the parliament buildings, the coffee shops where I met with friends, and the big indoor market where you can buy everything from flowers and vegetables to woven baskets and beaded necklaces.

After we got home, I asked them their impressions. They were surprised, they said, not to have seen a single beggar or emaciated child.

I was dismayed. Here were members of my own family, to whom I'd been writing in detail about life in Kenya's bustling capital, whose expectations had nonetheless been shaped primarily by what they were reading and hearing in the U.S. media. The news they had been absorbing was about famine and war, not the rapid increase in shopping malls catering to middle-class Kenyans, or the latest scandals and successes of Kenya's pop stars.

Their reactions told me a lot about what is wrong—and has been wrong for a long time—about U.S. coverage of Kenya and Africa as a whole. From what I've observed first-hand—first as a Peace Corps volunteer in the 1960s, and then during 10 years in the 2000s during which I taught journalism, consulted at a Nairobi newspaper, and occasionally wrote for *The Nation*—the shortcomings of foreign coverage of Africa go well beyond journalists' natural tendency to focus on "bad news."

The first problem is that most white foreigners come to Africa with a set of assumptions based on outmoded and often racist views. These are constantly reinforced by books and films in which white Westerners are the main (and usually heroic) protagonists, while Africans are, at best, supporting players.

Such accounts have a long and disturbing history. The earliest European voyagers to Africa returned home with reports that portrayed Africans as shrewd traders and skillful bargainers. But, as American academics Dorothy Hammond and Alta Jablow documented in a 1970 study, once the slave trade got under way, the need to justify it led to a distinctly different tone and content: "African behavior, institutions, and character were not merely disparaged but presented as the negation of all human decencies," they wrote.[4]

The second problem with coverage of Africa, which I explored during a semester at Harvard's Shorenstein Center in 2010, is that foreign correspondents' perceptions are largely shaped and then reinforced by the narratives spun by aid organizations. This is a case where the shrinking of international newsrooms in recent years has made a bad situation worse.

It's in the interest of such aid groups, which began their explosive growth in the 1970s, to paint Africa as full of misery, since—as some of them in candid moments admit—more misery equals more donations. "When you're fundraising you have to prove there is a need," the head of one large U.S. non-profit organization told me. "Children starving, mothers dying. If you're not negative enough, you won't get funding."

Lauren Gelfand, whom I met when she was a correspondent for *Jane's Defence Weekly* in Nairobi, told me that when she took a year off from journalism to work for the global antipoverty non-profit Oxfam, she found that most reporters were stretched too thin to do time-consuming stories. "If reporters were going to cover a development story, it had to be easy," Gelfand said. The simplest sell, she said, was a celebrity visit to an aid project.

Daniel Dickinson, a former BBC reporter who later became a communications officer for the European Union, told me that, "The big difference in the past five to ten years is the expansion of the internet," which demands a constant supply of new material. Add to that the growing financial constraints, he said, and "more and more [journalists] are taking the content we offer them."

It's more than lack of time and resources that leads to poor reporting; it's also the proclivities of the journalists themselves. Martin Dawes, a UNICEF official for West and Central Africa, told me that foreign journalists often came to him or his colleagues but ignored African officials. "It means that the chances of Africans to show an engaged response is limited," he said. "They are written out of their own story."5

I doubt that significant change will occur in coverage of Kenya or any other African country until they become economic powerhouses like China or South Korea.

Recently, I read in Kenya's leading daily paper about how the demand in East Africa for technical training is so great that South Korea's Advanced Institute of Science and Technology is setting up a graduate-level sister university in Nairobi. It was the kind of story that was unlikely to be picked up by foreign correspondents—and it wasn't.

For now, though, the past is still the present. Thinking about changes in foreign reporting about Africa over the past 50 years, I am forced to conclude that there haven't been many. Yes, there have been some outstanding and sensitive foreign journalists. But the fundamental fact remains that for most Americans, journalists included, Africa is still the "Dark Continent"—a place of heroic Western aid workers and starving Africans, with dollops of corruption and witchcraft thrown in. And until that changes, foreign reporting is going to remain, at best, inadequate.

SYLVANA FOA: MISSING ADVENTURES, NOT ASSASSINATIONS

The life and work of a foreign correspondent has changed drastically over the past 50 years. In many ways I miss the romance and adventure of the life I led covering war, coups, floods, earthquakes, and assassinations around the world.

But, honestly, I'm glad to be out of the business. Being a foreign correspondent just isn't as much fun anymore. The job of a foreign correspondent has become incredibly stressful. The excitement may still be there, but the quality of life has deteriorated significantly.

When I was abroad, we filed day leads for the afternoon papers and night leads for the morning papers. But when your last story was sent to the telex office, you could head to the opium den or the bar without worry of being scooped.

No more.

The new communications technology makes it possible to file written, audio, and video reports in real time. The explosion of 24-hour media outlets on cable TV and the internet has created an insatiable 24/7 news cycle that constantly demands more and more, and newer and newer material. Every newspaper has a website and expects their correspondents to keep it updated.

Today, if you are on assignment overseas, you are on call 24 hours a day. You do not have a life. And there are other, uglier ramifications. The competition has become even more cutthroat. The rush to get stories out first erodes a correspondent's ability to ignore rumor and meticulously check the facts. The insistent demands for new information and instant analysis diminish reporters' capacity to put stories in context.

Another drawback of journalism today is the increasing likelihood of death. It is one thing to have spent the night in a ditch with bullets whizzing over your head, to have dodged stones thrown by a rioting mob, to have nearly choked to death on tear gas, and to have stumbled upon a corpse with its throat cut on your office doorstep. It is another to get killed.

When I began my journalism career in 1970 as a stringer for *Newsweek* in Saigon, more experienced hacks taught me two important rules of the game. The first was to always walk down the middle of a road in a war zone because the shoulders were probably mined. The second was immediately to learn the words for "journalist" and "press" in the local language.

Both rules stood me in good stead, and I emerged from years of conflict reporting with only two small shrapnel wounds and the ability to shout "press" in a dozen languages—from Arabic and Khmer to Vietnamese and Farsi.

Neither rule is much help today as more and more frequently journalists are not the accidental casualties of conflict. They are the targets. The Newseum Journalists Memorial (newseum.org/journalistsmemorial) highlights—with names, photos and biographies—many of the thousands of men and women who have died doing their jobs. About half are journalists killed covering war. Others were murdered while reporting equally risky stories—investigating corrupt Russian oligarchs, Mafia murders, Latin American drug lords, human trafficking, and man's inhumanity to man.

Journalists are constantly reminded, "No story is worth getting killed for."

Veteran correspondents like to think they are immune. Take Kurt Schork, a widely admired Reuters correspondent. Schork had reported on conflict in Bosnia,

Kurdistan, Chechnya, East Timor, and Kosovo before he went to cover the civil war in Sierra Leone. All that experience was not enough to keep him alive. Schork and cameraman Miguel Gil Moreno de Mora, with the Canadian national news organization APTN, were gunned down in May 2000, bringing to 12 the number of journalists killed covering the fighting in Sierra Leone.

It has not stopped. Among those murdered since Haitian journalist Jean Dominique, husband of my classmate, Michèle Montas, was assassinated in 2000 when he refused to stop criticizing the government:

- Daniel Pearl, a correspondent for the *Wall Street Journal*, was brutally beheaded by Al-Qaeda operatives in Pakistan in 2002.
- Freelance journalist James Foley was kidnapped by ISIS in northwestern Syria in 2012 and beheaded nearly two years later.
- Marie Colvin, a correspondent for the *Sunday Times*, was covering the siege of Homs in February 2012 when Syrian government forces tracked her cell phone signal and shot a shell packed with nails directly at her location. She died together with French photographer Remi Ochlik.

It is getting worse at an alarming rate. In 2017 and 2018 alone, 121 journalists died doing their jobs, according to Reporters Without Borders. The majority were murdered. The vast majority were citizens of the country where they were killed. And that is the third reason I am glad to be out of the foreign correspondent business.

Today, my chances of getting a well-paid overseas assignment would be minuscule. Few media organizations can afford the expense of maintaining internationals abroad. After graduating from the J-School in 1969, I flew to Saigon on my own. By the next morning, I had talked myself into a job and a spot on the *Newsweek* masthead. After a few years of stringing for *Newsweek* and United Press International, both offered me full-time jobs. *Newsweek* offered Atlanta at a hefty salary. UPI countered with Hong Kong at starvation wages. I took Hong Kong.

Today, if either news organization still maintained foreign bureaus, they would just hire a local journalist.

In the legendary days of 50 years ago, every big newspaper, wire service, news magazine, and television network had foreign bureaus in major cities around the world. Today, those bureaus are few and far between. Even the wire services are cutting back drastically.

This is because most media outlets, newspapers in particular, are struggling financially as advertisers decide they get more bang for their buck on the internet. The first casualties, when the going gets tough, are the travel budgets for overseas correspondents. Then they cut the correspondents and hire local talent. Then they close their foreign bureaus altogether and rely on reports from freelancers, blogs, and even tweets.

Local journalists are much cheaper to keep on staff. In every foreign bureau I have ever worked, the internationals were extremely dependent on local staff. The locals provided translation during interviews, their expertise gave perspective to each story, they advised on the reliability of sources, and through their own contacts, they opened doors through which no foreigner could have passed.

In most cases, local journalists are young, energetic, and ambitious. The only real drawback is that, for the most part, they are writing in a language that is not their mother tongue. That is why media organizations have desk editors ... oh, right, they are being cut too.

Fifty years ago, many editors were reluctant to byline "foreign" names. They did not think their readers would trust a story written by a local. My byline was regularly Americanized to Sylvia Fox or simply omitted. This was particularly true when I was reporting from Southeast Asia. Then some editors were sure my byline was a misspelling of Souvanna Phouma, the prime minister of Laos.

This has changed. Today, more and more of the bylines one sees in the best newspapers are those of a local staffer. That is a change for the better, and news organizations that recognize the value local journalists bring to their reports should be saluted. That is easy for me to say, because I am no longer looking for a foreign assignment.

KENNETH TIVEN: CNN'S REACH AND RETREAT

At the end of the twentieth century, the idea of expanding American-style broadcast news around the globe burned bright on the 14th floor of CNN's Atlanta headquarters. Ted Turner wanted CNN to lead the way. CNN's success with the coverage of the fall of the Soviet Union, with the end of the Berlin Wall, and with the first Gulf War coverage from Baghdad had convinced Turner and his team that quicker distribution and growth were available outside the USA, because in America the penetration of cable households was not in their hands.

At the urging of my boss, Burt Reinhardt, then vice chairman of CNN, I flew to Turkey from Germany where I was helping manage NTV, a German news channel, also a joint venture with CNN. At the time I was CNN's go-to man for joint news ventures outside the United States. I had already done projects in Australia and Spain as well as Berlin. Our Turkish partners were having difficulty agreeing on how to get started. Reinhardt told me to make something happen NOW.

Which is how I found myself in the kitchen of Mehmet Birand's Istanbul home in early 1999, a large sheet of brown kraft paper covering the table. With a black marker, I listed the things to do and outlined the systems that would work best for a faultless launch to move the project, called CNN Türk, from theory to actual television broadcasts. Birand enthusiastically agreed, and urged about 10 of his senior staff to ask questions. When the meeting finished, Birand had everyone sign the paper.

Birand, who died in 2013, was famous in Turkey as a courageous journalist. He started working initially for newspapers owned by the Dogan Group, which was the partner in this television venture and was at that time NTV's designated managing editor. In the late 1970s, turbulent political times in Turkey had led to a military dictatorship under which the news media suffered. At that point in his career, he had been arrested and jailed. It did nothing to dim his belief that a journalist had an obligation to question officials at every level about what they did. He was tough as nails but equally charming on camera and off.

We organized CNN Türk around a workflow that had considerable quality control and clear responsibilities, unusual for Turkish media of that time. The launch party was a gala event. In retrospect it was the high point of good relations between the media and the government. Over the next two decades in Turkey and elsewhere around the world, increasingly right wing and repressive governments have harassed and pressured media companies and reporters to write what the government wants people to read and hear.

In Germany, NTV hired former East German journalists who had grown up in the Russian system, but several of them had difficulty reporting without being told first what to report in substance and tone. My experience creating news channels in Germany, Turkey, Spain, Bulgaria, Serbia, India, Pakistan, Uganda, Nigeria, Kenya, South Africa, Madagascar, and Australia taught me that in many societies younger journalists are too respectful—afraid perhaps—to ask questions considered difficult or even rude of leaders in politics, business, or social organizations. This inherent "distance" means that critical reporting goes undone.

After the launch of CNN Türk, we had instances where the Turkish government wanted us to shut down the channel for a week as a penalty for breaking one or more obscure rules based on the Turkish constitution's prohibition on anything that disrespects the nation. I cannot speak for what has happened since I left after the first year, but CNN Türk has been a frequent target of government displeasure.

"The United States has traditionally been a beacon of press freedom and defender of journalists, but a barrage of anti-press rhetoric from President Trump undermines the role of the press in a democracy and potentially endangers journalists," says Robert Mahoney, deputy executive director of the Committee to Protect Journalists. "Labeling reporting you don't like as 'fake news' sends a signal to authoritarian leaders globally that it's OK to crack down on the press."[6]

Authoritarian regimes and global conflicts have turned journalism into a deadly pursuit, almost as dangerous as being the security guard for cash in a transit truck. Nearly 2,300 journalists and media staff were killed between 1990 and 2015, according to the International Federation of Journalists.[7] Another indicator of attacks on the "free press" are the hundreds of journalists who have been arrested or detained for doing their jobs. Turkey is a leader in doing this, as is Eritrea.

Equally troubling, the media is cracking down on itself because of diminished revenue from the impact of business shifting to online advertising. Newspaper revenue from website operations hardly makes up for the print losses, especially in classified advertising. Advertiser revenue paid for the product and made publishers in many situations very wealthy. That has precipitously crashed with the shift to digital advertising.

Media companies reflexively cut staff to save money, meaning less content in the product to cause people to buy it. Among the first people to go in many instances are the correspondents operating away from the home office. Dependency on the Associated Press is hurt because as the name implies, it depends on its newspaper and TV clients for help. This is the classic downward spiral.

When it comes to coverage of key places outside the U.S., fewer and fewer media organizations have meaningful numbers of reporters at work there. It goes downhill from here because newspaper circulation has cratered in some nations and is slipping everywhere else.

That does not mean there is less "news" consumption because lots of information is available on smartphones and the internet. However, as the U.S. election of 2016 demonstrates, this is not information produced by any agreed-upon standards of journalism. This information may do more damage than good in explaining to an electorate the impact of the decisions it might make.

We all understand that the digital information revolution changed many things. Perhaps we did not completely recognize the unintended consequences for democracy.

TERRY WOLKERSTORFER: ON TELLING THE TRUTH

Three months after graduating from the J-School, I was on the overnight foreign desk of the Associated Press at 50 Rockefeller Plaza, editing dispatches from Vietnam. A few months after that, I joined the AP's Saigon bureau.

It was, I believe, one of the great journalism teams of all time. My colleagues included reporters like Peter Arnett, Richard Pyle, and George Esper and photographers like Horst Faas, Henri Huet, Hugh Van Es, Dang Van Phuoc, and Nick Ut. A bunch of them either had won, or would go on to win, Pulitzer Prizes.

In the years since, I have asked myself more than once, "Why would a reasonable man or woman (and there were women) want to do such a thing?"

I think there are two answers: First, Vietnam was the biggest story in the world. How could you call yourself a journalist and not want to be there? And

Figure 6.2: Terry Wolkerstorfer, reporting from the Parrot's Beak of Cambodia in 1970, eyes weapons that came down the Ho Chi Minh trail intended for use by Viet Cong troops in South Vietnam. As an AP reporter, he helped break the story of the U.S.-South Vietnamese "incursion" into Cambodia. Source: *Courtesy of Terry Wolkerstorfer*

second, I believed in the American people's right to know what was going on. I thought I could help tell the truth.

And we did try to get at the truth and to tell it, even when that made the generals in Saigon and the politicians in Washington unhappy. In the end, I think we made a difference.

Some years after the war, my friend Lt. Gen. John Cushman, then retired, took me to his luncheon club in Annapolis, Maryland, where I discovered that all the members were retired generals and admirals. When I was introduced as someone who had served in Vietnam as both a soldier and a journalist, one old general pounded on the table and shouted: "Fucking media lost the goddamn war!"

I guess it depends on your point of view.

From a journalist's point of view, it was what my late friend Richard Pyle—who served as AP bureau chief in Saigon and Tokyo and as a correspondent in the Middle East during the Gulf War—called "the golden age of war reporting."

We had access, transportation, functional communications (the AP bureau had a closed-circuit teletype link to New York), and a complete lack of military or government censorship. Essentially, we could go anywhere and report on anything.

News reports and photos could appear in American, Asian, and European newspapers within 24 hours of the event—TV reports within 48. That may seem slow in the digital age, but it gave news reports from halfway around the world an immediacy and an impact they never had before. Ordinary people had the war at their breakfast tables and in their living rooms.

It wasn't just the golden age of war reporting, it was the golden age of international reporting in general. Major newspapers, magazines, and TV networks were rolling in cash and it was prestigious to cover foreign news with your own staff. Some enlightened editors and news directors saw it as their responsibility to inform readers, listeners, and viewers of international developments. And some even saw it as a potential attraction for audiences.

The result was that major American news organizations developed a global network of bureaus, mostly staffed by U.S.-based reporters. That, of course, all changed with the explosion of news sources on the internet, and the redirection of advertising dollars. As my classmates have pointed out, the result is that news budgets get cut, staff gets cut, bureaus get closed, and international news becomes a smaller piece of the daily news budget.

Major media companies, many of which took seriously their responsibility to nurture an informed citizenry, are now to a very large extent owned by corporations whose interest in media is purely financial.

As one of our J-School classmates put it some years ago, "Unfortunately, the news business is becoming less about news and more about business." When the owner's primary concern is the bottom line this quarter and the stock price this week, then the focus becomes giving the people what they want to see or hear—not what they need to know to be productive citizens. Hence, more entertainment, more sports, less news. Particularly less international news, which is the most expensive to produce.

There's also a political element: "America First" means less need to know what's going on in the rest of the world, especially as others see it. And President Trump's constant denigration of the mainstream news media has given dictators around the world the sense that it's perfectly OK to crack down on honest reporting in their countries.

As Karen Rothmyer and Sylvana Foa point out above, one positive element in the budget cutting and bureau closing is that many American news organizations now rely on local reporters rather than foreign correspondents. They're cheaper, of course. But they're better informed, they have better sources, they're more likely to understand things from the local perspective—and they look like the people they're reporting on.

One of the downsides, however, is that much foreign reporting, especially in the most dangerous and complicated situations, is now being done by young and relatively inexperienced freelancers and stringers with little preparation and almost no support—not even, in many cases, medical insurance.

Because those young writers are the future of foreign reporting, efforts are underway to improve their training and support. Mary Stucky, founder of Round Earth Media, is leading the way. She's training aspiring journalists in programs in Morocco and South Africa, pairing them with local reporters, and getting their stories broadcast or published both in the country where they're working and in the U.S.

Also through Round Earth Media, young American professionals are being paired with journalists in Latin America. Two of them recently won the prestigious Peabody Award for radio reporting.

In a partnership between the University of St. Thomas in St. Paul, Minnesota, and PBS's *NewsHour*, called the "Under-Told Stories Project," veteran correspondent Fred de Sam Lazaro and young associate producer Simeon Lancaster do just that: visit far corners of the world to tell stories most of us have never heard about.

So there's hope for those of us interested in international news.

MICHÈLE MONTAS-DOMINIQUE: IS THE PHOENIX RISING?

We are at a time of incredible challenges as technology transforms journalism, bringing instant news from the far corners of the world to within our reach at a time when intelligent context is desperately needed to "understand the world." Will the media, paradoxically, become an added casualty of the present political climate, turning increasingly inward?

From his post at the publication *India Legal*, Inderjit Badhwar, another member of the J-School Class of 1969, does not see it happening. He writes in the Indian magazine *Outlook*, ". . . mainstream American media, under vicious attack from political forces and a president who dubbed it the 'enemy of the people,' has arisen like a phoenix from a long slumber, all guns blazing, gaining traction and credibility."[8]

And with that in mind, my wish is for a young correspondent abroad to be told one day that the truth he or she covered matters. Or, as the retired general put it to Terry Wolkerstorfer, years after the Vietnam defeat: "Fucking media lost the goddamn war!"

NOTES

1. Conflicts where the U.S. is launching extensive military incursions include Afghanistan, Syria, Libya, Somalia, Niger, Yemen and Pakistan. American Special Operations deployed in 149 countries in 2017 according to Tom Engelhardt, *The Nation*, January 4, 2018.
2. Priya Kumar, "Foreign Correspondents: Who Covers What," *American Journalism Review*, last modified December/January 2011, https://ajrarchive.org/article.asp?id=4997.
3. Mya Frazier, "Rethinking Foreign Reporting at the AP," *Columbia Journalism Review*, last modified February 19, 2019, https://www.cjr.org/business_of_news/the-associated-press-foreign-reporting.php.
4. Dorothy Hammond and Alta Jablow, *The Africa that Never Was: Four Centuries of British Writing about Africa* (Twayne Publishers, 1970), 21–23.
5. Interviews with Lauren Gelfand, Daniel Dickinson and Martin Dawes are all in Karen Rothmyer, "They Wanted Journalists to Say 'Wow,'" Joan Shorenstein Center on the Press, Politics, and Public Policy, last modified January 2011. https://shorensteincenter.org/wp-content/uploads/2012/03/d61_rothmyer.pdf.
6. Graham Ruddick, "Global Press Freedom Plunges to Worst Level this Century," *The Guardian*, last modified November 29, 2017, https://www.theguardian.com/media/2017/nov/30/press-freedom-at-all-time-low-journalist-safety-article-19-v-dem-study?CMP=twt_gu.
7. "IFJ 25th Report on Journalists and Media Killed," International Federation of Journalists, 2016, 6, accessed May 18, 2019, https://www.ifj.org/fileadmin/user_upload/25_Report_Final_sreads_web.pdf. For other organizations that track journalist and media staff deaths, with varying numbers depending on methodology, see the International Press Institute's "Death Watch," https://ipi.media/programmes/death-watch/; the Committee to Protect Journalists, https://cpj.org/data/; and Reporters Without Borders, https://rsf.org/en/barometer.
8. Inderjit Badhwar, "That Eighties Scoop Show: Indian Journalism Needs a Shot of the Past," *Outlook*, last modified October 30, 2018, https://www.outlookindia.com/magazine/story/that-eighties-scoop-show-indian-journalism-needs-a-shot-of-the-past/300826.

CHAPTER SEVEN

Criminal Justice: The Journey from "Give Me Rewrite!"

TED GEST

Many Americans formed their image of police and court news reporting from *The Front Page*, the classic comedy set in the pressroom of Chicago's Criminal Courts Building. The 1928 play features hard-drinking, poker-playing reporters competing for the latest scoop on a jailbreak and other crime news of the day. But that old-timey, smoke-filled scene was due to change in the 1960s as the nation, its politicians, and its reporters began grappling with rising crime rates.

Crime, of course, has always been a favored topic of the news media. "Allowing for changes in language usage, there is a continuum in crime reporting from the penny press era of the 1830s to the yellow journalism of 1900 to the jazz journalism of the 1920s to the tabloid TV-tinged journalism of the 1990s," wrote crime reporter David Krajicek in *Scooped! Media Miss Real Story on Crime While Chasing Sex, Sleaze, and Celebritie*s.[1]

Barry Goldwater, in his unsuccessful presidential bid of 1964, was among the first to make crime a headline of his campaign. In his acceptance speech at the Republican National Convention, the conservative Arizona senator vowed to make "enforcing law and order" a priority, saying he would "do all that I can to see that women can go out on the streets of this country without being scared stiff." Goldwater was talking about the beginning of a huge modern-day rise in crime in the United States that first became evident in the decade of his candidacy.

To give a sense of the scale, about 160 violent crimes were committed per 100,000 people in 1960, according to an annual Federal Bureau of Investigation count of crimes reported to police departments. That rate steadily rose to 758 per

100,000 at its height in 1992 amid urban strife over drug dealing. Even with the widely reported decline in violent crime since that time, by 2018 the rate still stood at 369 per 100,000 people, more than double the 1960 total.[2]

With this striking increase in victimization, it was not surprising that reporters increasingly focused on crime when I started my career after graduating from the Columbia University School of Journalism in 1969.

POLICE REPORTING—A REWRITE JOB

Like most journalists, I didn't start out with the dream of being a police reporter, but being put on the police beat was something of a ritual for new reporters. Many local newspapers would assign newcomers to the crime beat, partly on the theory that it would give them a crash course on the city they were about to cover. The idea was that they would quickly learn local geography and where the dangerous and safe areas could be found. Besides, it was seen as a rookie assignment.

My work started in my hometown, St. Louis. Typical of big cities at the time, St. Louis had two newspapers, the morning *Globe-Democrat* and the afternoon *Post-Dispatch*.

I was fortunate to land a job at the *Post-Dispatch*, the paper founded by Joseph Pulitzer, whose bequest helped establish the Columbia J-School in 1912. It was an afternoon newspaper—still owned by the Pulitzer family—with its story lineup for the day's paper put together starting at 4 o'clock each morning. (I later served as an assistant city editor starting at that hour, which I blame for a lifetime of rising early.)

The newspaper published three editions, with the first copy deadline at 8:30 a.m. This meant that reporters had only a few hours to put together stories from news releases, police reports, and other sources. One of the prime sources was the competing *Globe-Democrat*, many of whose stories we would rewrite after making a quick check for accuracy.

My arrival at the *Post-Dispatch* coincided with the establishment of a night staff to prepare stories that had emerged since the last edition of the previous day's newspaper. I was assigned to that crew, which covered a disproportionate number of crime stories.

The paper long had been based in downtown St. Louis, but an increasing amount of news was being made in the growing suburban areas, especially a sprawling jurisdiction called St. Louis County, which comprised nearly 90 independent municipalities and a vast unincorporated area. That's where I was assigned a year or so after my night staff stint. One of my jobs was to track crime. The main challenge was that there were several dozen police departments to monitor. One of them was Ferguson, which was just another of many suburbs back then, but

Figure 7.1: Ted Gest pounds on a typewriter as an assistant city editor at the *St. Louis Post-Dispatch* in the 1970s, in the era before computers. He has no recollection of why he was wearing a helmet but assumes that's why a passing staff photographer snapped the picture. Source: *Courtesy of Ted Gest*

which became infamous world-wide in 2014 when one of its police officers fatally shot unarmed black teenager Michael Brown in the street on a Sunday afternoon, prompting riots and national demands for police reform.

Back in the 1970s, well before the internet, I found that reporters were operating in ways reminiscent of the *Front Page* era, but it was not so colorful as the smoke-and-liquor-infused Chicago Criminal Courts Building. Our typical coverage of crime in St. Louis County consisted of reporters from the *Post-Dispatch* and the *Globe-Democrat* sitting in a tiny office in a government building, periodically phoning a list of police departments and asking what news had come up since a previous call several hours earlier.

It was a remarkably poor way to cover crime, but we were forced to do it. There was no way that any one reporter could personally visit dozens of police departments daily in an area of 523 square miles, far larger than the adjacent city of St. Louis, which is only 66 square miles.

We were dependent on the departments telling us about news, using their own definitions. Frequently, whoever answered the phone at a local police department would withhold information, presumably on the grounds that the latest violent crime still was under investigation. (I have wondered whether, if a Michael

Brown-type shooting had occurred back in the 1970s, the Ferguson Police Department would have disclosed it promptly to a reporter calling from several miles away).

Even if a police department mentioned a newsworthy incident (and in those days it was most often an auto accident involving a fatality), it was difficult to prepare a good story by telephone. Most often, a police dispatcher was merely reading a report written by someone else, which could not convey vivid details and often not even accurate facts. On a truly major story, reporters and photographers would be sent from downtown St. Louis to the scene, but that was unusual. Most of what passed for crime reporting in those days was based on second-hand accounts. Often adding to the confusion, we suburban-based reporters would then phone in the reports to "rewrite men" (and a few women) downtown, meaning that details could be lost or mangled in the process.

My experiences in St. Louis County were hardly unique. J-School classmate Dick Riley tells similar tales from his days as a reporter for the Associated Press, where he worked nights at the police "shack," the second and third floors of a building over a gun shop on Center Market Place in lower Manhattan, directly behind police headquarters on the border between Little Italy and SoHo. (Press operations outside the home office were often referred to as "shacks," whatever their location or physical description.)

Riley recalls that the night-side shack crew in the 1970s consisted of a former railroad cook working for the *New York Post* who routinely pretended on the phone that he was from the *New York Times* (the cops despised the then-left wing *Post* as a Commie rag); the real *New York Times* reporter, who rarely opened the door of his office and whose workload was light (the *Times* typically covered crime out of their main offices, then in midtown Manhattan on West 43rd Street); and the *Daily News* reporter, known as "the Inspector" because he dressed, acted, and often impersonated a high-ranking officer, right down to the miniature Inspector badge on his tiepin.

"This is Doyle from downtown," he would bark into his phone all night long, calling precincts around the city when a potentially newsworthy crime and its location appeared on the police teletype.

Riley, who worked at the shack periodically, never saw a female reporter in the office during his time there, though women later would become a routine sighting there. In fact, women rarely were assigned to night shifts at all, even in the central office.[3]

Better reporting of crime news was possible in cities with a centralized police department where reporters could talk to key officials face to face, but the coverage-by-phone routine was typical in U.S. journalism. It still is necessary a half-century later in many places, given that there are about 18,000 police departments around the nation and a shrinking number of reporters covering them amid layoffs and newspaper closings in the twenty-first century.

Most of us in those days focused on individual crimes, the primary job of reporters on the police beat, but as crime rates increased in the 1960s and 1970s so did public interest in policy issues surrounding crime and what might be done to reduce it. Many Americans were afraid of being victimized, partly because of the non-stop media coverage.

The federal government became more involved with what had been almost exclusively a local issue. After Goldwater talked about crime in his presidential campaign, President Lyndon Johnson appointed a commission to study criminal justice and Congress passed a law in 1968 that set up an agency in the Justice Department to help states and cities deal with crime.[4]

As a cub reporter, I assumed the beat of covering a new entity in the St. Louis area called the Law Enforcement Assistance Council that decided how to spend a new pot of federal aid. This effort intensified when the Justice Department designated St. Louis a "high impact" city that would be given $20 million to test various anticrime strategies.

It was an eye-opening experience for me as I sat in meetings with officials from across the criminal justice system discussing how they could improve their operations. This was far different from interviewing a police officer about a single criminal case, as interesting as that crime might be. Now I was learning first-hand that the criminal justice system really wasn't much of a system as the public probably believed. On the front end, the police weren't necessarily coordinating what they were doing very well with the prosecutors, judges, probation officers, and prison wardens who would have to deal with cases that started with an arrest and ended, most often, in a jury conviction or guilty plea.

While it was absorbing to see from the policy perspective how the justice system really worked—or didn't work—it was frustrating to write about criminal cases through a "rewrite" process that hadn't changed from the *Front Page* days. And as a member of the newspaper's night staff who had told my editors that I was interested in the courts, I was doing just that, taking phone calls from two veteran reporters who covered the federal and state courthouses. These reporters did not write stories themselves. Rather, they would dictate highlights to reporters like me who would actually do the writing. Clearly, much was lost in translation, sometimes even basic facts.

I recall getting a story from one reporter in which the first name of the main subject, a figure in a criminal court case, didn't establish the person's gender, probably a name like Pat or Terry. I was chagrined the next day when I saw that the headline on our item mentioned that a man had been sentenced while the *Globe-Democrat* reported that it was a woman. I don't recall either paper ever publishing a correction and I don't know which headline was accurate.

More broadly, the public wasn't served very well by seeing stories that weren't written by the person who actually reported them.

Perhaps the low point for me came one afternoon in early 1970 when I got a call from our federal court reporter saying he had a good story for the next day's paper: a judge he was covering was named that day to the U.S. Supreme Court. Unlike today, Supreme Court vacancies were not topics of intense speculation, with the news media publishing lists of possible nominees. So I thought that my colleague must be joking. It turned out that he wasn't. Harry Blackmun of Minnesota, a judge on the U.S. Court of Appeals for the Eighth Circuit based in St. Louis, had been chosen by President Richard Nixon for the high court.

Our reporter had spoken briefly to Blackmun, who was at the courthouse that day, but the conversation produced nothing substantive to write about, just a vague statement that he was pleased to be nominated. We had a major national news story but lacked the background on Blackmun and his judicial philosophy. (Blackmun promptly returned home to Minnesota and editors had to dispatch a reporter to do a proper story about his nomination.) I complained to the city editor that we had failed remarkably to cover this important story in our home town. I said I'd be interested in taking over the federal court beat and doing a better job.

It took two years, but I got my wish and started that job on May 1, 1972 after the long-time reporter who had covered Blackmun retired. The next day, FBI director J. Edgar Hoover died and I had my first chance at a big story for which I sought out recollections of the legendary lawman from local agents.

Covering the courts was both exhilarating and tiring. I was responsible for keeping track of news in two large buildings, the federal courthouse and the Civil Courts Building across the street, which housed not only many state trial judges but also the state court of appeals. Long before the efficiency of the internet, the job was somewhat haphazard, requiring me to cover interesting trials as well as flip through new court cases and judicial rulings as they were filed. It was easy to miss a story if a blockbuster lawsuit was filed just minutes after I made a routine check, I would just have to pick up on it later.

Yet, there was a clear advantage to walking a beat before the internet: you talked to sources in person, from judges to clerks to FBI agents to prosecutors. Now, by contrast, it's possible to follow U.S. Supreme Court opinions and those in many lower courts by computer, writing stories about rulings with no human contacts.

Unlike my predecessor, who didn't really know Harry Blackmun, I made it my business to get to know judges as well as I could, frequently popping into their chambers to chat about cases and other developments. I understood that these conversations were off the record. Once I got to know judges and they saw that I would report responsibly, they would confide to me when and possibly how they were likely to rule on a major case so that I could be prepared for it.

This kind of inside knowledge paid off when one of the judges I knew well, U.S. District Judge William Webster, was appointed director of the FBI by President

Jimmy Carter. He didn't give me any national security secrets, but I had good access to the FBI when I later was stationed in Washington, D.C.

For five years at the *Post-Dispatch*, I spent my days trying to dig up stories on general trends in the law as well as covering individual cases. It often wasn't easy, but I made it a point to write my own stories when I could and not depend on the problematic rewrite process. Soon after I started covering courts, we were able to use telecopiers, which were first marketed in the 1960s as an early version of what are now called fax machines. Because it took about four minutes to transmit one page, I was able to keep up with the machine, typing a new page and feeding it to the device before the telephone connection was broken. The result was much better journalism, allowing me to report on the context and nuances of cases in a way that usually couldn't be done by talking to a reporter in the main office on the phone.

Because telecopier transmission was unwieldy, at the end of most days I traveled to the newspaper's main office, about six blocks away, to write my stories for the next day's paper. It made for some very long days, with sometimes as many as seven or eight stories to file. Some I had reported during the day for earlier editions of the paper, so I had to come up with a "second-day lead"—some angle that I hadn't featured in the original story.

The prevalence of computers and smartphones has made the process of journalism much easier, even as the availability of fewer reporters to cover more news has increased the demands of daily work.

THE POLITICS OF CRIME

In the 1970s, most Americans got their crime and justice news from local newspapers and television if they were not experiencing it in their personal lives. Crime was always a big topic of local news, but there was relatively little national news about the rising problem. Things began to change in the mid-1980s, when the crack-cocaine epidemic focused attention on the role of drugs in violent crime. Wars among urban drug dealers helped fuel a sharper increase in the national crime rate that peaked in the early 1990s.

By that time, I had moved to Washington, D.C., to report for the weekly newsmagazine *U.S. News & World Report*, where I paid attention to national trends. After a stint covering Jimmy Carter's White House, I began covering "legal affairs," which the magazine defined as including the Justice Department and the Supreme Court. Partly because of my background in St. Louis, I followed what government officials were doing about crime, much of which revolved around major crime bills passed by Congress between 1984 and 1994.

Crime policy was becoming much more of a political issue at all levels. In 1988, Vice President George H. W. Bush defeated Massachusetts Governor Michael

Dukakis for the presidency, partly on the strength of mocking Dukakis' policy of giving weekend furloughs to prisoners like Willie Horton, a convicted murderer who committed a brutal rape while on such a release in 1987.

Four years later, Bill Clinton saw that a crime-fighting platform could make him a winner. He made a federal project to hire 100,000 local police officers a major plank in his successful 1992 run for the White House, defeating incumbent Bush. Clinton's ascendancy came at just the time when crime totals in the U.S. were reaching their highest levels ever.

It wasn't the raw numbers but a series of horrible incidents that focused attention on the problem. In his review of media crime coverage, crime reporter David J. Krajicek traces the furor to the kidnapping of Polly Klaas, 12, from her California home during a slumber party in 1993.

It's the kind of crime that rarely happens, but when it does, it strikes fear in the mind of any parent. The saturation coverage of the case on network television "had a huge influence on national opinions about crime," Krajicek wrote.[5]

Then came a public mass shooting of the kind that was still rare in late 1993, when an armed man walked through a commuter train on Long Island, killing six and wounding 19.[6]

One result of these and other dramatic crimes was a series of magazine cover stories on the issue. *Business Week* wrote on the cost of "rampant crime" in December 1993, quickly followed by *Newsweek, U.S. News* and *Time*. My contribution was a cover story for the January 17, 1994 issue of *U.S. News* headlined "Violent Crime: What You Really Need to Fear." (I plead guilty to helping continue the trend, writing a cover story for the March 25, 1996 issue, called "Crime Time Bomb.")

Journalists were at the center of the action as politicians competed to say what they would do about street crime in what was then the height of the "tough on crime" era. This continued through the 1996 presidential campaign, when incumbent Bill Clinton and challenger Bob Dole fought over the "war on drugs." (I wrote a story in our September 30, 1996 issue headlined "Popgun Politics. Both candidates are laying claim to the crime issue, and neither is playing it straight.")

Reporting on individual crimes, as journalists mostly did in the decades before the 1980s, was fine if they got the basic "who, what, when, where, and why" correct. Insightful reporting on crime and justice should go much farther, trying to assess the underlying causes of various crime problems and what might be done about them.

Such explanations actually baffle many of the experts, including academics who spend their professional lives studying crime. It is difficult to come up with cogent explanations for many crime trends, so criminologists frequently cite a combination of factors, such as demographics (a higher or lower number of young people in the population who commit a disproportionate number or crimes), street wars over markets for popular drugs, economic conditions generally, the ups and downs of organized gangs, or the availability of firearms.

By the time of the crime rate peaked nationally in the early 1990s, few reporters could claim to be experts on the issue. One result was that journalists depended almost entirely on local police chiefs to interpret crime trends. Not surprisingly, the chiefs were quick to take credit when crime rates in their areas dropped, but when crime was on the rise, they typically cited factors beyond their control, like demographics or the economy.

The news media tend to report uncritically the views of political leaders on many public issues, crime prominently among them. So it was in the 1990s that news stories repeatedly discussed calls for more police officers, more prisons, and ideas like sending accused juveniles to adult courts where they would be treated more severely. It was during this period that the "three strikes" movement grew rapidly, with states passing laws that required life terms behind bars after a third criminal offense.

It is impossible to say for certain what role the news media played in the adoption of what turned out to be questionable anticrime policies, many of which were being re-examined in the first two decades of the twenty-first century, when it was common for critics to declare that the "criminal justice system is broken." What is clear is that several organized efforts emerged to improve the quality of reporting on crime and justice issues.

I had attended one of those efforts in the fall of 1996, when the Ford Foundation, the Edna McConnell Clark Foundation, and the *Columbia Journalism Review* co-sponsored a national conference for journalists and experts to discuss the state of knowledge about crime and justice with the goal of improving media coverage. I volunteered, along with Krajicek, to continue working on the national issue of covering crime. With several others at the conference, we formed the organization called Criminal Justice Journalists which I have headed starting from its beginning in 1997 to the present. It has included several hundred reporters nationwide and an advisory board of 15 journalists.

The group assumed control of a Listserv called Cops and Courts Reporters, where journalists can post queries and exchange coverage tips. It has sponsored dozens of panel discussions, often in conjunction with the national group, Investigative Reporters and Editors, and others.

In 1998, a group of investors started a website called APBNews.com (short for "All Points Bulletin") devoted to crime coverage. The site had ambitious plans, spending an estimated $1 million per month and hiring 140 staff members. APBNews produced good journalism, winning seven major awards in 1999 and 2000, but it folded in June 2000 when its investors balked at spending more money after a crash of the high-tech NASDAQ stock index.

In 2005, I worked with Jeremy Travis, then president of the City University of New York's John Jay College of Criminal Justice, to establish a Center for Media, Crime and Justice in an effort to create a permanent hub for journalists interested in this subject. The center then started a website called *The Crime Report* (www.thecrimereport.org), which incorporated a daily news digest on criminal justice developments nationwide that I had launched independently in 2003. Over the years, the center has held training programs for more than 1,000 journalists on a wide range of subjects. It also has given annual awards for coverage of criminal justice topics by print media.

Another criminal justice journalism effort was launched in 2014 when journalist and later hedge-fund manager Neil Barsky started a website called *The Marshall Project* (in honor of former Supreme Court Justice Thurgood Marshall). The website in its first five years produced many notable stories, including one that won a National Magazine Award, employed 27 full-time journalists as of 2019, and has attracted about 100 significant funders.[7]

Both *The Crime Report* and *The Marshall Project* helped propel coverage of criminal justice as a specialized subject apart from occasional reports in newspapers, TV, magazines, and websites.

A BROADER LOOK NEEDED

Covering individual crimes and crime trends is just part of the crime beat reporter's job. The entire justice system is a much broader subject, including bail, prosecutors and defense attorneys, the courts, jails, prisons, probation and parole, and sentencing. Another major topic of reporting should be the "collateral consequences" of involvement in the justice system—the negative impact on defendants' abilities to be educated, find jobs, housing, and medical care.

Relatively few reporters make a career out of covering police agencies, and even fewer have specialized in courts and the corrections system, meaning that news coverage over the decades has ranged from sporadic to non-existent, absent a major scandal or prison riot. As just one example, many journalists don't know the difference between jails and prisons, a mistake frequently made in headlines even by major news organizations. (Jails house pretrial defendants and those sentenced to short terms in custody, usually year or less; prisons house longer-term convicts and usually provide many more programs collectively known as rehabilitation.)

As internet news flourished and traditional print newspapers and network television broadcasts struggled to retain readers and viewers in the second decade of the twenty-first century, the overall state of crime and justice news reporting was something of a contradiction. On one hand, a greater volume of news about criminal justice was available than ever before for those who want to search for it in both the mainstream media and on such websites as *Slate*, *BuzzFeed*, and the *Huffington Post*. On the other hand, local newspapers that once had reporters routinely hanging out at police stations and courthouses were doing less enterprise reporting. This means that in many states and regions, the public does not know how well or how badly criminal justice systems are operating because reporters are not there to investigate.

One area where journalists have played a major role in recent times is reporting on cases of wrongful convictions. A National Registry of Exonerations sponsored by three organizations counted more than 2,400 wrongful convictions in the U.S. as of 2019.[8] Many stories of such injustice have been brought to light by newspapers, magazines, and websites. One organization that has specialized in this field is the Medill Justice Project, founded at Northwestern University's Medill School of Journalism in 1999. The center, which in 2019 was incorporated into a new organization called the Medill Investigative Lab, has sponsored research in 18 states and Washington, D.C.[9]

One significant flaw in coverage of criminal justice, however, involves the age, race, and gender of the victim. The annual murder total in the U.S. in the last 50 years has ranged from about 15,000 to nearly 25,000, according to the Federal Bureau of Investigation. The news media takes note of only a small fraction of these cases, greatly favoring those involving young, female, white victims and perpetrators over those involving poor blacks. Northwestern University sociologist Zach Sommers was quoted in the *Washington Post* in 2018 as saying that such stories are "a natural trope" in American society, a variation of the classic "damsel in distress" tale that has been reinforced by movies, books, and culture.

As Sommers sees it, "white viewers and readers may think, 'that could be my daughter, my sister, my neighbor.' There's a built-in emotional attachment."[10] Among such victims have been Chandra Levy, an FBI intern who vanished in Washington, D.C. in 2001 and whose remains were eventually found in Rock Creek Park, and 14-year-old Elizabeth Smart, who was abducted from her Salt Lake City home and managed to escape nine months later.

IS CRIME OVER-REPORTED?

What have we learned from five decades of journalism in an era of high crime rates? One thing is that crime remains one of the most covered topics in U.S. journalism. There are no precise numbers on crime news in any medium, but Krajicek reports that as of the late 1990s, crime news made up about one-third of the content of daily newspapers and as much as half of local television newscasts.[11]

Andrew Tyndall, whose Tyndall Report has monitored the three major television networks' evening news broadcasts since 1988, calculated that at the peak of the modern crime wave in the early 1990s, the three broadcasts devoted 2,500 minutes to the topic per year. That number had declined to 1,616 minutes by 2018—about 200 minutes more than were devoted to foreign affairs coverage. Still, crime and justice-related stories were the most frequent subjects of the top 20 stories in terms of minutes, also exceeding the ever-popular and visual topics of the weather and wildfires.[12]

It is difficult to say exactly what impact this deluge of coverage has had on the public, but it seems evident that over time, the drumbeat of crime news has made many people more fearful and has exaggerated the level of violence nationally.

For many years, the Gallup survey has asked Americans if there was an area within a mile of their home where they are afraid to walk at night. Nearly half of respondents said "yes" in the peak year for positive responses to that question, 1982. The number had declined to about 30 percent by 2017, after many years of the crime rate itself actually falling.[13]

When Americans are asked whether the problem of lawbreaking is getting worse nationally, they regularly respond that crime is rising even while government data show the opposite. An analysis of 22 Gallup surveys about national crime between 1993 and 2009 —years when crime rates were declining—found that 60 percent of respondents in 18 of those surveys said crime had gone up the previous year.[14]

Pew Research Center surveys found a similar pattern. In late 2016, 57 percent of registered voters said crime in the U.S. had become worse since 2008, even though FBI and U.S. Bureau of Justice Statistics data show that violent and property crime rates dropped by double-digit percentages during that period.[15]

What could the media do to provide better crime and justice coverage? The best and most doable option in an era of tight news reporting resources might be to supply more context to readers and viewers, such as distinguishing between crime rates in specific neighborhoods and those of the community as a whole. The national obsession with rankings, partly driven by my own former employer *U.S. News & World Report*, has included the nation's "most dangerous cities" lists, which do not drill down to neighborhoods and give a false impression of some cities as a whole. Another problem is the media's tendency to give prominence to "bad news," such as an increase in crime, rather than giving equal or greater play to a decrease.

What difference does it make if the public thinks crime is worse than it really is?

Psychologists Paul Thibodeau and Lera Boroditsky of Stanford University write that the news media tend to talk about "crime waves, surges or sprees. A spreading crime problem is a crime epidemic plaguing a city or infecting a community. Crimes themselves are attacks in which criminals prey on unsuspecting victims. And criminal investigations are hunts where criminals are tracked and caught."[16]

Over the years, politicians have tended to respond to such views by enacting punitive policies that have resulted in the world's largest prison population and a high rate of new crimes committed by inmates who have spent years behind bars with few attempts at rehabilitating them.

How crime is portrayed also may exacerbate racial stereotypes. According to The Sentencing Project, a criminal justice reform organization, "Many media outlets reinforce the public's racial misconceptions about crime by presenting African Americans and Latinos differently than whites—both quantitatively and qualitatively. Television news programs and newspapers over-represent racial minorities as crime suspects and whites as crime victims."[17]

There are signs that public views are moderating. For example, fewer Americans support capital punishment and more back attempts at helping inmates re-enter society successfully. Some of the changed public opinion must be attributable to different and improved media coverage, but popular views have not changed radically.

The sad fact is that basic, day-to-day news coverage about crime remains much like it was when I started covering the beat some five decades ago: an unrelenting string of stories about acts of violence, many of them now embellished by video.

It is heartening that the nation's overall crime problem has subsided since the bloody 1990s. It is disheartening that in many respects, the news media's treatment of the issue has not kept pace.

NOTES

1. David J. Krajicek, *Scooped! Media Miss Real Story on Crime While Chasing Sex, Sleaze, and Celebrities* (New York: Columbia University Press, 1998), 71.
2. "Crime in the United States 2018," Federal Bureau of Investigation, accessed November 24, 2019. https://ucr.fbi.gov/crime-in-the-u.s/2018/crime-in-the-u.s.-2018/topic-pages/violent-crime.
3. Dick Riley, excerpt from unpublished essay written for Columbia Journalism School Class of 1969, 50th reunion, 2019.
4. For most of its early existence, the agency was named the Law Enforcement Assistance Administration. See Ted Gest, *Crime & Politics* (New York: Oxford University Press, 2001), 20.
5. Krajicek, 20.
6. Krajicek, 21. Colin Ferguson committed these crimes on a commuter train on Long Island on December 7, 1993.
7. The Marshall Project, accessed May 14, 2019, https://www.themarshallproject.org/.
8. The National Registry of Exonerations, accessed May 14, 2019, http://www.law.umich.edu/special/exoneration/Pages/about.aspx.
9. Medill Justice Project, later Medill Investigative Lab (no website as of November 2019).
10. "Colorado Murders Signal a Return of the News Media's 'Damsels in Distress' Trope," *Washington Post*, last modified August 21, 2018, https://www.washingtonpost.com/

lifestyle/style/colorado-murders-signals-a-return-of-the-news-medias-damsels-in-distress-trope/2018/08/21/c818aede-a557-11e8-97ce-cc9042272f07_story.html?utm_term=.ab70b-9c9e61a.
11. Krajicek, 7.
12. "Tyndall Report 2018 Year in Review," accessed May 14, 2019, http://tyndallreport.com/yearinreview2018/crime/.
13. Frank Newport, "Americans Fear of Walking Alone Ties 52-Year Low," Gallup, last modified November 2, 2017, https://news.gallup.com/poll/221183/americans-fear-walking-alone-ties-year-low.aspx.
14. Jim Norman, "Americans' Concerns about National Crime Abating," Gallup, last modified November 7, 2018, https://news.gallup.com/poll/244394/americans-concerns-national-crime-abating.aspx.
15. John Gramlich, "5 Facts about Crime in the U.S.," Pew Research Center, last modified January 3, 2019, https://www.pewresearch.org/fact-tank/2019/01/03/5-facts-about-crime-in-the-u-s/.
16. Paul H. Thibodeau and Lera Boroditsky "Metaphors We Think With: the Role of Metaphor in Reasoning," *PLOS One*, February 2011, accessed May 14, 2019, http://lera.ucsd.edu/papers/crime-metaphors.pdf.
17. Nazgol Ghandnoosh, "Race and Punishment: Racial Perceptions of Crime and Support for Punitive Policies," The Sentencing Project, last modified September 3, 2014, https://www.sentencingproject.org/publications/race-and-punishment-racial-perceptions-of-crime-and-support-for-punitive-policies/.

CHAPTER EIGHT

Medicine: From Gee-Whiz to Hard-Edged

RICHARD KNOX

The half-century between 1969 and 2019 was a time of transformation in the life sciences, medical care, public health, and the journalism that chronicled those changes. I was privileged to be among the journalists charged with reporting and explaining these developments.

The beat was hardly new in 1969, when I became a medical writer straight out of the Columbia University School of Journalism. In the 1930s, a few enterprising reporters in scattered newsrooms had carved themselves a niche, writing about medicine or a combination of physical science and medicine. But the late 1960s marked an inflection point—a shift away from a credulous style of reporting, heavy on gee-whiz and "human interest," toward a more skeptical and hard-news conception of the beat.

The five decades since have seen an explosion of coverage encompassing medicine, biomedical science, public health (global and domestic), new and complex ethical issues, the burgeoning business of health care, equitable access to it, and more. The accelerating pace of medical advances awakened editors to the need for reporters able to translate and explain these unfolding developments.

I didn't set out to become a medical writer. All I knew was that I wanted to specialize in *something*, and not politics or sports. Simply, I wanted more autonomy to choose my subjects, insofar as any newsperson can hope for, and I wanted to develop some familiarity with the subject matter. So it was by sheer good fortune that the *Boston Globe* called the spring of graduation to ask if I might want to be a medical writer. "Seems kind of narrow," I remember thinking. In the end, I chose the *Globe* over business writing at the *Chicago Sun-Times*. It had little to do with medicine's appeal; I had fallen in love with Boston when, fresh out of the Midwest, I'd interned at the *Globe* the previous summer.

It took all of about two weeks to discover (1) how radically wrong I was about the narrowness of the beat; (2) what a fabulous stroke of luck it was to be covering medicine in Boston, then and now one of the best places in the world to catch the wave of oncoming medical developments; and (3) how much I loved doing it.

I ended up doing it at the *Globe* for 31 years before moving to National Public Radio's science desk in 2000 for another 15 years, never losing my bedrock conviction that health is the subject "with the greatest impact on ordinary Americans' lives," as economist Paul Krugman has observed.[1] Or, as I've often reminded my editors, everybody has a body.

SHEDDING NAIVETÉ

By the time I landed on the medical beat, big cultural changes were elevating its rank in the news mix. The space race, which began in 1957 after the Soviet Union launched a beach ball-sized satellite called Sputnik, helped inaugurate a new era in government funding of science in general and the National Institutes of Health (NIH) in particular. ("If we can put a man on the moon . . .") By 1969, the NIH was in full tilt and biomedical research, building on the 1953 discovery of the double-helix structure of DNA, was generating enormous expectations that scientists were on the verge of understanding the molecular mechanisms of life. Cures of virtually all diseases seemed within reach, and that optimism fueled the careers (and colored the prose) of those of us on the medical beat.

It took a while for news editors to recognize the growing importance of medical news. Old-hand newsroom denizens thought we were pretty exotic and wonky, and didn't always consider our output worthy of page one. Even the *New York Times*, which had a stable of science writers, had no science desk or editor in 1969. "There was no real structure to organize the coverage," says Lawrence K. Altman, who joined the *Times* that year—one of the first medical reporters to hold a medical degree.[2]

At the *Philadelphia Inquirer*, medical writers were scattered—on the New Jersey desk, the city desk, or the suburban desk—covering parochial stories such as hospital closings or local outbreaks. It wasn't until the early 1990s, when Dotty Brown, a fellow 1969 J-School classmate, honchoed an internal "What's Missing?" committee at the *Inquirer* that the paper was persuaded to launch a medical/science desk to champion stories and provide guidance on how to play medical news.[3]

Despite some recalcitrance, publishers and major broadcast outlets around the country got behind the expansion of medical coverage. Throughout the 1970s and

Figure 8.1: *Boston Globe* medical writer Richard Knox (right) and Jerry Bishop of the *Wall Street Journal* listen to an explanation of medical research at a 1994 meeting of the American Heart Association. Understanding the complex science was one challenge; getting good play for their stories was another. Source: *Courtesy of the American Heart Association*

into the 1980s, mainstream media outlets routinely sent reporters to meetings of major medical organizations, not to mention many second-tier conferences and single-topic meetings. So I got to know a roving band of smart and savvy colleagues on the same beat.

"The desire to cover the latest, newest, most wondrous thing kept us very busy, well-employed, and flush with travel money," recalls Joann Rodgers, who wrote about medicine and health for the Hearst newspapers and later wrote books and directed public affairs for the Johns Hopkins Medical Institutions. This traveling band of medical journalists was a priceless education for a newbie like me. We competed with each other to get the story, but we also benefited from each other's probing questions and perspectives—and our shared pursuit of accuracy. "It began to occur to us that the stakes were so high in terms of the impact on human health and illness and the potential to foster fear and worry so great that we'd better get it right," Rodgers says.[4]

At the same time, I often felt uneasy as I covered medical meetings on tight deadlines. It was tempting to be seduced by an intriguing and plausible presentation that didn't have the most solid scientific basis without time to check it out with critics or skeptics. I wasn't alone. "To be honest, we had a huge naiveté about it," Rodgers acknowledges. "We all drank the Kool-Aid to some degree."

Gradually, we honed our skepticism and stepped back from the cheerleading, but it didn't occur often enough in the 1970s. "It took too long to develop a critical eye," says Joanne Silberner,[5] who has covered medicine and health for *Science News, U.S. News & World Report,* and NPR. The fault wasn't all in ourselves. After all, we had to sell those stories to editors and justify the expense of a week away. That pushed many of us toward a more enthusiastic account of new discoveries than they deserved.

We also had to do a complicated dance with our sources. Their careers depended on acclaim from their peers and, increasingly, from the public that subsidized the research. (In the case of drug industry-funded research, substitute "the stock market.")

"The medical community itself wasn't very skeptical," Altman says. "They believed what was presented at those meetings. And when they got sharp questions from the journalists, it often was the first time they got questioned about what they were doing."

THE "INGELFINGER RULE"

Dr. Franz Ingelfinger, who took over the helm of the venerable *New England Journal of Medicine* in 1967, took note of the rising tide of medical stories in lay media. His ambition was to make his the world's leading medical journal. Although his specialty was gastroenterology, Ingelfinger had the instincts of a newsman or a master marketer. He realized he could assure big play for the weekly journal's studies by offering pre-publication copies to medical reporters with an embargo of 5 p.m. on Wednesdays. That allowed evening television broadcasts first crack while making news about the studies available for the next morning's papers. It worked like a charm. Before long, the journal's stories were part of daily news budgets more Thursdays than not and the *New England Journal of Medicine* became a household name.

It was a good deal for journalists too. The world's most selective medical journal[6] publishes only one of every 20 articles it receives. Each is reviewed and endorsed by a panel of anonymous "peers"—experts in the relevant field. That gives some comfort to journalists whose job is to vouch for the study's credibility. (Over time, however, we would discover that the *New England Journal* and other esteemed journals could be duped by authors who were less than rigorous or even fraudulent.)

The embargo policy, which punished reporters who broke it by denying them pre-publication copies, imposed a predictable order on the release of much medical news and provided a fair playing field. Except for rare occasions when a journalist didn't abide by the embargo, we didn't have to worry about being scooped by a competitor.

But Ingelfinger had another aim besides getting noticed in mainstream media. He hated being scooped by the medical "throwaways"—trade newspapers lavishly supported by drug company ads—whose reporters picked up on presentations weeks or months before the *New England Journal* could complete its cumbersome peer-review process.

Thus was born the Ingelfinger Rule,[7] as it was dubbed. It admonished researchers who hoped to be published in the *New England Journal* not to talk to journalists about their work in advance of publication. For researchers, getting studies into top medical journals is the coin of their academic realm, the key to future grants and tenure. But the rule, quickly adopted by most other journals, caused headaches for journalists who heard public presentations of newsworthy research at medical meetings, only to run into flat refusals by researchers to answer questions or provide context.

With the advent of electronic publication, journals began to post peer-reviewed articles online to coincide with meeting presentations. Moreover, journals often make new data with time-sensitive implications publicly available with no embargo. And today some biomedical scientists even post "preprints" of their research, work-in-progress that has not undergone peer-review vetting.[8] Those who favor the trend say it promotes cross-fertilization among researchers, improving and accelerating the process. Opponents say, among other things, that when the research has implications for health and medical care, it can unleash bad information harmful to patients.

"It's exactly what Ingelfinger was worried about," says Dr. Ivan Oransky, vice president for editorial at *MedScape.com* and president of the 1,400-member Association of Health Care Journalists.[9] "With preprints, there won't be any embargoes and articles won't even be peer-reviewed. On the other hand, I think a lot of reporters are more sophisticated now."

Beyond the debate over the rules of the road lies a more fundamental issue that medical reporters began considering in the 1980s: Were we paying too much attention to medical journals at the expense of broader, more meaningful takes on subjects relevant to our audience? "There began to be a lot of discussion about not just regurgitating journal articles—that they were dominating our coverage," recalls Nils Bruzelius,[10] who was the *Boston Globe*'s health and science editor from 1986 through 1999. Some argued we should never cover journal stories, but Bruzelius (and I) disagreed. "This is how things change in science and medicine," he argued. "We can't ignore that. We should try as well as we can not to oversell stories, to contextualize them."

WANTING TO BELIEVE

The dilemma of when medical developments become news, and how to play them, is eternal. In all news coverage, the shiny new thing grabs the lion's share of attention. The tendency is often amped up in medical reporting because the public wants to believe in medical progress—in breakthroughs. Moreover, editors often don't want to hear cautionary tales about the incremental nature of research, the flaws in an exciting new study, or the potential downsides of a flashy new technology. Medical reporters want to believe, too. After all, we've reported on a string of genuine advances from open-heart surgery to organ transplants and magnetic resonance machines to bona fide cancer cures.

The mid-1980s served up a steady diet of allegedly imminent breakthroughs. Margaret Heckler, then U.S. Secretary of Health and Human Services, promised in 1984 that researchers would invent a vaccine against the AIDS virus within two years. Dr. Steven Rosenberg of the National Cancer Institute garnered mega-coverage for his supposedly pathfinding success in curing cancer with a chemical called interleukin-2. In 1984, an infant named Baby Fae received a baboon heart transplant at Loma Linda University, a landmark operation the *New York Times* called "a bold surgical effort that could have a wide impact on the treatment of failing hearts."[11] And in Texas, Utah, and Kentucky, surgeons began implanting artificial hearts into the chests of dying patients.

Gary Schwitzer, who covered the artificial heart program at Humana Hospital in Louisville for CNN, got fed up with daily briefings for the pack of journalists hungry for updates on artificial heart recipients. "I remember calling [my editors] and saying, 'Can I just back away from this hourly drivel and start doing some issue-oriented stories? When will we start talking about allocation of resources or who will pay for this?'" Schwitzer says.[12] "I would get a pat on the head and be told 'great idea.' But nothing would change."

As the medical beat evolved, many of us became immunized against the word "breakthrough," since it's impossible to know at the outset whether a touted innovation will transform patients' lives or be a big dud. In 2019, an effective vaccine against AIDS is still nowhere in sight. Rosenberg's early work with interleukin-2 didn't cure cancer, and only decades later has it been subsumed into a branch of cancer treatment called immunotherapy that's beginning to pay off for patients. Xenotransplants—suturing animal organs into people—have gone nowhere. And permanent artificial hearts don't whir and click in the chests of twenty-first century patients, although a temporary version of the device has been implanted in more than 1,800 people waiting for transplant.[13]

But even if hype of medical innovation is a problem without any real solution, some have attempted to guard against it. Schwitzer ended up founding *Health News Review*, a website that closely analyzed medical stories in mainstream media, calling out hype, pointing out flaws and criticizing lapses such as failures to specify who funded research being covered. *Health News Review* critiqued 2,600 medical news stories between 2005 and 2018. "We just scratched the surface," Schwitzer says. In 2017, the website published stories from patients "telling us of the harm they experienced as a result of misleading coverage," Schwitzer says. "It was one of the things of which I'm most proud."[14]

The watchdog website earned the respect of medical journalists for its fair criticism and helpful guidance on the bases every medical story should cover. Unfortunately, its foundation support expired. So despite what Schwitzer calls "loud gnashing of teeth about our demise," no other funder stepped forward.

MONEY AND MEDICINE

During the 1970s and beyond, large economic forces transformed the entire medical enterprise, catapulting journalists into areas beyond discoveries and sexy new technologies. Federal policies, including the Great Society programs of 1965—Medicaid for the indigent and disabled and Medicare for those 65 and over—helped fuel an explosion of national health care spending. Exciting new drugs and medical technology turbocharged the trend. National spending on health care more than tripled in inflation-adjusted dollars between 1970 and 1980.

These developments changed the focus of reporters who followed health care. "Coverage of everything got more skeptical," says Bill Salganik, a J-School Class of 1969 classmate who covered health care as a business reporter for the *Baltimore Sun*. "Instead of science gee-whiz stories on the traditional health beat, it was 'how does the system work?'" he says.

Opportunities to make big money began to blur the lines between doctors obligated by their Hippocratic oath to keep individual patients' needs foremost and doctors whose judgment was (at least potentially) swayed by their own financial ties. A number of my *Globe* stories in 1971 and 1972 documented how Harvard kidney specialists founded a chain of for-profit dialysis centers, capitalizing on a new federal law that opened Medicare payments to patients with end-stage kidney disease. The doctors lost their Harvard faculty appointments but their company grew into the nation's largest dialysis chain and was later sold to a German corporation for $2.3 billion.[15]

New funding sources also reshaped the medical research enterprise and the non-profit academic institutions where they were largely based. The chemical company Monsanto made front-page news in 1975 with an unprecedented $23 million grant to two Harvard researchers who had the novel idea that cancerous tumors might be vanquished by shutting off their blood supply.[16] (Years later the concept resulted in drugs that help some cancer patients, but don't "eradicate any type of cancer," as a 1998 *New York Times* article predicted.)[17]

As "the money side of medicine" loomed ever larger, recalls Cristine Russell, who covered medicine at the *Washington Post*, reporters began to take notice. "I always asked researchers where they got their money from. Many were offended and said things like, 'It doesn't matter, I'm doing great science.'"[18] Eventually, as journals were embarrassed by exposés of financial conflicts among their authors, they began imposing rules of disclosure and journalists began reporting sources of funding.

UNCOVERING ERRORS

Financial conflicts of interest weren't the only emerging problems that led medical journalists into investigative territory. In 1975, I got wind of a cardiac surgery team serving two Boston-area community hospitals whose patients had unusually high mortality rates. A cardiac catheterization technician at one of the hospitals, frustrated by his hospital's refusal to do anything about it, agreed to share mortality data he collected. Eventually we were able to show that the team had an astonishing 52 percent mortality rate over a seven-year period—at a time when anything over five percent was considered beyond the pale.[19] Their rate at another hospital was in the mid-20-percent range.

The day after we broke the story, the head of the surgical group resigned on the eve of his installation as president of the American College of Cardiology.

It was, in fact, a hidden national problem. A number of heart surgeons told me they knew of many other hospitals with excessive heart surgery mortality. But no one would talk on the record. It would be another 13 years before New York became the first state to require cardiac surgeons to report their mortality rates to a public database. Surgery-related death rates fell substantially as a result.[20]

Later—two decades later—our reporting on another egregious lapse in the quality of medical care would also shake up hospitals and change the way some routine things are done. The story involved consumer health specialist Betsy Lehman, who wrote a popular *Boston Globe* column called Health Sense. Lehman, the mother of two young girls, had breast cancer that recurred despite full-on primary treatment. As the quintessential health consumer herself, she researched her options and chose an experimental treatment at the Harvard-affiliated Dana

Farber Cancer Institute, one of the nation's 70 elite federally designated cancer research centers. Coincidentally, her husband was on the Dana Farber staff.

The therapy was intense and heroic. So it was no surprise that Lehman and another woman undergoing the treatment became deathly ill as they struggled to overcome the toxic chemotherapy while imprisoned in special germ-free isolation rooms. What was shocking was that Lehman, who was doing much better and scheduled for discharge home in days, died suddenly. The other woman required intensive care for months due to heart damage but survived.

Weeks later, the Dana Farber staff figured out why. Both women had mistakenly received four times the planned high dose of chemotherapy. When the hospital discovered it, they informed Lehman's husband, who told the *Globe's* health and science editor—because he was a friend, not because he was seeking coverage. (In fact, we had to persuade him to let us do the story.)

Nils Bruzelius, that editor, notes we most likely would never have learned about the mistake if Lehman had not been a *Globe* medical writer. The assignment fell to me. The first story, headlined "Doctor's Orders Killed Cancer Patient,"[21] ran on page one on March 23, 1995.

For the rest of that year we explored what had gone wrong at Dana Farber. For instance, there was no pharmacy system to catch excessive dosage orders, routine training of nurses in the details of experimental treatment protocols had lapsed, and other quality assurance mechanisms were missing. We also looked at how common medical errors were at other institutions and how systemic error-prevention and follow-up responses were lacking.

The Betsy Lehman case became the touchstone of a movement to prevent medical errors. Five years later the National Institute of Medicine published a landmark report, *To Err Is Human: Building a Safer Health System*, that estimated medical errors kill from 44,000 to 98,000 American hospital patients a year. The very first sentence references Lehman's death. A 1999 survey showed that the report was "the most closely followed health policy story of the year."[22]

A DISEASE LIKE NO OTHER

In the summer of 1952, in Hoopeston, Illinois ("Sweet Corn Capital of the World"), a playmate of mine died of polio—one of 60,000 American children infected that year and one of 3,000 who died.[23] The boy's death sent my mother into a panic. I wasn't allowed to swim in the public pool or use the playground. Then, three years later, I lined up in my underwear with other fourth graders to get a shot of the new Salk polio vaccine (later replaced by the oral Sabin vaccine). As vaccination became universal, the scourge disappeared. The United States hasn't seen any polio transmission since 1979.[24]

Thanks to vaccines and antibiotics, it seemed for a couple of decades that epidemics were permanently in our rear-view mirror. Then, in the summer of 1976, a newly recognized type of pneumonia, incubated in a dirty air conditioning system, hospitalized 200 people attending an American Legion convention in Philadelphia, killing 34 of them. "I think Legionnaire's disease was the first time journalists covered an outbreak [of an emerging infectious disease] at the time it occurred," says Altman.

Suddenly, it seemed, new—or at least newly recognized—infections were emerging with disturbing regularity. The list includes Lyme disease, West Nile, Ebola and Marburg hemorrhagic fever, toxic shock syndrome, hantavirus pulmonary syndrome, SARS coronavirus, new strains of influenza, and Zika virus.

But none would test our journalistic mettle like the AIDS pandemic that began in 1981. "A mysterious epidemic ... is suddenly afflicting sexually promiscuous young men, most of them homosexual," I wrote in my first story on the disaster in December of that year. "So far the puzzle has baffled the nation's leading specialists in infectious disease ...."[25]

By 1995, more than a half-million Americans had been diagnosed with AIDS and the global caseload had reached 18 million. AIDS was unlike any other story we had ever covered. It was a medical story because the horrific effects of immune collapse needed to be explained, along with the burdens the disease imposed on doctors and hospitals. It was a public health story because people needed to know how HIV was spread—through exposure to bodily fluids during sex, by sharing of needles among injection drug users, and by transfusion of contaminated blood. Just as important, we needed to explain how HIV *didn't* spread—not by handshakes, hugs, sneezes, or by sharing close quarters, food or toothbrushes.

Sexual transmission of HIV called for us to report on intimate practices previously taboo in public discourse. And since many infected with the human immunodeficiency virus were homosexual or bisexual and others were injecting drug users, we ventured into topics that offended sensibilities and triggered prejudices. Sex education became a battleground, as those who argued for frank talk and promotion of teenage condom use fought those who believed with equal passion that sexual abstinence was the right message.

"It became the first big public health story that checked all the boxes of what was crucial in medical journalism," says Joann Rodgers, who covered the epidemic for the Hearst newspaper chain. "It checked the epidemic box, the fear box, the tragedy box, the ethics box, the homophobia and racism boxes, the lack-of-a-pharmaceutical-answer box. Suddenly medical journalists became political reporters. We became investigative reporters because of the false claims that were made. It was a fantastic story."[26]

It often felt more like a calling than a story. AIDS imposed a special obligation to promote understanding, combat fear, and call out prejudice. It demanded sensitivity to people with AIDS (not "victims of AIDS"). Many AIDS activists, of course, were from the gay community, requiring another layer of sensitivity of a kind many journalists hadn't practiced before.

"There was so much distrust and general angst and sadness," recalls Susan Spencer, a J-School 1969 classmate who covered AIDS for CBS News between 1986 and 1991. "For me, as a straight woman, it wasn't easy to overcome." But looking back, she calls the period one of the most gratifying of her career. "I honestly felt we were making an important contribution."

The darkest times lasted 14 years. Then in 1995, researchers devised cocktails of antiviral drugs that transformed patients' prognosis from inexorably fatal to manageable. The new regimens transformed our coverage, too. Suddenly the number one question was how to deliver costly life-saving drugs to tens of millions of the already infected, most of them in sub-Saharan Africa.[27] There seemed to be little hope that most HIV-infected people would benefit.

Six years after the new drug regimen was invented, a top official in the George W. Bush Administration said expanding treatment to the most affected regions was infeasible because Africans couldn't be depended on to take the drugs on schedule. Many Africans "don't know what Western time is," Andrew Natsios, administrator of the U.S. Agency for International Development, told the *Globe*[28] in 2001.

By this point, I had joined NPR's science desk. I'd heard that Harvard's Dr. Paul Farmer was treating people in Haiti with the new anti-HIV drug cocktail. Since Haiti was this hemisphere's nearest equivalent to the impoverished sub-Saharan countries heavily afflicted with AIDS, I persuaded my editor to send me down to check it out. Farmer's group had trained a cadre of local people to deliver the AIDS drugs on foot to far-flung patients and make sure they were taking the pills. We met the first Haitian patient to get the regimen, a six-foot-tall, 33-year-old man named Francois St. Ker who weighed barely 100 pounds when he took the bus from Port-au-Prince back to his native village to be buried there. But thanks to the new drug regimen, he didn't die. To dramatize his turnaround, St. Ker took me to a backyard storage shed to show me his brightly colored coffin.

Eleven years later, back in Haiti to report on the nation's raging cholera epidemic, I looked up St. Ker. He told me he had been faithful about taking his HIV medicine. "Every day! Every day! I manage myself," he said. "I need to see the future of my children. I am a miracle! I compare myself to a second Lazarus." And the shiny coffin? "We sold the coffin," he replied. "Somebody else use it, not me."[29]

Such evidence caused the Bush Administration to do an about-face on delivering anti-HIV drugs to the most affected countries. In his January 2003 State of the Union message, Bush announced a $15 billion emergency program to treat and prevent AIDS in poor countries. By 2015, the annual number of AIDS deaths in the world was almost half the 2.1 million death toll in the peak year of 2005.

THE STRUGGLE TO COVER EVERYONE

In the spring of 1988, as Massachusetts Governor Michael Dukakis was running for president, he persuaded his state legislature to pass a landmark law that guaranteed health insurance to every citizen in the commonwealth. Then George H.W. Bush won the presidency. And Dukakis' Republican successor as governor promptly dismantled the Dukakis plan. The collapse of the Dukakis plan showed that health care for all is elusive, even in a politically progressive state with an uninsured population below the national average.

President Bill Clinton learned the same hard lesson. When he was elected in 1992, the time seemed ripe for health care reform. When Hillary Clinton convened her Committee of 500 to write the plan in 1993, nearly three-quarters of Americans supported a big change. But a year later, more Americans opposed the Clinton plan than supported it.

The collapse of the Clinton plan was for me personally depressing. Having covered the issue for years, I harbored a belief the U.S. health system was (and is) inherently unfair and in need of reform. I suspect that many health reporters, who for decades now have devoted so much time to covering the issue, have that bias to some degree.

Professor Robert Blendon and his colleagues analyzed why support for the Clinton plan fell away.[30] Its complexity was hard for most people to grasp (and for reporters to explain) so it was easy for opponents to spook insured Americans by asserting the plan would take away their choice of insurer, doctor, or hospital. (The plan would actually have expanded privately insured Americans' choices.) Beneath these fears, many Americans had become deeply cynical about government's ability to improve their lives or act in their interests.

But the effort to expand health coverage is a long game and public opinion does change. For evidence, look again to Massachusetts where a longer-lasting universal health insurance law was enacted in 2006. Romneycare—as some call it after then-governor Mitt Romney, a Republican—became the template for the federal Affordable Care Act, widely known as Obamacare. Passed in 2010, Obamacare is still standing as of this writing despite fierce opposition and mis-characterization that are bound to persist.

MEDICAL REPORTING: CUTS AND CURES

The questions that now loom over medical reporters are the same that cloud all of journalism: Can in-depth reporting on research, epidemics, health care, and costs—among so many medical issues—continue? In what form? How will it be paid for? Who will read, listen or watch, and how will they access it?

Newsrooms of all kinds are feeling pinched, but the data are most striking for the post-millennium newspaper industry. Between 2006 and 2018, ad revenue plunged almost 71 percent, from $49 billion to $14.3 billion.[31] More than half of all newspaper newsroom jobs disappeared between 2008 and 2018—from 71,000 to 37,900.[32]

Reliable data aren't available on the number of medical writing positions that vanished (from newspapers or any medium). But one 2009 survey of 256 health care journalists found that 40 percent reported a decline in the number of health reporters in their organization, and nearly all said bottom-line pressures in news organizations were seriously hurting the quality of health news.[33]

Another bellwether is the decline of weekly newspaper health and science sections. Ninety-five U.S. newspapers featured weekly sections in 1989, according to the *Columbia Journalism Review*.[34] Six years later, the number had plummeted to 34. By 2012, there were only 19. More recent data are unavailable, but it's probably safe to say, as a headline in *Editor & Publisher* put it, "They're Almost Gone."[35]

The *Boston Globe* had one of the earliest health and science sections, with a staff at its peak of nearly a dozen reporters and editors. When circulation plummeted in the 2000s, the weekly section went to the chopping block after a quarter-century run. "The managers decided they wanted less science reporting," says Carey Goldberg, a *Globe* medical writer from 2002 to 2009. "It seems crazy. Boston has more NIH funding than anywhere."[36]

Television coverage of medicine and health has also suffered. Jeanne Blake, a communications consultant with a focus on the biotech industry, counts herself lucky to have covered medicine for WBZ-TV in Boston during the early years of AIDS. "I reported over 500 AIDS stories for WBZ, and we did impactful hour-long specialists," she recalls. "Our evening news pieces were sometimes four and five minutes long. Now reporters are lucky to get 40 seconds."[37]

NPR, where I worked for 15 years, is the acknowledged leader in non-commercial media with 29 million weekly listeners. But it, too, has had to adapt to a fragmented media market. The network has shifted from the longer, sound-rich pieces long its hallmark toward shorter (and cheaper to produce) reporter-host conversations.

As medical coverage in legacy media gets squeezed, what's taking up the slack? Initially, to a large degree, blogs rushed into the vacuum. Web surfers have hundreds of medicine- and health-related news blogs to choose from—some of which spew misinformation potentially harmful to patients and public health, such as anti-vaccine posts responsible for a resurgence of measles.

Blogs are hardly the only alternative. Podcasts have sprung up, some devoted to health-related content. But whatever their merits, podcasts don't fill the need for day-in and day-out coverage of health and medical news. One stand-out in that category is Kaiser Health News (KHN), an editorially independent arm of the

Kaiser Family Foundation (KFF), which has leveraged its $650 million endowment to become a national leader in promoting informed health care policy. It disseminates reliable data, does nonpartisan analysis, sponsors polling, and offers journalism fellowship to health reporters.

The foundation launched KHN in 2009. It publishes authoritative news on the web and also provides print and radio stories to news outlets without charge. By 2019 it had a staff of more than 50 experienced reporters and editors.

In the past, news outlets were chary of allowing outsiders to produce content. But that dissipated as news budgets shrank and high-quality content became available from organizations like KHN without ties to industry or other self-interested parties. Like other non-profit journalism enterprises such as *ProPublica*, KHN partners with other health care-oriented foundations to foster regional outposts and collaborations.

"There's been a complete shift in the relationship between news organizations and nonprofit organizations," says the KFF's Penny Duckham,[38] who founded and manages its media fellowship programs. "They're happy to partner on news stories to a much greater degree."

"Partnerships are all the rage," agrees Ivan Oransky, president of the Association of Health Care Journalists. "It's a way forward, but maybe not *the* way forward." One challenge will be steering clear of conflicts-of-interest.

Boston has birthed a different alternative. After Boston Red Sox owner John Henry bought the *Boston Globe* from the New York Times Company in 2013 at a fire-sale price, Carey Goldberg implored him in WBUR's *Cognoscenti* blog to restore the newspaper's former rigor in covering medicine, health, and biomedical science. "If this is a 'scientific hub,' shouldn't the pages of our biggest newspaper reflect that?" she wrote. "Shouldn't medicine and technology and education … dominate the headlines far more than they do?"[39]

Within a year, Henry conceived an innovative venture to cover medicine. "I realized that while Boston and Cambridge were indeed the epicenter of life sciences," he wrote on its launch, "this fascinating world was not being covered by a serious, stand-alone news organization committed to the kind of in-depth journalism that has been a hallmark of the *Boston Globe*."[40]

"Stand-alone" is the key word. Rather than restore the *Globe* to its former eminence in this realm, Henry launched a website dubbed *STAT* (medical jargon for "right now!"), a new company which neatly side-steps thorny issues related to unions, pensions, and salary levels.

"You don't have to worry about print or delivery or anything like that," says *STAT* executive editor Rick Berke,[41] a former *New York Times* editor. "You can just build it in a way that's digital-first and make it as appealing and shareable online as possible." With a staff of about 50, including experienced medical and science writers, the site has attracted more than a million page-views per month. But its finances are anchored by a subscription service—STAT-Plus, aimed at professionals. That might imply that online medical journalism needs to become a niche venture to be economically viable.

Still, there's some reason to think the hemorrhaging of medical writing jobs may have slowed. Duckham of the Kaiser Family Foundation says that talking to health reporters in 2019, "you don't get the feeling that newsrooms are crumbling around their ears." Oransky is also cautiously optimistic. "What I've seen is a lot of growth in smaller outlets, particularly in public media," he says. "It feels like every year we learn about a new program or project or new online publication."

"Terrible things have happened in the profession, but counter-intuitively, lots of good things are happening too," says Larry Tye,[42] a former *Boston Globe* medical reporter who has built a second career writing nonfiction books.

Tye reports no shortage of applicants for a nine-day Health Coverage Fellowship he founded in 2001 with funding from Blue Cross-Blue Shield of Massachusetts. "Every year we get more applicants, maybe five for every spot in the program." Increasingly they come from new-ish outlets such as *Politico*, *ProPublica* and other non-profit news and investigative shops. "When media outlets have any kind of resources, they're smart enough to know that one of the things audiences demand is health coverage," Tye says. "Everybody's worried about their own health or their parents' or their children's."

Former *Washington Post* reporter Cristine Russell, now a Harvard lecturer, agrees. "It's still probably the most popular across-the-board subject that readers, viewers and listeners want to hear about. I don't think the Golden Age of medical reporting is past. I think it's being recreated."

The next Golden Age, if and when it arrives, is likely to get a turbocharge from the medical science now beginning to emerge from academic labs and biotech startups that are closing in on ways to cure diseases by correcting faulty genes—the promise born way back in 1953 with the discovery of DNA's structure. Future medical reporters will then have plenty of stories to write about how to deliver and pay for such wonders.

NOTES

1. Paul Krugman, "Republicans Really Hate Health Care," *New York Times*, March 26, 2019, https://www.nytimes.com/2019/03/26/opinion/republicans-really-hate-healthcare.html.
2. Dr. Lawrence K. Altman, interview with author, March 5, 2019. Subsequent quotes from Altman are also from this interview.
3. Unless otherwise noted, any information or quotations from members of the Columbia University Journalism School, Class of 1969, were obtained through emails or interviews between September 2018 and April 2019.
4. Joann E. Rodgers, personal interview, February 2, 2019.

5. Joanne Silberner, personal interview, March 18, 2019.
6. "Top Twenty Medical Journals," Syberscribe, last modified October 24, 2018, https://www.syberscribe.com.au/blog/top-twenty-medical-journals/.
7. Marcia Angell, M.D., and Jerome P. Kassirer, M.D., "The Ingelfinger Rule Revisited," *New England Journal of Medicine* 1991, 325: 1371–1373, accessed on May 15, 2019, https://www.nejm.org/doi/full/10.1056/NEJM199111073251910.
8. Jocelyn Kaiser, "Are Preprints the Future of Biology? A Survival Guide for Scientists," *Science*, last modified September 29, 2017, https://www.sciencemag.org/news/2017/09/are-preprints-future-biology-survival-guide-scientists.
9. Ivan Oransky, interview with author, February 24, 2019. Subsequent quotes also from this interview.
10. Nils J. Bruzelius, personal interview, February 27, 2019.
11. Lawrence K. Altman, "Baboon's Heart Implanted in Infant on Coast," *New York Times*, last modified Oct. 28, 1984, p. 1
12. Gary Schwitzer, interview with author, February 20, 2019.
13. "7 Things You Should Know about Artificial Hearts," SynCardia, accessed April 16, 2019, https://syncardia.com/patients/media/blog/2018/08/seven-things-about-artificial-hearts/.
14. Gary Schwitzer, interview with author, February 20, 2019.
15. Barry Meier, "German Merger for Grace's Dialysis Unit," *New York Times*, last modified February 5, 1996, https://www.nytimes.com/1996/02/05/business/german-merger-for-grace-s-dialysis-unit.html.
16. Walter V. Robinson, "Harvard, Monsanto Form $23 Million Research Team," *Boston Globe*, last modified February 2, 1975, 1, https://bostonglobe.newspapers.com/image/436009101/?terms=Harvard%2Bresearchers.
17. Gina Kolata, "Hope in the Lab: A Special Report; A Cautious Awe Greets Drugs that Eradicate Tumors in Mice," *New York Times*, last modified May 3, 1998, 1, https://www.nytimes.com/1998/05/03/us/hope-lab-special-report-cautious-awe-greets-drugs-that-eradicate-tumors-mice.html?searchResultPosition=1.
18. Cristine Russell, interview with author, February 21, 2019. Subsequent quotes from Russell are from this interview.
19. Richard A. Knox, "Heart Surgery Death Rates Probed at Malden Hospital," *Boston Globe*, last modified February 23, 1976, 1, https://bostonglobe.newspapers.com/image/436561486/?terms=.
20. Mark. R. Chassin, "Achieving and Sustaining Improved Quality: Lessons from New York State and Cardiac Surgery," *Health Affairs*, July/August 2002, accessed May 15, 2019, https://www.healthaffairs.org/doi/full/10.1377/hlthaff.21.4.40.
21. Richard A. Knox, "Doctor's Orders Killed Cancer Patient," *Boston Globe*, last modified March 23, 1995, 1, https://bostonglobe.newspapers.com/image/440848770/.
22. Drew E. Altman, Carolyn Clancy and Robert J. Blendon, "Improving Patient Safety—Five Years after the IOM Report," *New England Journal of Medicine* 351: 2041–2043, last modified November 11, 2004, https://www.nejm.org/doi/full/10.1056/NEJMp048243.
23. Jason Beaubien, "Wiping Out Polio: How the U.S. Snuffed Out a Killer," National Public Radio, last modified October 15, 2012, https://www.npr.org/sections/health-shots/2012/10/16/162670836/wiping-out-polio-how-the-u-s-snuffed-out-a-killer.
24. "Polio Elimination in the United States," Centers for Disease Control and Prevention, accessed April 16, 2019, https://www.cdc.gov/polio/us/index.html.

25. Richard A. Knox, "Mysterious Disease Afflicts Gays," *Boston Globe*, last modified December 10, 1981, 3, https://bostonglobe.newspapers.com/image/436883460/.
26. Joann E. Rodgers, interview with author, February 6, 2019.
27. "Global HIV & AIDS Statistics—2018 Fact Sheet," UNAIDS, accessed April 16, 2019, http://www.unaids.org/en/resources/fact-sheet.
28. John Donnelly, "Prevention Urged in AIDS Fight: Natsios Says Fund Should Spend Less on HIV Treatment," *Boston Globe*, last modified June 7, 2001, 8, https://bostonglobe.newspapers.com/image/442174166/?terms=Andrew%2BNatsios.
29. Richard Knox, "Treating HIV: From Impossible to Halfway There," *All Things Considered*, NPR, July 3, 2012. Accessed April 16, 2019, https://www.npr.org/2012/07/03/156154794/treating-hiv-from-impossible-to-halfway-there.
30. Robert J. Blendon, Mollyann Brodie and John Benson. "What Happened to Americans' Support for the Clinton Health Plan?" *Health Affairs*, Summer 1995, accessed May 1, 2019, https://www.healthaffairs.org/doi/full/10.1377/hlthaff.14.2.7.
31. *Newspapers Fact* Sheet, Pew Research Center, last modified July 9, 2019, https://www.journalism.org/fact-sheet/newspapers/.
32. Ibid.
33. *Survey of AHCJ Members*, Kaiser Family Foundation/Association of Health Care Journalists, March 2009, accessed April 16, 2019, https://www.kff.org/wp-content/uploads/2013/01/mh031109pres.pdf
34. Sara Morrison, *Columbia Journalism Review*, January–February, 2013, accessed April 22, 2019, https://archives.cjr.org/currents/hard_numbers_jf2013.php
35. E&P Staff, "Remember Newspaper Science Sections? They're Almost Gone," *Editor & Publisher*, last modified January 10, 2013, https://www.editorandpublisher.com/?s=newspaper+science+-sections.
36. Carey Goldberg, interview with author, March 6, 2019.
37. Jeanne Blake, interview with author, January 24, 2019.
38. Penny Duckham, interview with author, March 20, 2019.
39. Carey Goldberg, "Memo to John Henry: Push the Globe to Cover the 'New' Boston," WBUR *Cognoscenti*, last modified September 3, 2013, https://www.wbur.org/cognoscenti/2013/09/03/boston-globe-carey-goldberg.
40. John W. Henry, "Why I Started STAT," Statnews.com, last modified November 4, 2015, https://www.statnews.com/2015/11/04/why-i-started-stat/.
41. Rick Berke, interview with author, March 18, 2019.
42. Larry Tye, interview with author, March 20, 2019.

CHAPTER NINE

Business: How Big Media Missed Small and Personal

DAVID E. GUMPERT

I was full of excitement when I started my professional journalism career in the summer of 1969 as a staff reporter for the *Wall Street Journal* in New York. Who wouldn't be? I was going to work for a national newspaper on an upward growth trajectory whose paid circulation had just recently passed one million.[1] There was just one little blip—it came each morning in the form of a daily moment of high anxiety when I did what so many other people did nearly without thinking: open the business section of the *New York Times*.

If the *New York Times* had a story related to my beat or area of coverage and it contained information I hadn't yet reported about a particular large corporation or business trend, well, I was in trouble—enough trouble that I could lose my job. The *New York Times* was seen as our most important competitor and the editors of the two publications monitored each other like hawks. Maybe because each was a daily publication, they took each other more seriously than, say, the other major business publications of the era like *Fortune* and *BusinessWeek*.

Day in and day out over the next 50 years, the two dailies would obsess over each other and penalize or even dismiss reporters over missed scoops. Unfortunately, while they were keeping close tabs on each other, they were late to the party—or even no-shows—to the explosive demand for business news from a variety of new quarters.

Two of the biggest explosions occurred in the areas of personal finance and entrepreneurship. In late 1970, Maryland Public Broadcasting launched Wall Street Week—the first TV show aimed at informing the small investor on the outside about what was going on inside major boardrooms. In 1972, Time Inc.'s *Money* magazine hit the stands, a major new consumer publication devoted to personal investing and personal finance. That same year, a New Jersey entrepreneur and direct marketing expert, Martin Edelston, started Bottom Line Inc., which published *Boardroom Reports* and *Bottom Line*. They focused on providing business executives and ordinary consumers with practical tips on making and saving money. Both *Money* and the Bottom Line publications grew rapidly, attracting many hundreds of thousands of readers.

One of the biggest bombshells to hit the investing world occurred in 1981 when investment banker Michael Bloomberg unveiled a stand-alone computer terminal that allowed bond and stock traders to monitor the action in real time. Before too long, those terminals became ubiquitous in brokerage firms around the country—not to mention many newsrooms—as both stock traders and journalists raced to stay up on fast-breaking business news. The fast-growing company also moved into business journalism with its own publications and radio stations.[2]

By the end of the 1970s, two major publications devoted to small business and entrepreneurship had launched as well. *Entrepreneur* magazine started in California in 1977 to keep tabs on hot new start-up business opportunities. In 1979, *Inc.* magazine started out of offices on Boston's waterfront to cover fast-growing smaller businesses.

A THIRST FOR BUSINESS NEWS

The newfound interest in business news wasn't confined to the start-up publications. Established daily newspapers around the country were sensing the thirst for business news as my Columbia University Journalism School classmate Leslie Berkman discovered not long after graduating in 1969. As she recalls, the big dailies were slow to quench that thirst:

> "When I arrived at the Orange County Edition of the *Los Angeles Times* in 1973, I believe the up-and-coming edition had not one reporter assigned to business news. This was despite industrial parks sprouting around the county's expanding airport and office and mega retail complexes taking shape in Costa Mesa and Newport Beach, already the preferred home of business titans who were beginning to transfer their corporate headquarters south from the congestion of Los Angeles.
>
> "In those years, it was difficult to find a young, ambitious reporter eager to write business stories for metropolitan newspapers. Business was considered a stodgy beat that focused on the stock market and corporate earnings. Business stories were stuffed behind sports, apparently because editors thought they appealed to wealthy business executives—mostly white males with stock portfolios who also kept abreast of football and baseball.

"But probably nowhere in Southern California was the missed potential of business development and trend stories more evident than in Orange County in the early 1970s, and I grabbed the chance to become the regional edition's first economic and business reporter. Soon, downtown editors decided to build a separate business staff for the edition to take a deep look at the county's booming entrepreneurial, financial, medical, retail, and housing sectors. We also explored workplace issues that mattered greatly to middle income families who were our readers, such as the plight of aerospace engineers thrown out of defense jobs at the end of the Cold War."[3]

Los Angeles Times deputy business editor Dan Beucke recalled that in the 1970s, "business news was concentrated in the 'trade' papers, the *Wall Street Journal* being the closest that most non-financial readers would come to serious coverage of economic and business matters. But as metro papers reaped the advertising rewards of an exploding post-war economy and their own regional oligopolies, publishers began investing in stand-alone business sections. And hard-nosed metro reporters and editors turned an eye toward financial topics."

In 1975, Beucke recalled, John Lawrence, then bureau chief of the *Los Angeles Times'* Washington, D.C. bureau, was brought back to Los Angeles where he oversaw the expansion of business coverage, including the launch of a standalone section and the hiring of an impressive staff, alongside business editor Paul Steiger.

"In a job interview I had with Steiger in 1982," said Beucke, "he explained that one of the first things he and Lawrence did was aim their reporters at high-impact original stories and let the wire services handle routine stock market coverage and corporate news. As a result, the staff—which grew to 60 and included such up-and-coming talent as Marty Baron[4]—was able to turn its attention to pieces that took a closer look at business people and transactions."[5]

Other newspapers were also slow to embrace business reporting. Karen Rothmyer, a member of the J-School Class of 1969, recalls visiting the *Detroit News* in the mid-1980s while on a reporting assignment: "I went to Detroit to do a story about Gannett's takeover of the *Detroit News*" she recalls.

> "I made an appointment with someone on the paper's business desk. But when I went into the newsroom and asked where I could find the person, I was told to go across the hall. That, it turned out, was where the *News'* business department (advertising, circulation, etc.) was also located. It spoke volumes about how business news was perceived—it was not quite legitimate, or at any rate not in the same category as crime and politics."

But competition has a way of grabbing editors' attention. Not only were PBS shows like Wall Street Week and flashy personal investing magazines like *Money* pulling at consumers' attention, but local television was as well.

John Cross of the J-School Class of 1969 recalls working in the 1970s with classmate Kenneth Tiven to develop business and investing news for a major Pittsburgh television outlet WPXI-TV. "Our news included home interviews with workers, on-the-spot economics coverage of major events with the chief economists of Mellon Bank and Pittsburgh National Bank, major business series on industrial espionage, women-in-high-places with a look at women priests, women executives, and women in self-started businesses," Cross recalls. "From there we went into some predictions about what would happen to the city as we did a number of series, venturing to cover stories in high tech, medicine and the infant robotics industry."

Leslie Berkman attributes the newfound consumer hunger for business and financial news in part to the demise of the traditional defined benefit pension plan—supplanted in many cases by 401Ks and IRAs filled with stocks and bonds. "Workers found themselves dependent on market performance for their retirement and turned to business page forecasts and analyses as they tried to build their nest eggs," she recalls. "In a similar way, skyrocketing volatility in Southern California home prices turned many average-income people into real estate investors and even 'flippers' who read the business pages during market upsurges for an adrenalin boost and during market busts to search for buying opportunities or to learn the extent of their losses."

REBELLING AGAINST BIG

The conventional economic wisdom during the 1960s and 1970s was that large corporations not only dominated the business landscape, but that their dominance would continue to expand. Congress even held hearings during that time in which federal policymakers and economists expressed concerns that an ever more predatory atmosphere was making it nearly impossible for small businesses to compete against the behemoths.[6]

Early in my tenure at the *Wall Street Journal*, I turned heads among the top editors when I declined an offer to transfer to its Detroit bureau. This bureau was probably second in influence within the *WSJ* news empire (behind New York) because it covered the Big Three automakers, as they were known then—General Motors, Ford, and Chrysler—and the sprawling network of suppliers that fed them. They were three of the largest corporations on the planet, and pretty much everything a reporter wrote about them was guaranteed major billing in the paper.

Something within me rebelled against being part and parcel of the corporate world that dominated then. Perhaps it had something to do with growing up in a world of small business; my father owned a retail men's wear business on Chicago's Michigan Avenue. I worked in his store several summers and came to appreciate that the owner did everything, including gift-wrap packages, sweep the floor, and personally deliver completed customized orders to customers' offices and homes.

After rejecting the Detroit move, I angled for a transfer to the *WSJ*'s Boston office. I sensed that my natural inclination toward writing about small business and entrepreneurship might be easier to justify there than in New York or Detroit, since Boston, with its Route 128 superhighway circling the city, was quickly becoming a high-tech hub along with its West Coast equivalent, Silicon Valley. I also calculated that one way to avoid the cutthroat *WSJ-NY Times* rivalry was to report more on smaller fast-growing businesses and less on well-established corporations like AT&T, General Motors, and General Electric. My approach worked, and by the start of 1971 I was reporting from the *WSJ*'s four-reporter Boston bureau.

Sure enough, I was quickly thrust smack dab into the middle of the Boston area's go-go business culture. One of my major responsibilities was covering one of the country's fastest-growing public companies, Digital Equipment Corp., a maker of "minicomputers," as small computers were known in that time before PCs. It was rapidly taking over abandoned manufacturing mills in the sleepy town of Maynard, Massachusetts, and turning them into manufacturing plants to keep up with its breakneck growth.

I found myself interviewing the "father of American venture capital," Georges Doriot, one of Digital Equipment's early financial backers, about this newest form of financing for America's most promising emerging businesses. In addition to covering Digital Equipment, I reported on other companies with equally strange names like Data General, Prime Computer, and American Science and Engineering that had equally ambitious fast-growth trajectories.

While the *WSJ* was definitely showing more interest in publishing stories about the young, burgeoning tech companies than the staid *New York Times*, both publications reserved the bulk of their precious editorial space for news about the nation's largest corporations—the auto companies and predominant manufacturers like General Electric and conglomerates like Textron. Yet in the background, a few publishers were taking note of the blossoming interest in entrepreneurship that I was reporting on.

By the late 1970s, I was hearing from two such publishers from opposite ends of the publishing world. One was a "bible" of corporate executives—the *Harvard Business Review (HBR)*. An arm of the Harvard Business School, its focus was on the managerial challenges facing major corporations in developing effective corporate, marketing, manufacturing, and human resource strategies. But its publisher, Ralph Lewis, a veteran executive from one of America's largest accounting firms, was noticing the budding interest in smaller, fast-growing ventures and he wanted *HBR* to be part of this new world.

I had gotten to know Ralph from covering news developments at a couple of large Boston-area corporations where he was on the board of directors. During my interviews with him, we compared notes on small business and entrepreneurship.

Eventually, he invited me to become an editor at *HBR* and help launch a new special section devoted to small business and entrepreneurship.

But wait! Right around the same time in 1978, another Boston-area publisher was seriously exploring a new magazine devoted to covering fast-growing small businesses. He was Bernie Goldhirsh, and at the time I met him for lunch at a fish restaurant on Boston's harbor front, he was the publisher of a glossy magazine he had launched a few years earlier, *Sail*. It targeted sailing enthusiasts and was doing so well that it had offices in the newest hot area of Boston, the waterfront Commercial Wharf.

Bernie was in his late 30s when we sat down to lunch that day in the spring of 1978. He was slight and dark-haired, and seemed a tad self-conscious; to me he was a spitting image of Dustin Hoffman in *The Graduate*, the hugely popular movie of a decade earlier about a new college graduate uncertain of his next steps in life who gets seduced by a friend's mother.

Bernie spelled out his vision: a new magazine to celebrate successful entrepreneurs like himself, currently entrepreneurs had no publication that spoke directly to their interests in subjects such as recruiting top employees and raising investment funds. He wondered what I thought of its tentative title: *Inc*. I told him I liked it. In fact, I liked the whole concept.

He was searching for a founding editor and wondered if it might be something for me. I told him that even though I had a few years of serious business reporting experience, I didn't have the kind of managerial or leadership experience to confidently assume the top spot of a glossy new magazine he was about to pour millions of dollars into. I also told him that Ralph Lewis had already offered me an editorship at *HBR*, which I was about to accept. I said I'd be monitoring *Inc.*'s progress closely, and perhaps one day I'd come to work for him.

Shortly after I joined *HBR*, my new colleagues and I christened the new small business section I would oversee "Growing Concerns." For the first time, *HBR* was publishing articles about business planning for early-stage businesses, the travails of minority-owned businesses, how small businesses could effectively compete for top employees, and the pressures associated with selling a small company. I networked with professors at top business schools around the country, encouraging them to investigate issues of interest to owners of smaller businesses, which led to them writing research-based articles on the loneliness of business owners, how ideas for new businesses germinated and sprouted, and whether entrepreneurs succeeded primarily because of inborn talents, among other subjects.

In the meantime, over on Boston's waterfront, Bernie Goldhirsh was publishing *Inc.* magazine with an eye to turning colorful and successful growth-oriented entrepreneurs into celebrities. He hit the jackpot with his first issue in April 1979 with a major story about two brash Silicon Valley entrepreneurs, Steve Jobs and Steve Wozniak. Apple Computer was only two years old and in 1978 had sales of just $15 million, the magazine reported. But the piece reflected the founders' unbridled optimism in its heading: "From the very beginning, Apple Computer was born to grow." The founders' projection for the next year was $100 million in sales.[7]

That same year, 1979, marked one additional milestone for business journalism, except this one emanated from the academic realm. A young economist at the Massachusetts Institute of Technology (MIT), David Birch, released research data on business creation that was completely at odds with the conventional wisdom of the time—that small businesses rather than large corporations created the vast majority of new jobs in the U.S.[8]

In a related step, Babson College in 1981 launched an entrepreneurship research conference that within a few years was attracting dozens of academics from around the world to its spring gathering in Wellesley, Massachusetts to present their findings about trends in small business financing and the personality traits of entrepreneurs, along with trends in small business job creation.[9]

By 1989, *Inc.* was reporting that researchers and economists were debating small business' true role in job creation.[10]

Academia's focus on small business jobs and financing helped propel ever more media coverage of the segment. Together with *Inc.* and *Entrepreneur* magazine—which was focused on hot new business opportunities—weekly newspapers like *Crain's Chicago Business*, *Boston Business Journal*, and the *Los Angeles Business Journal* had sprung up to cover local small businesses and were growing rapidly. *Working Woman* magazine, which had launched in 1976, was seeking articles on women-owned businesses, a number of which I had the opportunity to write as a contributing editor.

By the late 1980s, I had fulfilled my prediction to Bernie Goldhirsh about joining *Inc.* magazine—I left *HBR* to become a senior editor, working out of its labyrinth of low-ceilinged cobbled-together offices on ancient Commercial Wharf. During spring and summer, the salty smell of the ocean wafted through the cubicles.

Not only was *Inc.* a cool place to report for work every day, but it was also the nerve center for journalism having to do with entrepreneurship and small business during the 1980s and 1990s. It eventually recruited David Birch, the MIT researcher, to write a regular column on "The New Economy," where he reported on the growth trends of small manufacturers and real estate.

Inc.'s true strength was highlighting the drama associated with the rise and fall of the nation's most interesting entrepreneurs. For example, it featured on its January 1987 cover a photo of Mitch Kapor, whose Lotus Development Corp. rivaled Apple Computer in its hyper growth record. The heading: "Walking Away from It All: Lotus' Mitch Kapor on Calling It Quits." And in October 1987, it was as if *Inc.* had come full circle, with a cover article picturing John Sculley, the new president of Apple Computer, with the heading: "Why I Fired Steve Jobs."

I was caught up in the drama as well that year, ghost-writing a column by successful entrepreneurs known as "Executive Forum." It featured the first-person stories of CEOs on topics like "The Secrets of Guerrilla Management"[11] and "How I Learned to Love Negotiating."[12]

Inc. didn't just report on the country's most exciting small businesses, though. It did something pioneering for the times: It used exclusive in-person conferences to foster a sense of community. It did that by inviting and regaling at an annual conference the owners of the companies listed in its *Inc.* 500 compilation of the fastest-growing private companies. These were glitzy affairs, at special locations, but they were also highly emotional. I attended conferences in New Orleans and Salt Lake City, observing first-hand how excited business owners were when they were honored at fancy dinners—so excited that many even brought along their children or parents.

Following the 1993 conference in Columbus, Ohio, *Inc.*'s editor, George Gendron, wrote this in the magazine:

> "Something extraordinary happens when you bring together in one room almost 1,000 leaders of *Inc.* 500 companies past and present. You can actually feel the entrepreneurial energy that is our nation's ultimate competitive advantage. As I stood at the podium preparing to open this year's *Inc.* 500 conference, in Columbus, Ohio, I found myself marveling yet again at what that energy can do. Six years ago, after all, most of the companies on the 1993 list were struggling to get started. Today they employ more than 50,000 people and generate more than $8 billion in sales.
>
> "This year's conference featured three days of speeches, seminars, roundtables, and workshops led by some of the country's most accomplished business thinkers and doers, on themes ranging from the art of building strategic relationships to the art of keeping personal relationships intact while building a fast-growth company. First, however, came the traditional opening-night sporting event, a game of touch football at Ohio State University Stadium. Governor George Voinovich joined *Inc.* 500 CEOs and the magazine's staff on the field, while Hall of Famers Sam Huff, Gale Sayers, Sonny Jurgensen, Paul Hornung, Ray Nitschke, and Paul Warfield watched from the sidelines. Midway through the second half, *Inc.* reporter Karen Carney hauled in a pass on a short down-and-out pattern. 'Now *that's* one for the record books,' said Governor Voinovich. 'The first woman on the receiving end of a completed pass in Ohio State Stadium.' Welcome to the new economy."[13]

There was an ulterior journalistic motive in those annual conferences: By virtue of gathering in one place the top newsmakers in small business, *Inc.*'s editors gathered intelligence, anecdotes, and dramatic personal stories to drive *Inc.*'s news pages for months and months afterwards.

Inevitably, the newspaper and magazine attention given over to small business attracted the interest of book publishers as well. By the early 1990s, I had written or co-authored five books about various aspects of small business—a resource guide and four business planning guides. One sold in excess of 100,000 copies.

The small business phenomenon continued to show strong media "legs" heading into the 1990s. In 1991, Time Inc. and American Express launched a new small business publication, *Your Company*, later renamed *Fortune Small Business*.[14] *Red Herring*, a slick magazine devoted to chronicling hot technology companies, started in 1993.[15]

Inc. and *Red Herring* were wonderful outlets for dozens of freelance business writers because the publications sought out serious, well-researched articles and were willing to pay attractive rates to get such content. *Red Herring* in particular was attracting so much advertising related to the emergence of fast-growing technology companies that it recruited dozens of freelance business writers to turn out articles about the latest wrinkles in venture capital and private company financing.

THEN CAME THE PARTY POOPER

In retrospect, the period of 1970–1995 was a golden age for business journalism. Another member of the J-School Class of 1969, Paul Sturm, spent that period working as a writer and editor at *BusinessWeek*, *Forbes*, and *Newsweek* magazines, and recalls the period with amazement:

> "In those glory days, business magazines were popular and grandly profitable. A full-page ad in *Forbes* cost perhaps $50,000, and the all-in cost of producing a page was less than $10,000. *Forbes* regularly sold more ads than anyone else—something like 2,000 pages annually, if I recall correctly. No wonder Malcolm [Forbes] had a yacht, a London townhouse, a French chateau, and a Moroccan palace. How better to wine and dine the advertisers?

> "Numbers elsewhere were a bit different but similar. While *Forbes* turned business news into entertainment, *BusinessWeek* was more meat-and-potatoes, with many foreign bureaus and a large staff. When I left in 1989, I was one of the three top editors and we had more than 200 journalists on the payroll. Still, *BusinessWeek* was regularly among the largest contributors of profits at McGraw-Hill."

> "It was generally understood that the business magazines as a group (*Forbes, Fortune, BusinessWeek*) were more profitable than the newsweeklies (*Time, Newsweek, U.S. News & World Report*). Lower costs, of course. And a higher CPM[16] rate."

But then came the internet, beginning in 1995, and everything changed. The internet upended long-standing business models from travel agencies to stock brokerages to book selling—and business journalism. Advertisers once limited to high-cost placements in newspapers, magazines, and television now had seemingly limitless low-cost promotional and advertising opportunities on the internet.

Classmate Leslie Berkman clearly recalls how the new realities roiled the *Los Angeles Times* Business Section as classified and display advertising revenues took a big hit:

"I took one of the earlier buyouts at the *Los Angeles Times* in 1995. Since then, there have been many more buyouts and layoffs leading to smaller business and other departments. The Orange County Edition building where I worked for 22 years was shuttered and only a few reporters and editors still covered the local news that had been its staple. The editorial staff throughout the paper unionized in part to stop the loss of jobs.

"However, the decline of the *Los Angeles Times* appears to have halted under the leadership of Dr. Patrick Soon-Shiong, a Los Angeles biotech billionaire who bought the paper in June of 2018 and talked about plans for expansion. He also moved the paper from its iconic downtown headquarters to suburban El Segundo."

Managing Editor Scott Kraft reportedly told a luncheon of *Times* retirees in March, 2019 that since Shiong took control, the editorial staff had grown by about 110 staffers, including some veterans who were rehired, for a total staff of about 523. But even with further expansion anticipated, the paper's goal was not to return to its peak staffing level of 1,200, *Times*' executives said.

According to Dan Beucke, the deputy business editor: "What has changed the most at the *Times* (since the boom times) are the loss of resources that resulted from a dramatic reduction in advertising and the necessary refocusing of a smaller newsroom. Today the *Times* business staff is less than half the size it was at its peak. Under a new owner, the *Times* aspires to a digital subscription model. So, as the newsroom rebuilds, it has shifted from a strategy of at least attempting to cover all beats to one in which we have to be even more selective about identifying topics and stories that will make a difference in our community (and convince people to subscribe)."

The same relentless trends took a bit longer to hit *Inc.* magazine. It continued during the 1990s to rack up steady profits, reported to be about $20 million annually. But poor health forced Bernie Goldhirsh to sell the magazine in 2001 to a German company, Gruner + Jahr, for a reported $200 million.[17]

Two years later, Goldhirsh died of brain cancer. I attended a memorial service for him in his picturesque Massachusetts hometown of Manchester-by-the-Sea, which turned out to be a reunion of sorts for dozens of writers and editors who had served at *Inc.* over the years. Much of the conversation was about *Inc.*'s tough times. There had been layoffs, and the editor of 22 years, George Gendron, had just resigned.

Two years after that, in 2005, Gruner + Jahr offloaded *Inc.* for a reported $35 million—less than 20 percent of what it had paid Goldhirsh just five years earlier. The new buyer was Joe Mansueto, the CEO of investment publisher Morningstar.

At least *Inc.* was still around in a slick paper format. *Working Woman* had ceased publication in 2001. *Red Herring* folded its print publication in 2007, and *Fortune Small Business* was history by 2009. Even broadcast was hit—PBS' Wall Street Week ended its 30-plus years' run in 2002.

The internet would continue to remake and realign the business journalism landscape. After folding its print version, *Red Herring* would continue with an online version of the magazine. In addition, all sorts of new publications offering at least some business coverage would spring up on the internet. They weren't "magazines," but rather "blogs" and "podcasts" and "websites"—outlets like *Huffington Post* (www.huffingtonpost.com) for general business news, *Techcrunch* (www.techcrunch.com) for technology news, and *SeekingAlpha* (www.seekingalpha.com) for investment news.

The traditional journalism survivors of the internet-inspired shakeout, such as *Inc.*, the *Wall Street Journal*, the *New York Times*, *Fortune*, and the *Los Angeles Times*, have mostly tried to fight back by investing heavily in a strong internet presence, seeking to make business news more entertaining and celebrity-oriented than ever.

John O'Dell, a member of the *Los Angeles Times* business staff and an editor from 1984 until 2007, put it this way:

> "News organizations have been forced by the rise of social media to become faster, breezier in style and more responsive to perceived popular appetites than ever before.... That means that smart business editors have identified regional areas—entertainment and sports business for the *Los Angeles Times*, for instance—in which they can shine covering companies and people their readers aspire to emulate, and perhaps envy a bit.

> "The trend toward personality-oriented coverage and public fascination with figures such as Bill Gates, Steve Jobs, Elon Musk, Warren Buffet, et al. also has made business news more interesting and accessible to many. And editors desperate to grow—or just maintain—circulation and viewership have seized on this and boosted their business coverage from an afterthought to a main part of the package."[18]

He adds: "I certainly can recall a dramatic rise during my years on the business staff at the *Los Angeles Times* in coverage of investment scams, high-profile business people's personal lives and earnings, and consumer-helpful topics such as goings on in the banking and investment fields."

The big challenge for any publication trying to make it on the internet has been how to make money. Many blogs and podcasts are offered for free by individual consultants and journalists who hope to cash in separately by writing books, giving speeches or doing private consulting rather than directly from their regular online news. No longer do established print publications have the advantage of controlling expensive and complex printing presses and distribution channels that once kept competitors at bay. Very large online sites, like *Huffington Post*, could generate revenues via the old television formula of offering free content to viewers while charging advertisers to reach ever-larger audiences.

On top of the free-content sites, established publications face an even larger source of competition: the social media. Places like Facebook, Twitter, and LinkedIn have millions of users with special interest groups who are regularly chatting and providing their own takes on the news—"user-generated content." Owners of small businesses can find an assortment of articles by other business owners about marketing and sales and finance, all created for free by business owners and consultants interested in bringing attention to themselves.

Increasingly during the 2000s, the *Wall Street Journal*, *Los Angeles Times*, and *New York Times* among other established mainstream publications decided to erect paywalls charging readers to see content, much like the subscription model of print newspapers and magazines in a previous age.

While the traditional publications seem to have been able to stop the hemorrhaging of online readership through adroit use of their well-established brands, they generally haven't been able to replicate their golden years of the late twentieth century. Paul Sturm, who helped Morningstar get its start in 1984, explains things this way:

> "None of the traditional business magazines, with the possible exception of *Forbes*, is a serious web player. In contrast, Morningstar has a thriving website (120,000 folks as of April 2019 paid $24 a month to subscribe) and the company sells ads against a couple of million monthly visitors. We even employ a few journalists (some hired from *WSJ*), but it all began with a clearer understanding of how to use the technology to serve the needs of investors.
>
> "This is what the mag guys missed. From the beginning, many of them had on-line options. But no one got it right. In contrast, Bloomberg cleaned up by providing market coverage for professionals. It used to be Dow Jones (owner of the *Wall Street Journal*) vs. Reuters. Now Bloomberg dominates the market, and the lock that holds everyone is a private email system and the ability to build custom charts. Who knew? There is a real cost to being an embedded success, and the business publications paid dearly."

For veteran business reporters like me, it's all been head turning and confusing. I recall the days when I would cover a corporate annual meeting for the *Wall Street Journal* and at the end of the meeting literally race a reporter from Reuters, our usual day-to-day competitor, to the pay phones to report breaking news from the event. Today, such information is released electronically, together with transcripts of follow-up calls with securities analysts, so not only journalists but individual investors can immediately scour the data and not only comment about it on various sites but make quick investment decisions.

And that is significant. As wrenching as the changes have been for business journalists, they have been beneficial in many ways for the public at large. People have a wider variety of sources and resources at their ready disposal to evaluate what's going on in the world of business. It may not be as well-curated as it once was, but it's out there.

For better or worse, one aspect of business news has remained unchanged: the *Wall Street Journal* and the *New York Times* still obsess over each other's coverage. I'm sure some young business reporters at the *WSJ* still sit in dread at their computers each day, worrying that a scoop from the *New York Times* will suddenly show up on their screens and prompt an angry message, or worse, from a senior editor.

NOTES

1. "Dow Jones Timeline," *The Wall Street Journal,* accessed February 15, 2019, http://online.wsj.com/public/resources/documents/info-DJTimeline0706.html.
2. "Michael Bloomberg," *Encyclopedia.com*, last modified February 15, 2019, https://www.encyclopedia.com/people/history/us-history-biographies/michael-bloomberg.
3. Unless otherwise noted, any information or quotations from members of the Columbia University Journalism School Class of 1969, were obtained through emails or interviews between September 2018 and February 2019.
4. Marty Baron served as editor of the *Boston Globe* from 2001 to 2012 when he became editor of the *Washington Post*.
5. Leslie Berkman, member of the J-School Class of 1969, interview with Dan Beucke, January 21, 2019.
6. D. E. Gumpert, "Future of Small Business May Be Brighter Than Portrayed," *Harvard Business Review* 57, no. 4 (July–August 1979): 170–188.
7. Norman Sklarewitz, "From the very beginning, Apple Computer was born to grow," *Inc.*, last modified April 1, 1979, https://www.inc.com/magazine/1979/04/apple-born-to-grow.html.
8. "David L. Birch," *Wikipedia*, last modified June 15, 2018, https://en.wikipedia.org/wiki/David_L._Birch.
9. "Babson College Entrepreneurship Research Conference," *Babson College*, accessed February 15, 2019, http://www.babson.edu/academics/centers-and-institutes/the-arthur-m-blank-center-for-entrepreneurship/babson-college-entrepreneurship-research-conference.
10. John Case, "The Disciples of David Birch," *Inc.*, last modified January 1, 1989, https://www.inc.com/magazine/19890101/5491.html.
11. Fred M. Gibbons, "The Secrets of Guerilla Management," *Inc.*, February 1, 1987, 124.
12. "How I Learned to Love Negotiating," *Inc.*, September 1, 1987, 124.
13. George Gendron, "Highlights from Our Annual Inc. 500 Conference," *Inc.*, last modified August 1, 1994, https://www.inc.com/magazine/19940801/3033.html.
14. "Fortune Small Business," *Wikipedia*, last modified February 8, 2019, https://en.wikipedia.org/wiki/Fortune_Small_Business.
15. "Red Herring," *Wikipedia*, last modified November 5, 2018, https://en.wikipedia.org/wiki/Red_Herring_(magazine).
16. The CPM rate is the advertiser's cost for every 1,000 impressions on a webpage.
17. Keith J. Kelley, "Inc. Is Getting New Editor," *New York Post*, last modified April 12, 2002, https://nypost.com/2002/04/12/inc-is-getting-new-editor.
18. Leslie Berkman, member of the J-School Class of 1969, interview with John O'Dell, January 16, 2019.

CHAPTER TEN

Covering the God Beat in a Time of Change

TAMMY TANAKA

Fresh out of the Columbia University Journalism School in 1969, I was hired as a staff writer for Religion News Service (RNS). It was an exciting prospect given that my stories would go to media all over the country since RNS is like an Associated Press for religion news, with major news organizations publishing the stories it reports.

But unlike its staff of religion specialists covering mainline Protestants, Orthodox Christians, Roman Catholics, Evangelicals, and Jews, I was given an unusual assigment: covering "other." Editor-in-chief Lillian R. Block was prescient in recognizing that at a time when the Hari Krishnas were seen as a sideshow to the Beatles, Americans were seeking spiritual fulfillment in new ways. So I began writing stories about religion in everyday life, features which attempted to understand the spiritual underpinning of an ever more diverse America.

During the next 50 years, religion writers would face a vastly changing spiritual landscape as a predominantly Christian country transformed into what is today described as one of the most religiously diverse industrialized nations in the world. Media spotlight on the hippies and their flights into nirvana and transcendental ecstasy would inspire waves of Americans to seek their own personal experience of God, spawning a spirituality movement that continues to evolve. "Religion" would come to encompass not only the major world faiths, but pantheism, agnosticism, atheism, secular humanism, mind-body-spirit groups, a "feminist Godhead," and more.

The "new morality," with its open views about sex and LGBT lifestyles, emerged in the 1960s and later would be countered in the 1970s by a new "born-again" awakening of charismatics and evangelicals—and the rise of the politically activist Religious Right, determined to protect their traditional religious values which they believed should also be those of the nation.

Over the decades, religious differences would become intertwined with political schisms, dividing America in ways that would continue into the Donald Trump presidency. And religion writers, among others reporters, would be challenged to explain some of the biggest stories of the era, from Fatwas to pedophilic priests to religiously motivated acts of terrorism.

"The intersection of religion and politics accounted for only one out of every 25 discussions of religion in the 1970s but one out of every eight in the 1990s," according to the Center for Media and Public Affairs, which analyzed religion coverage between 1969 and 1998 by such news organizations as the *New York Times*, *Washington Post*, and *Time* magazine.

A major weakness in the mainstream media coverage was that "fully 95 percent" of the religion stories contained "no spiritual dimension," the report concluded. "Theological and spiritual questions are rarely presented as newsworthy, either in their own terms or in relation to broader social issues." The United States, the report noted, "remains by far the most religiously observant of all advanced industrial nations, yet people of faith have often complained that the centrality of religion to everyday life in America is not fully reflected in the media images that shape the common culture of its citizens."[1]

That concern continued into the new millennium when religion reporting would be dominated by two major stories: news of Muslim extremists in the aftermath of the September 11, 2001 attack on the U.S., and the uncovering of long-standing, widespread instances of sexual abuses by Catholic priests and other clergy. The *Boston Globe's* 2001 reporting won a Pulitzer, became a major film, and led to exposés around the country and the world, resulting in Pope Francis issuing rules in 2019 for dioceses to systematically report abuse and cover-ups.

WRITING ABOUT "OTHER"

When I first started my job at RNS, the largest secular newsroom devoted to religion coverage in the country, editor Jim Woodworth steered me away from covering hard news on the religion front, saying I'd "get slaughtered" by religion experts who would discover my ignorance on mainline theology and doctrines. Instead, I wrote features on Buddhism and mysticism. Once I reported a story on the Hare Krishnas, a Hindu sect who were often seen on the busy streets of New York in the 1970s, dancing and chanting the name of Lord Krishna, which they said filled the air with the good vibes of the Godhead. They had a center with a restaurant that served sanctified food, blessed by Krishna, which I enjoyed with the devotees after joining them in dancing and chanting.

Woodworth also sent me out searching for stories with unexpected religion angles such as addiction, mental health, family life, and gender roles—stories he thought people would be interested in. My 1972 story of a visit to a Gamblers Anonymous meeting described the group recovery session popularized by Alcoholics Anonymous and its 12-step program, which has become a popular therapy to deal with any addiction. Group meetings typically include the serenity prayer:

> "God, grant me the serenity to accept the things I cannot change,
>
> Courage to change the things I can,
>
> And wisdom to know the difference."

Writing on mental health and religion in 1973, I learned that an aspect of mental illness may involve a spiritual starvation—a feeling of meaninglessness in life, essentially a religious problem. Many news organizations over the decades failed to recognize readers' hunger for more spiritual content, what my J-School colleague Susan Miller described as "opportunities squandered." She tried to address those needs in her roles as an editor at several mid-sized papers and as vice president for Scripps Howard.

"When I was handed the religion page along with 16 other duties as assistant city editor at the *Bremerton* (WA) *Sun* in 1974," Miller said, "I decided to make it local and interesting. By then, I'd decided that the four pillars of 'newsworthiness' I'd been taught—proximity, prominence, unusualness, and human interest—were flawed.

"People didn't need weird vegetable stories—they needed something relevant to their everyday lives so I wrote about local people with universal religious/ethical/moral problems," she said.

In her 1993 essay, "Opportunity Squandered," written while vice president for Scripps Howard Newspapers, Miller argued that "the number of people affected by a topic is just as proper a measure of newsworthiness as 'unusualness' is." Stories about "ethics and values" she wrote, were among subjects of particularly high interest to women.[2]

When Miller became editor and publisher of the *Monterey County* (CA) *Herald* in 1994, she said, "I worked with the features editor to carve out space each week for religion/ethics/morals and recruited a local Episcopal minister for a 'Dear Abby' column. I said I'd never seen a 'Dear Abby' on religion, but I wanted one. Could he do an ecumenical column on the kinds of questions that clergy get asked all the time?

"He did a couple of sample columns," she said, "and we were off and running. He covered topics like how to respond when your child wants to marry someone of a different faith, or how to handle an ethical problem at work, or what constitutes a 'just war' by the United Nations' definition. I'm a firm believer that these topics can be made of a general, non-denominational interest. We all face /moral dilemmas fairly frequently. We just don't call them that."[3]

Studies by the Pew Research Center, Journalism & Media, support Miller's view that broader ethical and spiritual stories touching people in personal ways get little attention from the media. "When religion did make news, it was often because of accusations about extremism or intolerance," its 2011 review of 46,000 stories from major news sources found.

"An analysis of the past five years of religion coverage suggests that interest in religion tends to be heavily event-driven, at least at the top of the media agenda. In 2008, for instance, Pope Benedict XVI's visit to the United States accounted for about 37 percent of all religion coverage during that year, though the visit itself lasted for only six days in April. And 82.3 percent of the stories about the visit were published or broadcast within that six-day window."[4]

RELIGION AND POLITICS

Dominating news coverage in recent decades has been the intersection of religion and politics, with a pivotal confrontation occurring in 1977. That November, I was in Houston for *RNS* when Phyllis Schlafly, a Republican and constitutional lawyer, led a coalition of an estimated 15,000 religious conservatives who descended on the city for a massive Pro-Life, Pro-Family counter-rally to the National Women's Conference. A major goal of the Houston women's conference, which attracted 2,000 delegates and upwards of 20,000 spectators, was to generate support to pass the Equal Rights Amendment, which would have given women equal rights under the U.S. Constitution.

Schlafly claimed that the ERA would harm more than help women, such as taking away men's legal requirement to pay child support. Those arguments energized the opposition and fueled the ERA's defeat. Schlafly is now credited by some as unifying and mobilizing a powerful conservative political force, sometimes called the "Religious Right," which four decades later helped put Donald Trump in the White House. The political activism of both the Religious Right, which generally focuses on conservative morality and family issues such as abortion, women's roles, and homosexuality, and the Religious Left, which is more focused on social change, set an increasingly combative tone to coverage of both religion and politics in the country.

Marjorie Spruill, an authority on the women's rights movement and author of *Divided We Stand: The Battle Over Women's Rights* and *American Values That Divided a Nation*, concluded that the 1977 women's conference was not the beginning of "something bigger" for the women's movement—but rather for the Religious Right. "Houston built their confidence," she said.[5]

Soon after, conservative movements such as the Moral Majority founded by televangelist Jerry Falwell emerged. By 2016, his son, Jerry Falwell Jr., chancellor of Liberty University, was a leading conservative evangelical who supported Donald Trump for president.

"The formation and growth of the Religious Right hasn't been clearly explained," said veteran religion writer Darrell Turner, a former RNS colleague, adding that the movement is often mislabeled simply as "evangelicals."

"The mainstream media sometimes made it seem as though all evangelicals are on the political right, overlooking those such as [social justice champions] Tony Campolo and Jim Wallis who are more on the left on certain issues of theology and politics. In recent years, evangelical leaders have either distanced themselves from that title or tried to find substitutes, such as 'Jesus follower.'"

More generally, the political activism of the Religious Right focuses on conservative morality and family issues such as women's roles and homosexuality, which are also divisive issues within many denominations.

"Religious groups that find themselves divided on the issue struggle with how to show love and acceptance of gay people while their scriptures have traditionally been interpreted as condemning a same-sex lifestyle," said Turner. He noted that religion writers have closely followed "the rise of same-sex lifestyles and the moves to accommodate them among religious groups that previously opposed them, and the ongoing conflicts surrounding the issue."[6]

Another result of the influx of new non-white immigrants and refugees after 1965 was to propel the "multicultural movement" with its reexamination of the historical view of America as a white Christian nation, greater respect and understand of ethnic and religious diversity and, at its extreme, attacks against "white privilege." Countering that movement, some religious conservatives believed America was a nation chosen by God for a divine purpose.

I found writing a fair story on polarized topics difficult. Religious conservatives and liberals focused on different issues. The Religious Right believed America had a divine origin and destiny and needed to be protected from the rise of atheistic communism and the new morality. The Religious Left was focused on reversing the rise of U. S. militarism and America's historic discrimination against racial minorities. It also believed Americans should turn to simpler lifestyles of piety and compassion for the needs of the poor.

Sometimes in covering social justice-related stories for RNS, I found it difficult to write a report that also met my own ethical standard of furthering world harmony and peace. Many of my stories emanated from Riverside Church in New York, then a center for social activism, where the Rev. William Sloane Coffin

Jr., a leading peace activist, was senior minister. Other stories came from the nearby National Council of Churches at its 19-story Riverside Drive headquarters known as the "God Box" or the "Protestant Vatican on the Hudson."

I also wrote stories about the Research Center for Religion and Human Rights in Closed Societies, which had an office in the God Box and was headed by the Rev. Blahoslav Hruby, a Presbyterian minister, and his wife, Olga, who brought media attention to persecuted Christians and Jews in Eastern Europe and helped them get visas.

An RNS editor once came to my desk with one of my Riverside Church stories in hand, saying "You really hate him [Wm. Sloane Coffin], don't you?" I was surprised, I thought I had written a carefully nuanced story. On another occasion, an editor chastised me saying, "Where's the conflict? There's no conflict here! There's no story!" My response, "Why does there always have to be conflict? Why can't reconciliation be the story?"

A PANDORA OF RELIGIONS

My RNS colleague, Darrell Turner, says that the growing awareness in the United States of religions outside the Judeo-Christian spectrum began to happen after passage of the Immigration and Nationality Act of 1965, which opened doors to non-Europeans and spurred an influx of Muslims, Buddhists, and Hindus. Since then, religion scholars and journalists have tried to explain the complexities of religion—that each of these groups has a diversity of beliefs and doctrines. "I think many reporters and readers both in those days and today have been unaware of the varieties of Christian evangelicalism and in the Jewish community—as well as among Muslims, Hindus, Buddhists, and other less familiar faiths," said Turner, whose RNS beat included evangelicals, Judaism, and cults.

He recalls that when Ayatollah Khomeini and other Shiite Muslims assumed power in Iran after the overthrow of the shah in 1979, many Western observers were surprised to discover that Islam is not monolithic. In later years, Darrell and other RNS staffers wrote about varieties of Buddhism and Hinduism, as well as such outgrowths of the major faiths such as the Bahá'í. "The fact that many people today continue to refer to `the Christians' or 'the Muslims' shows the importance of informed religion writing," Turner observed.

But the Sept. 11, 2001 terrorist attacks on New York and Washington did little to deepen American's understanding of Islam, as reporters' focus on conflict overshawdowed reporting on the nuances of the faith, such as distintinctions between Sunni and Shia Muslims. Or the efforts by American Muslims to have their beliefs understood.

For example, in her book, *A New Religious America, How a "Christian Country" has Become the World's Most Religiously Diverse Nation,* Diana L. Eck described how 11 national Muslim groups in America responded within hours after the 9/11 event in which Islamic terrorists drove their hijacked planes into the World Trade Center, collapsing the Twin Towers. Expressing their solidarity as Americans, the joint Muslim statement denounced the "vicious and cowardly acts of terrorism" and called for "the swift apprehension and punishment of the perpetrators." But their voices were drowned out by the devastating reports from "Ground Zero," and months later, people were still asking, "Why don't Muslim leaders say something?"[7]

The religious and political nuances of groups within Judaism and the Middle East also make for complicated journalism. "Judaism and politics have rarely been as intertwined as they are today both in the United States and in Israel," says J-School Class of 1969 member Stewart Ain, a long-time reporter for the *New York Jewish Week*. "As a result, many of my stories address the divide between the branches of Judaism—Reform, Conservative, Orthodox, and the Haredi or ultra-Orthodox. For instance, Orthodox Jews tend to be Republican and very supportive of President Donald Trump and his embrace of Israel's right-wing government. Conservative and Reform Jews tend to be Democrats and are critical of the Orthodox monopoly that dominates Jewish life in Israel.

"In writing about Israel, I avoid certain tripwires because our readers are from all branches of Judaism and I don't wish to upset anyone," Ain continued. "Thus, I will refer to the 'West Bank' rather than the 'occupied territories,' knowing that some of our readers believe the land is not occupied but rather is the Biblical land given by God to the Jewish people."

Another 1969 classmate, Amy Stone, helped in 1976 to found *Lilith*, a feminist Jewish magazine that very intentionally took on the tripwires within the Jewish world, especially the role of women. "In the heady days of deeply knowledgeable feminists challenging the patriarchal DNA of Judaism, the quarterly magazine was filled with breakthroughs," explained Stone. She took on the men's-only stance of the United Jewish Appeal's Young Leadership Cabinet, the Jewish Theological Seminary, which ordains Conservative rabbis, and other groups that belatedly opened their doors to women. "Over the decades, *Lilith*'s coverage of the creation of women's rituals has grown from experiments within Shabbat, weddings and births to rituals for divorce and miscarriage. With #MeToo, *Lilith* is reporting on long-time abuses of young Jewish women within the Jewish fundraising world, and for years, Lilith has regularly explored Jewish LGBTQ issues," Stone said.

An ambitious study looking back on 30 years of religion coverage by the nation's largest media from 1969 to 1998 analyzed thousands of articles and broadcasts by the *New York Times, Washington Post, Time, Newsweek, U.S. News & World Report,* and the ABC, CBS, and NBC evening newscasts. Led by S. Robert Lichter of the Center for Media and Public Affairs, it found that the "broad reach and rich diversity" of religion in America was reflected in "wide-ranging news coverage" by the secular media, but that the emphasis was largely on the political elements of religious ideas and institutions. Thus, the most heavily covered news involved public policy debates and conflicts with authority in church governance. The sharpest rises in coverage in the 30-year period were in the categories of "religion and politics" and "crime and wrongdoing."

The study also found that while the volume of news about the main Christian and Jewish groups remained the same, the volume of news abut relatively small Eastern and new religious movements grew substantially. A major weakness in religion covereage, the study concluded, was that "fully 95 percent" of the religion stories contained "no spiritual dimension."[8]

REPORTING ON NEW AGE RELIGION

> "Have hope! Though we seem to be living in an 'age of slaughter,' we stand at the threshold of a new epoch. Planet earth is giving birth to a new age. A new concept of spirituality is emerging which transcends splits between spirit and matter and sees the whole of Earth as a 'sacred living organism.'"[9]

This was my lead reflecting some of the ideas expressed at an interfaith conference I covered on "Christianity, Judaism, Islam, the Emerging Spirituality," held in New York in March 1983 at the Episcopal Cathedral of St. John the Divine. It was one of many stories I covered for RNS at the Cathedral, then a stimulating center for ecumism and exploration of the new spirituality.

The March 1983 event was the first major "new age" conference oriented to persons from Western faiths. Numerous new age events had been held in the previous two decades—but most were dominated by groups representing Eastern religions, psychic, and occult groups, as well as the human potential movement which later emerged as quests for "religion in every day life" and self improvement through integration of mind-body-spirit.

Attending the conference were some 250 people from varied backgrounds, including clergy and members from mainline denominations, un-churched people with renewed interest in religion, avant-guard religious leaders, students of mysticism, and new age thinkers from academia and the arts.

"Diversity is the name of the game, and unity is the name of the game," said the Rt. Rev. James Park Morton, the Episcopal Cathedral dean who opened the conference. He and others stressed that they weren't advocating for a brand new religion, but for the deepening of people's own faiths, growth of tolerance and respect for other beliefs, and the search for the "core meanings" of all faiths.

"We have treasures in the attic," said conference speaker Vivienne Hull, reflecting the common view that religions of the West as well as the East contain wisdom and paths to union with God. "There is a whole sacred heritage of humanity that must go forward with us."

Over the decades, public interest has soared on such topics as biblical prophecy, physical earth changes, UFOs and aliens. Change, too, is sweeping Christianity, according to Phyllis Tickle, who in 1992 became founding editor of the religion department for *Publishers Weekly*. Her 2012 book, *The Great Emergence*, for instance, claims that Christianity, among other religions, is going through a massive cyclical change as the public becomes increasingly distrustful of institutions. Tickle writes:

> "People under 40 right now have been born right smack-dab into a fully matured emergence, the Great Emergence. They can't change their sensibilities any more than they can change the color of their eyes. They're going to be non-hierarchal. They're going to be afraid of institutions. They're going to want to spread out horizontally. They want to be communal. They're going to be actively involved in social justice as they define it, and not in the usual Protestant way. They are connected to the world. They're 'glocal'—I hate that word—but they think glocally. All of those things are sensibilities that are ingrained now; they have no choice."[10]

"American religion is changing before our eyes," said Bob Smietana, a longtime religion writer who in 2018 was named editor-in-chief of RNS. The independent non-profit, founded in 1934, is now affiliated with the Missouri School of Journalism at the University of Missouri. He continues:

> "Old denominations are fading while new traditions are taking their place. Churches, synagogues, mosques and temples are reinventing themselves as our formerly mostly-white Christian nation is becoming increasingly religiously and ethnically diverse. Meanwhile, the numbers of 'Nones'—Americans who claim no religious identity—has skyrocketed. Yet faith still shapes every part of life for many Americans: what they wear ... who they marry, where they work ... where they spend their money, even what direction they face while praying. Deeply held religious views and values shape how Americans are born and how they die."[11]

An example of fulfilling a spiritual need without a religious imprimatur might be the 2014 book written by my 1969 J-School classmate Stewart Ain and his wife, *The Living Memories Project*, which focuses on how our loved ones lived, not how they died. "The act of doing research and writing the book proved therapeutic for both of us because we lost all of our parents during the process," said Ain. "As we learned how others kept the memory of their loved ones alive ... we learned that although a loved one is physically gone, he/she is always with you in some way." The book, he said, resonated with readers who have contributed their own living memories projects to their website.

The current interest in spirituality is not new, but the re-emergence of something that's always been there, according to scholars such as theologian Harvey

Cox,[12] author of the 1965 classic, *The Secular City*. They point out that many cultures past and present hold the "magical world view" that everything is alive with spirit, teeming with nature spirits, gods and goddesses.

Now, with new scientific findings that blur the boundaries of the secular and the divine, a new version of the magical world view is rising which sees all of humanity, the earth, and the universe as a living sacred whole, united by a higher spiritual law.

In 2001, as part of my research on complementary and alternative medicine, I attended a "prophets" conference" in New York. It featured speakers such as physicist Russell Targ, who had been part of "remote-viewing" ESP experiments for the CIA at the Stanford Research Institute; theoretical physicist Michio Kaku, who speculates that earthlings are in the basement or sub-basement of cultures in our galaxy; and geologist Gregg Braden, who has researched the "wisdom of the ancients" and asserted that the "Shift of the Ages has already begun." Another leader is Larry Dossey M.D., who studies the power of group prayers and meditation.

These topics are still considered too "far out" to be seriously covered by most of the mainstream media, but they are widely discussed in gatherings and "alternative" forums on the internet, attracting vast constellations of people who seriously believe in these ideas.

NEW OPPORTUNITIES FOR RELIGION WRITERS

"Many meaningful faith and value stories are waiting to be told, which creates great opportunities for these niche religion website startups," said Debra L. Mason, professor emerita of the Missouri School of Journalism and publisher emerita of Religion News Service, pointing to a void left by "the elimination of the religion beat at many media outlets."[13]

Still, membership in the Religion News Association, which Mason helped to build as the premier organization for religion writers and which is based at the Missouri journalism school, has held steady at about 400–500 members over the last 15 years. The group also offers free tools to train religion writers on its website, www.religionlink.com.

While print jobs for religion writers have declined, religion news has benefited from the internet, Ain of the *New York Jewish Week* observed. "The internet has permitted our newspaper's stories to be seen worldwide and we now have a large Israeli readership. The internet has also allowed us to post short video interviews with key Jewish leaders."

Columbia J-School professor Ari Goldman, who directs the school's Scripps Howard Program in Religion, Journalism, and Spiritual Life, in 2018 invited RNS editor Smietana to a "conversation" with students, where the two were upbeat about the future of the field.

"Right now is a great time to be a religion reporter," said Smietana. "Walk out the door, be curious, pay attention—and you can find a great story! What is the essence of religion reporting? It's about human beings, how they live. It's the story of people's lives."

In a polarized America, he said, such stories are critical. "We live in different universes—New York, California, Nashville . . . and we have to find ways to understand each other and get along better. The work of RNS is more important now than ever before," with a mission to build a "journalistic bridge" between people of different faiths, telling their important stories in interesting ways.

A Pew Center study in 2018 redefined religion's "different universes." Instead of looking at traditional institutions, the study focused on the "intrinsic connections between religion, race and politics in America." This new "religious topography" identified groups including the "Sunday Stalwarts," who are most involved in their religion and their churches and tend to be Republican; "God-and-Country-Believers," who are "less active in church groups," but "tilt right on social and political issues;" the "Diversely Devout," largely made up of racial and ethnic minorities who are also diverse in their beliefs; the affluent, highly educated "Solidly Secular;" and the "Religion Resisters" who, while spiritual, rebel against organized religion and tend to be Democrats.[14]

Religion experts still cover traditional topics, said Smietana, but there is "so much religion out there that's not being covered." A $4.9 million grant from the Lilly Endowment in 2019 to create a "Global Religion Journalism Initiative" will help matters. The money—one of the largest grants to religion coverage in decades—will fund salaries for 13 new religion positions at the Associated Press, RNS, and the non-profit publisher, The Conversation, to work collaboratively on multiple platforms.

Goldman, a former religion reporter at the *New York Times*, began teaching religion at the J-School in 1993 after writing *The Search for God at Harvard*. Among his goals is to make his students "religiously literate" by introducing them to the varieties of religious experience in the United States and around the world. His second goal, he said, is to teach students how to write about religion without falling back on stereotypes and clichés.

Regardless of their "beat," he says, all journalists need to know about religion. "It is one of the major motivating factors in American life," he tells students. "Based on religion, people make decisions about where to live, what to eat, where to send their children to school and even how to vote."[15]

Mainstream media appear to be awakening to the need for a better understanding of religion's complex landscape. Said *New York Times* executive editor Dean Baquet: "I think . . . the media powerhouses don't quite get religion. We don't get religion. We don't get the role of religion in people's lives. And I think we can do much, much better."[16]

NOTES

1. Lichter, S. Robert, Linda S. Lichter, Daniel R. Amundsen, "Media Coverage of Religion in America 1969–1998," *Center for Media and Public Affairs*, last modified April 2000, http://users.clas.ufl.edu/kenwald/pos4291/spring_00/relig2000.htm.
2. Susan B. Miller, "Opportunity Squandered—Newspapers and Women's News," *Media Studies Journal* (Winter/Spring 1993): 170–171.
3. Unless otherwise noted, any information or quotations from members of the Columbia University Journalism School, Class of 1969, were obtained through emails or interviews between January and March 2019.
4. Jesse Holcomb, "Religion in the News, *Pew Research Center*, last modified February 23, 2012, https://www.journalism.org/2012/02/23/religion-news-0/.
5. Dianna Wray, "The 1977 National Women's Conference in Houston Was Supposed to Change the World. What Went Wrong?" *Houstonia*, last modified February 2018.
6. Darrell Turner in email interviews with author, November 2018 to March 2019.
7. Diana L. Eck, *A New Religious America* (New York: HarperCollins, 2001), xiv.
8. Lichter, "Media Coverage of Religion."
9. Tammy Tanaka, "Inter-faith Gathering Fastens Gaze on 'New Age' of Religion," *Religious News Service*, March 8, 1983.
10. "Phyllis Tickle: Like an Anthill," *Faith and Leadership*, last modified August 30, 2010, https://www.faithandleadership.com/phyllis-tickle-anthill.
11. Bob Smietana email interviews with author, March and April 2019.
12. Harvey Cox, *The Secular City* (Princeton: Princeton University Press, 2013).
13. "Debra Mason, RCC 2012 speaker, comments on changes at RNS," *Religion Communicators Council*, accessed April 14, 2019, https://www.religioncommunicators.org/national-network-of-religion-sites-fills-gap-for-religion-news.
14. "The Religious Typology, a New Way to Categorize Americans by Religion," *Pew Research Center*, last modified August 29, 2018, https://www.pewforum.org/2018/08/29/the-religious-typology/.
15. Ari Goldman email interviews with author, March 18, 19, 2019.
16. David French, "If You Don't Get Religion, You Can't 'Get' America or the World," *National Review*, last modified December 14, 2016. https://www.nationalreview.com/2016/12/religion-american-media-coverage-dumb-reporting-sins/

CHAPTER ELEVEN

Book Publishing: Authors on the Front Line

CARLA FINE

Books are magical and enchanting: they have covers protecting your words and thoughts; they have a title page where you can write an inscription for readers; they have your photograph and biography on the back flap, a table of contents, a space for acknowledgments, and, if you can afford it, an index. When you tell people you write books, their first question is about the subject. You are an expert, deservedly or not.

The process of publishing books today, however, is not so enchanting. It is a process that has changed radically over the past 50 years, putting more responsibility and expense on the shoulders of writers. Where once publishers took care of everything from editing to marketing—often leaving authors free to simply write their story—authors today frequently must hire their own editors, do their own marketing, and create their own world of social media to publicize their book. Increasingly, they cannot even get the attention of publishers and are spending thousands of their own dollars to self-publish. At the same time, the world of self-publishing gives authors a platform to get their books out to the public without being restricted by the conventions of the traditional book publishing industry.

"While it's easier today to publish a book than it was years ago, it's more difficult to earn money from its publication," says David Hammer, an attorney who graduated with me in 1969 from the Columbia University School of Journalism. "The result is that non-professional writers have an easier time in publishing a single book on a specific topic but serious writers find it more difficult to earn a living as full-time authors."[1]

JOHN MONTELEONE

I started my work in book publishing in 1969, the year of our graduation. The late Dick Schaap, an adjunct professor at the J-School and a best-selling author, hired me to do reporting, editing, and audiotape transcriptions. I helped him prepare the manuscripts for several books that his company, Maddick Manuscripts, had under contract, including *I Can't Wait Until Tomorrow Because I Get Better Looking Everyday* by NY Jets Quarterback Joe Namath and *The Year the Mets Lost Last Place*, which chronicled the 1969 season in which the Mets won their first World Series championship.

After working for an independent publisher, I launched my own book-producing company, Mountain Lion, Inc. Through the years, I authored, edited, and packaged/produced books for adults, young adults, and children on sports and reference topics. In later years, I represented authors and published a limited number of titles under the Mountain Lion brand.

A noteworthy change that I have seen in book publishing is the shrinking shelf life of a published title. Today, books are like waves washing up on the shore—here on the bookstore shelf for a moment and then quickly gone, washed back out to sea and replaced. Like book retailers who want to turn over inventory, publishers likewise value the storage space in their warehouses. If a slow-selling title occupies space that a new title fresh off the presses needs, the former is soon gone (remaindered and sold as bargain book or simply destroyed).

The emergence of the e-book is a change—for the better, I think—because e-books help keep books alive. An e-book requires no warehouse space, costs less than hardcover or softcover editions, and keeps royalties flowing to the author long after he/she has toiled in bringing the manuscript to completion. Not all types of books lend themselves to an e-book format, so the change is limited.

Journalists have historically turned to book writing as a medium for conveying in-depth reporting, as did at least 25 of the 101 members of the Class of 1969, including me. I am the author and co-author of nine commercial trade books, all published by prestigious publishers in both hardcover and paperback and each represented by a top literary agent. Yet, only one of my books, *No Time to Say Goodbye: Surviving the Suicide of a Loved One*, published in 1997 by Doubleday, remains actively in print by the original publisher.[2] Now in its 23rd printing, the book has sold more than 100,000 copies and shows no sign of slowing down: *No Time to Say Goodbye* is available in hardback, paperback, e-book, Kindle, Audiobook (narrated by me), and has been translated into Korean, Japanese, and Portuguese. The book can actually be found on bookshelves in brick and mortar bookstores as well as in libraries throughout the country.

Yet, of all my books, this is the only one that earned back my advance from my publishers and for which I still continue to receive modest yearly royalties. I also earn money from speaking to groups about suicide loss, although many of my talks are given *pro bono*. Despite my track record, I am considered a "mid-list" author—meaning well respected, with books that sell and provide income but are not blockbusters or best sellers. My agent has warned me that she will have difficulty selling my current book proposal.

Why did *No Time to Say Goodbye* "succeed?" My other books were equally important, well written, well edited, well marketed, well represented, and many were written in collaboration with prominent authorities in their fields. They dealt with subjects that remain relevant today such as empowerment for girls, mentorship for African American youth, job opportunities for Latinos, and the achievement gap in American education. One of them actually was a follow-up book to *No Time to Say Goodbye*, addressing precisely the same subject (suicide loss) and co-written with one of the most prominent psychiatrists in the field. Yet, my later books sold only a few thousand copies in hardback and paperback, faded quickly from public view, and now are listed on Amazon at bargain prices with occasional sales that generate no royalties for me.

Based on my research about how publishing has changed in the last 50 years, as well as from my personal and professional experiences and those of many of my author-classmates, I believe that my publisher still continues to print *No Time to Say Goodbye* for several reasons. First, the book has an "evergreen audience:" people kill themselves every year and every year new survivors of suicide loss look for help and guidance. My book was one of the first published on suicide loss because of the stigma of the subject and the reluctance of publishers to talk about the subject of suicide; as such, it is considered a "classic" in the field. I wrote from personal experience—my first husband killed himself—and I wrote from passion, understanding, and a mission: I was "one" with my readers.

GARTH HALLBERG

Before I transitioned to writing full-time, I spent 30-plus years in advertising and marketing consulting. I've published one nonfiction marketing book (*All Consumers Are Not Created Equal*, Wiley, 1995), and two novels under my own imprint. I have another novel currently out with an agent and am deep into Opus #4, so writing is not a hobby but a second career, albeit a far less lucrative way of making a living.

Putting on my former marketing hat, the reasons that publishing has become a different business are clear. There's too much product available, thanks in large part to self-publishing on Amazon and Create Space. Demand is also down because of all the new technology-driven information and entertainment options. Distribution has become chaotic—bookstores are fading fast and the Amazon page is not trying to sell the author's book but any book that seems similar; publishers are public companies with bottom line concerns, driving a star system where only "bankable" authors who are "brands" make money. Editors are mostly acquisition experts, not story-shapers.

These changes have not benefitted authors. Given the upheaval in the industry, the biggest problem for any author is "discovery," a.k.a. brand awareness. And authors get little editorial guidance, are often asked to fund their own copyediting and proofreading, and to spearhead marketing efforts. And woe to the aspiring author who has the temerity to believe their book breaks new ground; the first question a publisher or agent will ask is, "What other books are like yours?" Genre is king. Welcome to the "Literary-Industrial Complex."

In addition, I used my journalism training to interview more than 60 people who had also lost a loved one to suicide, integrating their stories together with mine. And, most important, more than 20 years after its publication, *No Time to Say Goodbye* still connects with its readers.

While my first book succeeded for reasons quite specific to its content, my others did not for reasons more related to changes in the world of book publishing.

In the 50 years since I graduated from the J-School with the goal of being a published author, book publishing has turned into a completely new industry—the "Literary-Industrial Complex," as my classmate Garth Hallberg, a published author who has spent many years in marketing, calls it.

Although the changes may seem discouraging at first to a future book author, these very changes also offer many new and exciting opportunities. What has not changed over the past 50 years is that writing books is exhilarating, frustrating, and adventurous, and that being an author changes not only your life but also the lives of your readers as well.

CHANGES OVER THE YEARS

My father, Benjamin Fine (Columbia University J-School, 1933), was the education editor of the *New York Times* for almost 30 years and a Pulitzer Prize winner. He wrote 24 books. I have a most vivid memory of him sitting at his manual typewriter—now on the shelf over my desk—tapping out text on the keys. He would encourage me and my sister Janet (J-School Class of 1975 and author of four books) to write books. "You will always be able to capitalize on calamity," he kind of joked—but not really. "Whatever happens to you, you can write about it. And, if you're lucky, others will read what you have to say."

But somewhere along the line, book publishing changed. According to the Authors Guild, the nation's oldest and largest professional writers' organization, full-time mid-list and literary writers are on the verge of extinction:

> "While mainstream publishers enjoy the cachet and increased sales that stem from publishing award-winning authors, in general they remain risk-averse, chasing 'blockbuster' and celebrity authors. To land and keep these top-selling authors, publishers are forced to pay six-figure advances and then spend enormous resources promoting the books to recoup the huge outlays. This leaves fewer resources for mid-list writers—the 90 percent—where most literary fiction and non-fiction authors fall."[3]

That comment comes from a 2019 report by the Authors Guild, published along with results of the largest survey to date of writing-related earnings by American authors. Canvassing 5,067 published book authors traditional, hybrid and self-published, the survey found that:

LEWIS FISHER

In 18 years, my Maverick Publishing Company published 49 regional general interest non-fiction books by 28 authors including myself until I sold it in 2014 to Trinity University Press. Since then, increasing changes in publishing, particularly in distribution, have further complicated profitability of small independent publishers, although individual authors with a guerrilla mentality can still make self-publishing work.

My successful exit from my company, to be sure, required titles with a uniformly high level of quality that also dominated a niche market. At the start, I had found myself in San Antonio, one of the nation's top travel destinations, which provided a self-renewing market for regional books. But San Antonio seemed to rely on oral traditions and tall tales to recall its storied past, and there was a lot more to be told. I sensed a market for professionally produced general interest nonfiction books about the city. I also saw a chance to skip the 10 percent royalties publishers pay authors and do the job myself. Why not get 100 percent of the net profits—or as much as 90 percent after giving other authors their (admittedly meager) share? Since getting started with a single self-published title is almost as much trouble as self-publishing two or three, I went for the whole show.

An important boost in profitability came from not having to bother with a distributor that charges commissions for actively selling books and ships to wholesalers who ship to bookstores. By having to worry little about national marketing, I could deal directly with wholesalers or do the shipping myself and, within the regional target area, I could also sell directly to independent bookstores, museum shops, and nontraditional outlets.

A downside of savings from a home office and garage warehouse was the slight grade up my driveway. The slope was too steep to move to the garage the full 2,000-pound pallets of boxed books that truckers lowered on a lift gate to the street in front of my house. Nearly half the boxes had to be taken off pallets and rolled up on two-wheel dollies. The rest could stay on, the driver pulling on his pallet jack and me pushing from behind.

If you decide to go the self-publishing route, just be sure you can hold your enthusiasm through the tedium, uncertainty and, literally, heavy lifting that it takes to profitably produce a book on your own.

- Literary writers experienced the biggest decline in book-related income (down 27 percent in four years) followed by general non-fiction (down 8 percent), raising serious concerns about the vibrancy of our continued literary heritage.
- More book authors, even those who consider themselves full-time writers, are forced to hold down multiple jobs to earn enough money to survive. This includes authors who have written books for decades and have survived on their writing in the past. In 2017, only 21 percent of full-time published authors derived 100 percent of their individual income from book advances and royalties, and only 57 percent of full-time published authors lived entirely on writing-related work, with speaking engagements, book reviewing, ghost-writing, editing, or teaching supplementing their book income.
- Even with this supplemental money, book authors who consider themselves full-time only earned a median income of $20,300 from their writing, well below the federal poverty line for a family of three or more, and considerably lower than the $25,000 median income that full-time authors earned in 2009.
- Yearly incomes for all book authors are at historic lows: the median income for a book author in 2017 was $6,080, down 42 percent from 2009. Earnings from book income alone—advances and royalties—fell even more, declining 21 percent to $3,100 in 2017 from $3,900 in 2013 and nearly a free-fall from the $6,250 in 2009.
- Roughly 25 percent of all published authors surveyed earned $0 in book-related income in 2017.
- Amazon now dominates the book industry, both as a seller of books and as a publishing house. Amazon currently owns 72 percent of the online retail book market, which includes both e-books and print books, and nearly 50 percent of all new book units sold in the U.S.
- Self-published authors' book-related income levels are $1,951, nearly 60 percent lower than traditionally published authors. Most self-published authors have limited options other than to accept Amazon's non-negotiable terms.

Academic and small/independent presses, while an option for book publishing, will likely not reap big rewards for writers either. According to Jennifer Crewe, president of the Association of University Presses, the biggest challenge remains the low sales of scholarly monographs, such as revised dissertations or scholarly books with a narrow focus in a small field.

"Libraries share copies and individuals don't purchase the new books in their fields as they did years ago," she explains. In addition, many academic and university

ALAN EHRENHALT

I was the executive editor of *Governing* magazine for 19 years. I've written three books, all commercial trade books. Having a long-time employer who was willing to give me time off made a big difference. For the first book, I got a paid, one-year book leave, which was wonderful. For the other two, I was able to get off one day a week for a year or so. Still, most of the work in each case had to be done while doing my day job. I used to get up early to work on the book. There's nothing like getting up at 5 a.m. to tell you whether you really want to finish a book or not. But I would set myself a fixed number of words each day and try to hit it, even if I didn't feel very inspired that particular day. If you can write 1,000 words a day, at the end of a year you have a pretty substantial book.

I sometimes tell people that landing a book deal is like selling a house—you only need one yes vote. I must have 25 rejections to go with my three acceptance letters. I also tell writers who are just starting out that an article in a good magazine can be the best way to break into the system.

All my books got mostly positive reviews, but only one was more than a modest seller. The three books together did a lot to help me define my image of myself as a writer, even though I had a full-time job as a magazine editor.

Writers are always complaining about inadequate publicity from the publisher, but in my experience, the most important thing wasn't publicity but distribution. If the writer (or editor) can persuade the marketers to order a healthy number of books, they will be visible in bookstores and people will buy them. If I could change my publishing fate in just one way, it would be to somehow get larger print runs. Of course, print runs may be less important now with Amazon, but even today I think it's important to have that stack of your books sitting there at Politics and Prose or Barnes and Noble.

presses also publish regional books on general topics of interest to people living in their state but with a sales potential too small for a commercial publisher to consider.

"Scholarly and trade books are only separate in terms of their audience size and sales prospects," Crewe says. "Yet, in the end, I think there will always be a market for scholarly books on topics with broad appeal that are accessible to general readers."[4]

The take away: professional writers are not doing well. Most of them are not really "full-time" writers since they can no longer live by writing alone. Their need to find outside work poses a severe hardship for them, but it also poses a threat to all of us. As James Gleick, author and president of the Authors Guilds warns, "When you impoverish a nation's authors, you impoverish its readers."

CAUSES FOR FALLING INCOME

The decline in earnings for book authors is a product of the growing dominance of Amazon over the marketplace. Amazon charges commission and marketing fees to publishers to essentially prevent their books from being buried on the site. Small and independent publishers, with fewer resources and less bargaining power, are particularly hard hit. Book publishing companies then pass these losses along to writers in the form of lower royalties and advances. Authors also lose out on income from books resold on Amazon.[5]

Roxana Robinson, author and past president of the Guild, says: "Maybe the worst blow to writers is Amazon's online secondary market. Within months of a new book's publication, 'new' and 'lightly used' copies are offered alongside the publisher's, for fractions of the price, in a sale that provides no royalties to the author. Writers can't survive without royalties. Copyright was intended to protect them from just this: the sale of their work without compensation."

According to the Authors Guild survey, other reasons for falling incomes for book authors include:

1. Lower royalties and advances for mid-list books, including the extremely low royalties paid on the increasing number of deeply discounted sales and e-books.
2. The blockbuster mentality of book publishers who grant celebrity writers massive advances and market them wildly at the expense of mid-list authors.
3. Many electronic uses, such as classroom course packs, Google Books and Open Library, now made on a royalty-free basis.

TED GEST

I covered anticrime policy for many years for *U.S. News & World Report* and I thought that my expertise combined with the high crime rates of the 1990s could be the foundation for a book. I went to a well-known agent who said she would give it a try but feared that it was too wonkish to be bought by a major publisher, even if it had good detail and analysis of what had happened. She was right. No mass-market publisher bought the book, although a respected academic firm, Oxford University Press, did buy it and *Crime and Politics* was published in 2001. Although various academics have said they have used it in classes, I don't think I ever made any profit from this, i.e., the royalties didn't exceed the advance.

4. Increased competition from Amazon's Kindle Unlimited program as well as the massive number of "new" books sold cheaply by Amazon resellers alongside the publisher's copies.

Richard Russo, a noted author and vice president of the Authors Guild, says:

> "There was a time in America, not so very long ago, that dedicated, talented fiction and non-fiction writers who put in the time and learned the craft could make a living doing what they did best, while contributing enormously to the American knowledge, culture, and the arts. That is no longer the case for most authors, especially those trying to start careers today."[6]

There is an upside to these statistics: More people are writing and publishing books than ever before. Of those surveyed, 33 percent published their first book in the past five years and the number of authors self-publishing books rose by 72 percent since 2013. The bibliographic website Bowker reports that more than one million books were published in the U.S. in 2017, up from 300,000 in 2009, and that two-thirds of those books are self-published.[7]

Many of those books are then recorded, with the possibility of royalties for authors. Audiobook sales are the fastest-growing segment in the digital publishing industry with over $2.5 billion dollars in sales in the U.S. in 2017. Of all listeners, nearly half are under 35 and 29 percent use their smartphones. A third listen to books in their car.[8]

Yet, writing books still requires resources and if you don't have money to support yourself or to self-publish, your book will not see the light of day.

What can be done to increase the earnings of book authors? Some recommendations of the Authors Guild include:

1. Congress should enact an exemption to antitrust law to permit publishers and self-published authors to negotiate collectively with Amazon, Google, and Facebook to equalize the bargaining power.
2. Resellers who sell new books should pay royalties to authors.
3. Publishers should pay higher royalties on e-books and deeply discounted books and they should destroy all bookstore returns to prevent them from getting into the secondary market.

THE SURGE OF SELF-PUBLISHING

Since 2000, the number of major book publishers has dropped from 36 to approximately five, largely due to the rise of online retail and e-books. But today's self-publishing market has actually grown in response to these changes.[9] Many published

DAVID GUMPERT

I self-published a book in 2015 titled *The Raw Milk Answer Book*. I had already published two books on raw milk via a conventional publisher, but the more I read, the more I became convinced that self-publishing could be a realistic alternative to traditional publishing's ever-smaller advances, minimal promotion, and tiny royalties. I raised $12,000 from a fundraising campaign from my blog followers, more than triple any advance I was being offered by conventional publishers. I also had the book recorded for distribution on Audible and produced a Kindle version. The keys to going it alone were twofold: having a serious "platform" and a serious following; I had an active blog that reported on food rights issues with about 4,000 followers.

How did I do it? In retrospect, two factors were most helpful: loyalty and commitment from my blog followers, and an array of "prizes" for those who contributed to the crowd-funding campaign including signed copies of the book as well as small-group tours of two raw-dairy farms for those who gave the most money.

Figure 11.1: After a career reporting on entrepreneurship, David Gumpert began writing books about purveyors of raw milk and other food producers. At a 2012 farm conference in Seven Springs, Pennsylvania, he is introduced to a prize-winning chicken. Source: *Courtesy of David Gumpert*

authors, including members of my Class of 1969, disappointed by traditional publishers (lack of visibility, being thrown over for ghost-written celebrity books, just being forgotten) have decided to go the self-publishing route.

Lewis Fisher, a J-School classmate who is a successful author and publisher, advises:

> "You may find trying to crash the barriers of mainstream publishers unappealing. It may be difficult to find an agent, and even then, the wait for a publisher's answer may try your patience. If accepted, there's another long wait for publication, and the result may not be up to your expectations. But if you have a firm grasp on a distinctive subject, feel sufficiently trained in the fundamentals of good writing, and grasp the elements that make up a first-rate book, then self-publishing may be for you."

Self-publishing requires a lot of detail work as well as entrepreneurial skills—or hiring someone with those skills—if the book is to get traction. The good news is that self-published books can be printed quickly and their quality is often indistinguishable from traditionally published books. And while authors forgo the prestige and marketing arm of a publishing house, they do get the gratification of being a published author and a larger share of whatever sales they can muster.

On the other hand, the author is responsible financially for the entire process: editing, copyediting, copywriting, book cover, release, distribution, and publicity. And because most mainstream media will not review a self-published book or interview the author, authors also need to create and maintain Twitter accounts, Facebook groups, email chains, etc. for any kind of visibility.

The average self-published print book sells only about 250 copies over its lifetime[10] and there's the inevitably of dealing with Amazon, whose influence in the world of book publishing is transformative. As the world's largest book retailer, it can decide which books to rescue from obscurity as well as which titles become best sellers. In addition, since Amazon entered the $16 billion-a-year consumer book publishing industry in 2009, it now publishes its own books with 16 different imprints in the U.S. alone.[11]

On the positive side, Amazon offers authors a huge potential audience. It has more than 100 million Amazon Prime members world-wide and members get deals that encourage reading, including Amazon First Reads and Kindle Unlimited e-book subscription plans. With smartphones and other electronic devices, everyone can have a personal portable library.[12]

Another upside for writers: many freelance professionals—editors, writers, proofreaders, indexers, book doctors—earn money from authors who self-publish and from self-publishing companies.

Also helpful to authors are the "hybrid publishers" who have emerged in the new book economy. Such companies take on the responsibility for publishing a book if the author shoulders some of the cost. Some are selective about their

DOTTY BROWN

After taking a buyout from the *Philadelphia Inquirer* after 30 years as a reporter and assigning editor, I started a blog called "Unretiring" in which I interviewed people about their transition from full-time work to what I called "the next great thing." After about a year of interviews, I thought I had enough for a book and approached an agent who told me, "I can't sell retirement books," so I gave up on the idea. Just then, an editor at Temple University Press asked me to write a book on the history of Boathouse Row, Philadelphia's iconic nineteenth century venue for rowing. No matter that Temple was offering me a small advance of $3,500; I was at that time in my life where money was not a deal breaker.

The book, which took three intense years of research and writing, used every skill I had acquired during my career: investigative reporting, interviewing, writing, storytelling, and thinking visually. The result was not just a book, *Boathouse Row: Waves of Change in the Birthplace of American Rowing*, but a life change. I suddenly was confronted with the need to learn new skills: marketing and public speaking. Fortunately, Temple University Press set up numerous speaking engagements during the book's first year. On my own, I set up a website and plunged into social media with Twitter, Facebook, and LinkedIn to promote my blog about the Row. I am now regarded as Philadelphia's expert on Boathouse Row—my new identity.

authors, much like traditional publishers; others, like the old "vanity presses," will print anyone's book for a fee. On her blog, Jane Friedman, author of *The Business of Being a Writer*, advises authors to check out how much the publisher will do for them, such as marketing and distributing the books to brick and mortar bookstores or other retail channels.[13] Although self-publishing authors can easily get distribution through Amazon, the more the hybrid publisher does, the more help for the author. In addition, a good hybrid publisher works with authors before and after publication, though the authors may have to pay to continue this relationship.

MARKETING YOUR BOOK

In both traditional and self-publishing, marketing is the key. Many times, authors have to begin marketing their book long before it is published or even written. Traditional authors usually rely on their publisher and its public relations department to contact the news media, handle social media, pay for advertising, find subscription reading and listening services, organize and fund book tours, promote books to book clubs, and so on. These services now are rarely provided to most authors and even celebrity authors usually pay out of their own pockets to market and publicize their books.

"Given the ease of book publishing today, the biggest challenge facing authors is rarely how to get published, but how to make their book visible and discoverable in a market with so much choice and competition," warns the Authors Guild. "You can't push the same buttons that were pushed in 2007 and expect the same level of sales or success that were achieved then." And no wonder, with more than 32 million books in print and approximately 50,000 new e-books released every month by Kindle.[14]

As a result, the concept of "having a platform" has become essential in book publishing. What is a platform? According to Nick Morgan, writing in *Forbes* magazine, it is getting enough people to care about you and your book, through social media, traditional media, word of mouth, bake sales—any way you can. "It's creating a community of people with a genuine interest in the idea you're putting forward," he writes. "It's the way in which you create a strong brand around you and the book and get the world to pay attention."

He also advises every author to build a network, both offline and online, to assist in the marketing and promotion of his or her book and to be alert to the changing digital and technical advancements that will attract attention to your book.[15]

John Monteleone, a J-School classmate who is a successful author and publisher, also emphasizes the significance of authors establishing a personal platform:

JOHN HENRY

In 2012, I was finishing the manuscript for a book about a lifelong interest of mine: the largest fleet of passenger steamers ever to sail on North America's inland waters. Presuming a limited audience for this book, I planned to self-publish it. Happily, fate intervened: The man who was advising me on illustrations for the book had a friend in Canada who suggested that since the passenger fleet in question was Montreal-based, I should send my manuscript to a publisher specializing in Canadian history, Dundurn Press in Toronto. Dundurn liked my writing and decided to publish *Great White Fleet: Celebrating Canada Steamship Lines Passenger Ships* in 2013. The book sold out all 2,000 copies and remains available on Kindle.

"I have seen many changes in book publishing, the greatest one being the rising importance of an author's platform, that is, the ability of the author to gain publicity and sell books via independent venues such as an author's website. It is often the most decisive factor in securing a publishing agreement. Publishers relentlessly strive to publish books that can be promoted beyond their ordinary channels. Thus, celebrities of all stripes—especially those who have huge television viewership—not only secure contracts but also snag large royalty advances. I think of these authors as the tall trees that blot out the sunshine that the saplings, that is, emerging writers, need to grow."

WHAT TO EXPECT IN THE FUTURE

In 2006, I wrote a book, *Touched by Suicide: Hope and Healing after Loss*, published as an original trade paperback by Gotham Press and co-authored with a prominent psychiatrist, Michael F. Myers, MD. Although we had a terrific editor, an enthusiastic agent, widespread distribution, marketing and publicity from the publishers, our book never earned out its modest advance. It is now available only on Amazon and Kindle.

Ten years after our book was published, Dr. Myers, who had authored seven other books and hundreds of articles, was unable to sell his book proposal on physician suicide to any publisher. His agent was told over and over that the subject occupied "too small a niche." Submitting the proposal to publishers on his own, he was also repeatedly turned down. At that point he turned to self-publishing.

In 2017, Dr. Myers went through Amazon to self-publish *Why Physicians Die by Suicide: Lessons Learned from Their Families and Others Who Cared*. After careful research, he chose a service to help him format his book, choose a cover, and get it printed and listed on Amazon. In 2019, it was selling for $14.95 (about $5 for the author) and he sells around 400 books each year.

Dr. Myers' expenses included a self-publishing service, a freelance editor/book doctor, and a publicity service that arranged for interviews, distribution, and media exposure for three months. Altogether it cost him about $15,000 to self-publish.[16]

Dr. Myers found that once his book came out, it did not seem to matter that it was self-published. It received a rave review in the *American Journal of Psychiatry* and other prestigious journals. Dr. Myers told me that unless you have a subject that is unique, the chance of getting an agent or publisher is low. He adds: "However, for the first-time author, it is worth the effort."

What is it like to go from being paid an advance for your work to paying others to publish your book? A well-known author once told me after finally self-publishing his latest book, "Either publishers are no longer interested in the subject I write about or I lost my fastball."

STEWART AIN

I co-authored with my wife Meryl Ain *The Living Memories Project: Legacies That Last*, published in 2014. Our book was a therapeutic venture for us, helping us to find comfort and strength after the death of our parents.

The experience was an exercise in frustration, despite the fact that the original book won an award that enabled us to garner quite a lot of publicity, including radio and television interviews on both local and network programs as well as numerous speaking engagements.

We initially signed a contract with an agent, whom we fired after six months and a couple of "near successes." Our second agent strung us along for another six months and was unable to sell the book. Both used the same excuse: No one wants to publish a book about death. We did not believe the book was about death, but rather an uplifting take on how to live your life after a loss. Despite our life experiences (losses), professional accomplishments, and our academic credentials, we were not considered to have enough of a "platform" for a major publisher, the kind of public recognition that might help sell books. Even though we both were published in newspapers, we had never published a book before, were not experts in the subject, and did not have a robust social media presence or following. Who has a platform? Someone like Facebook's Sheryl Sandberg, for example, whose book about her own loss became a best seller in 2017.

We did not want to self-publish and finally found a small publisher in the Midwest. In retrospect, this was an even more frustrating experience as we had to convince the publisher to put the book on Amazon, which she had never done before. We had to do all of the public relations and marketing ourselves and learned that media exposure did not translate into massive sales for folks like us without a "platform." While we got great feedback from those who read the book, listened to our speeches, or were involved in bereavement counseling, we never had the knowledge or time to do the marketing a successful book requires. Worse still, we were constrained by the publisher's practices. For example, she didn't engage a distribution company, as most publishers do. And she did not want to advertise on Amazon.

Since our book came out, other books on the same subject have been released by major publishers. While our book has become the cornerstone of an annual grief conference for professionals and people continue to give us positive feedback, we are disappointed that the book did not generate greater traction.

I asked Dr. Myers to put on his psychiatrist hat and talk about the ego element. "You *reframe* your experience," Dr. Myers advises. "Instead of seeing yourself or your work as a loser after so many rejections, you go for it yourself. It's a different world. Even in traditional publishing you may be disappointed if there's no publicity or distribution."

When I started writing books, my J-School professor and mentor Leonard Robinson warned me that the shelf life of a book is about the same as a carton of milk. It was all about getting your book in the stores because if people were not able to physically see your book, relate to its cover, touch it, and glimpse through its pages, they would never know that your book even existed.

Of course, technology has changed everything. And while individual books may today seem ephemeral, the vocation of writing is not. Nor has the gratification writers feel changed over the past 50 years. We touch the lives of many people through our words: we help bring about change and we expand on our own horizons and universes along with those of our readers.

STEWART AIN, continued

So what did we learn? One, we enjoy being published authors, and if you have a book in you, by all means, go ahead and write it. Two, there are more options now than when we published our book. Hybrid presses will publish and distribute your book through regular channels and most are not interested in a platform. Three, find out first what exactly your publisher expects from you, for example, purchasing a certain number of books, distribution, public relations, etc. Four, try to find a topic in which you have a platform. And five, after a while, move on and write another book.

NOTES

1. Unless otherwise noted, any information or quotations from members of the Columbia University Journalism School, Class of 1969, were obtained through emails or interviews between January and March 2019.
2. Carla Fine, *No Time to Say Goodbye: Surviving the Suicide of a Loved One* (New York: Doubleday, 1997).
3. "Six Takeaways from the Authors Guild 2018 Authors Income Survey," The Authors Guild, January 5, 2019, accessed on May 12, 2019, https://www.authorsguild.org/industry-advocacy/six-takeaways-from-the-authors-guild-2018-authors-income-survey/.
4. Leonard Cassuto, "Worried About the Future of the Monograph? So Are Publishers," *The Chronicle of Higher Education*, last modified April 2, 2019, https://www.chronicle.com/article/Worried-About-the-Future-of/246014.
5. Concepcion De Leon, "How Much Do Writers Make? Hint: Hang on to That Day Job," *The New York Times*, last modified January 17, 2019.
6. "Authors Guild Survey Shows Drastic 42 Percent Decline in Authors Earnings in Last Decade," Authors Guild, last modified January 5, 2019, https://www.authorsguild.org/industry-advocacy/authors-guild-survey-shows-drastic-42-percent-decline-in-authors-earnings-in-last-decade/.
7. "New Record: More Than 1 Million Books Self-Published in 2017," Bowker, last modified October 10, 2018, http://www.bowker.com/news/2018/New-Record-More-than-1-Million-Books-Self-Published-in-2017.html.
8. Michael Kozlowski, "Global Audiobook Trends and Statistics for 2018," last modified December 17, 2017, https://goodereader.com/blog/audiobooks/global-audiobook-trends-and-statistics-for-2018.
9. "Getting Started in Self-Publishing," *The Authors Guild Guide to Self-Publishing*, Authors Guild, 2018, accessed May 12, 2019, https://www.authorsguild.org/member-services/writers-resource-library/authors-guild-guide-e-publishing/.
10. "Overview: The Evolution of Self-Publishing," last modified April 16, 2018, https://www.sfwa.org/other-resources/for-authors/writer-beware/pod/#Overview.
11. A list of Amazon's imprints is available at "Our Imprints," Amazon Publishing, accessed July 28, 2019, https://amazonpublishing.amazon.com/our-imprints.html.
12. "How Technology is Changing the Publishing Industry," Jennings Business Valuation, last modified July 24, 2018, https://jenningsvaluation.com/2018/07/24/how-technology-is-changing-the-publishing-industry/.
13. Jane Friedman, "What is a Hybrid Publisher?" last modified December 7, 2016, https://www.janefriedman.com/what-is-a-hybrid-publisher/.
14. "Marketing and Publicity for Writers," *The Authors Guild Guide to Self-Publishing*, Authors Guild, 2018.
15. Nick Morgan, "Thinking of Self-Publishing Your Book in 2013? Here's What You Need to Know," *Forbes*, January 8, 2013.
16. Interviews with Michael F. Myers, MD, March 2019.

CHAPTER TWELVE

J-Schools: In the Wake of New Media

TOM GOLDSTEIN

As the teaching of journalism has expanded and diversified in the last half-century, the Columbia University School of Journalism has been an unusual trendsetter. At a time when journalism education, when it is taught at all, is almost always at the undergraduate level and typically as part of a broader "communications" curriculum, Columbia's journalism school since 1935 has taught solely on the graduate level and focused on preparing working journalists, not scholars of communication.

"Our school is different from 99.9 percent of the journalism schools in the United States." Former acting dean Frederick Yu, who himself had a doctorate, uttered those words several decades ago.[1] They resonate loudly today. Like so many venerated institutions, the Columbia University School of Journalism is larger than the sum of its parts. It derives its reputation less from the scholarship it produces—or even from the accomplishments of its graduates—but equally and more from programs ancillary to the educational mission of the school: the *Columbia Journalism Review*, the Pulitzer Prize (actually a direct offshoot of the main university), and a dozen other prizes. Columbia has been the convener of choice for important journalists. I believe that, more any other school, it has helped establish standards for journalism.

In the cruel cutthroat world of New York real estate, the clichéd watchwords are "location, location, location." The J-School has benefited immeasurably from its location in New York. The city of eight million people and eight million stories has been the laboratory for the students who have been guided in their studies by bona fide working professionals, who are available in great supply in Manhattan.

Unlike most other disciplines at Columbia, the J-School is not particularly known for the scholarship of its faculty. The irony is that over the years, it has had its fair share of important thinkers about journalism and communication, most recently the late Jim Carey, Michael Schudson, and Todd Gitlin. It has offered a doctorate since my days as dean of the J-School from 1997 to 2002. But the scholarship it produces is generally overshadowed by other factors.

The alumni body emits another mixed message. A look at its graduates shows many eminent journalists. But relatively few of its alumni have scaled the loftiest heights. One crude marker of this: In the 50 years since we graduated, Columbia graduates en masse have left only a modest imprint at the highest echelons of the leading newspapers in the country. If you look at four leading papers—the *New York Times*, the *Washington Post*, the *Los Angeles Times* and the *Wall Street Journal*—only two J- School graduates served as either editor or managing editor in the last half-century: Howard Simons, Class of 1952, was managing editor of the *Washington Post* when it reached exalted heights during the Watergate exclusives of the 1970s; Joe Lelyveld, a 1960 graduate, led the *New York Times* from 1994 to 2001 and again in 2003. (The dean serving in 2019, Steve Coll, although not a J-School graduate, also served as a *Post* managing editor.)

The school that our class of 101 entered in late summer of 1968 was unlike any graduate school of any type anywhere—a one-year master's program at the only Ivy League college that offered journalism courses. The campus was recovering from the protests that spring when student grievances—from complaints that university research was too closely connected to the prosecution of the Vietnam war to the ill-considered decision of the university to build a gymnasium on school land abutting Harlem—culminated in students occupying campus buildings before they were removed violently by New York City police.

The J-School had its own building, a gracious, seven-story structure designed by the exalted architectural firm of McKim, Mead & White. It occupied a prime piece of campus real estate at the main entrance of the university at the corner of 116th Street and Broadway, but it was pretty much isolated in terms of academics from the rest of the university. The school's well-liked and powerful dean, Edward Barrett, had resigned in August, just before we arrived.

For a school that prides itself on teaching pure journalism skills, (one dean, Joan Konner, referred to those who entered public relations as "fallen angels"), the school's early leaders were decidedly unusual choices. Its first director, Talcott Williams—nicknamed Talkalot because his fulsome introductions of speakers left them little time to speak[2]—had solid journalism credentials. The first formal dean, long-serving Carl Ackerman, came from the world of public relations—working at Remington Rand and Eastman Kodak before becoming assistant to the president of General Motors. Then came Barrett, who after a robust career at *Newsweek*, had worked as a high-level public relations executive, at one time defending the tobacco industry.

Barrett's unexpected departure left faculty member Richard Baker, just back from the Far East, as acting dean. Although he was a chain smoker, Baker projected calm and gentleness. He, too, had no background in newspapers to speak of. He was steeped in the study of religion. He inherited a feisty faculty, more comfortable with the norms of newsrooms than academia. Many professors had taken sides in the student protests the spring before; either they were aligned with the students, or they were not. That meant that some professors did not talk to others.

Some toyed with the idea of leaving Columbia. Unbeknownst to his students, a popular faculty mainstay, Penn Kimball, was interviewing for the deanship of the new graduate school of journalism at the University of California at Berkeley, a job that ultimately went to someone else.[3]

The J-School may have resembled a mess, but it was a thrilling mess for students. It was, after all, at the center of student protests, in the media capital of the world. What better place to train as a journalist?

Almost no one from our class had actually been on campus during the convulsive events of the spring of 1968. (I was an exception—I was there as an unhappy first-year law student), but as James Boylan noted in his 2003 book, *Pulitzer's School: Columbia University's School of Journalism, 1903–2003*, our class "began to enter into the spirit of 1968"—with Boylan himself as a prime victim.[4]

A new course, "The Role of the Journalist," had been introduced. It was a course about the history and ethics of journalism, a course ahead of its time, taught by Louis Starr, an early champion of the discipline of oral history, and Boylan, trained as an historian and the founding editor of the *Columbia Journalism Review*. Of all our teachers, Boylan was probably closest in age to the students. That meant nothing to us. According to Boylan, in his typical understated, self-effacing way, neither he nor Starr "was a theatrical lecturer." The students did not like the course, and they rebelled—peacefully. The subject matter of this course, "primarily historical, could be easily declared irrelevant, and was thus declared," Boylan wrote many years later.[5]

Students preferred to be taught by Larry Pinkham, a full-time faculty member, and by Richard Goldstein, a rising star as an alternative music and cultural critic. Goldstein had an uncommonly long, wispy ponytail and told his students that he graduated near the bottom of his class at the school three years earlier. He recounted how he had trouble being accepted as legitimate by staff members in the mailroom.

The new course was called "Subjective Reality" and it captured the pulse and energy of our remarkable academic year of 1968–1969. Its roots were contemporary journalism issues—the loosening of traditional boundaries, the questioning of objectivity, the expansion of journalism into different forms of media.

There were screenings with young filmmakers like the Maysles Brothers and D.A. Pennebaker, who were to become major figures in the world of cinema. Robert Christgau, the pop critic of the *Village Voice*, visited. Readings from Marshall McLuhan, Herbert Marcuse, and Tom Wolfe were assigned.

"It caught the spirit of the day," recalled Marty Gottlieb,[6] youngest class member who was to have a remarkable and eclectic career in editing. Gottlieb went back to the J-School in 1990 to teach as the Gannett Visiting Professor. He revived the "Subjective Reality" class with a co-teacher Amy Taubin, an insightful critic from the *Voice*. Pennebaker returned for a class "and there were plenty of other kindred guests," Gottlieb recalled. More than 50 students signed up.

The Class of 1969 was lucky to attend journalism school when it did. It came at the end of a decade of major newsworthy changes in the United States. Civil rights struggles became an enduring story. The women's movement emerged. Large swaths of the population took action against an unpopular war. Protests were legitimized. Popular culture was transformed. Our time at Columbia came just before reporters' good work helped expose the Watergate scandal. Journalism had become a legitimate career path for college graduates, and while journalism school was not a required credential to practice journalism, journalism education grew substantially.

With the exception of an experimental course like "Subjective Reality," the curriculum we encountered as students was pedestrian. It could be intense, but at bottom it was merely an extension of many undergraduate journalism programs across the country. That said, its guiding philosophy was forward thinking. Professors would tell us that we were being prepared for a world of changes in technology that no one could envision. They were right.

No one then envisioned the changes of the next half-century. But we were ready, at least in a rudimentary way. There were no computers in classrooms back then, but we learned to take pictures, splice film and work with audio. That meant we became comfortable—or at least familiar with—incorporating visual and audio components into our news judgments.

Fifty years after graduation, students in our class recall with fondness–giddy, at times–their year at the J-School. (See Class of 1969 Survey). As someone who has spent a large part of my working career as an academic administrator, often in touch with alumni, I have never seen such rapturous recollections. Many graduates of 1969 point to Columbia as their premier experience in higher education.

Here, too, contradictions abound. We may have loved it, but the school has been a frequent target for ridicule for the last century, an inviting bullseye in the country's media capital. Boylan wrote in the introduction to his book:

> "The school has been a visible presence in the world's most visible journalism community. It has been seen as a metaphor—or an epithet—for journalism education. It has been honored as the bearer of the gold standard in its field and condemned as a sham; it has been valued as an incubator of journalists who have risen to the top of their profession, and discounted as a holding tank for the mediocre; It has been seen as a standard setter and ethicist-in-chief; it has been condemned as a citadel of the establishment. Whatever the truth of these evaluations—and all have probably been true at one time or another—the debate over its merits and shortcomings has been strong, sometimes vehement, even into the twenty-first century."[7]

Journalism as an academic discipline is rather new, and journalism schools still have not gained the traction that law or business schools have. When the idea of a journalism school was originally conceived, the subject was typically viewed as part of the English department. This was not so at Columbia.

Had it not been for the aggressive lobbying of publisher Joseph Pulitzer or the $2 million he donated, it is doubtful Columbia would ever have offered journalism courses. No evidence exists of any independent clamor at the time by students or faculty to start teaching journalism.

Columbia was an early adopter of journalism education when the school opened in 1912, but it was not the first university where it was taught. The formal beginning of journalism education has been traced to 1869 at what is now Washington and Lee in Virginia.[8] At the turn of the twentieth century, several universities, especially land grant universities, soon bought into the idea of starting journalism programs. The University of Missouri opened the first journalism school in 1908. Eventually, the center of journalism education settled in the Midwest, half a continent away from the media mecca of New York City.

Since it began, Columbia has occupied a privileged position as the only Ivy League University with a journalism school. In recent years, Yale, Princeton and Cornell have begun to offer interesting—and oversubscribed—journalism classes as electives. It is still the case that no Ivy League school offers a journalism major to undergraduates or a graduate degree in journalism.

The J-School of 2019 is different in key respects from the school envisioned by Joseph Pulitzer, the cerebral and quirky publisher of assorted high-and low-market newspapers. He became the self-appointed high-minded philosopher of journalism education and in the past century, no one has replaced him. In 1904 he wrote, "My idea is to recognize that journalism is, or ought to be, one of the great and intellectual professions; to encourage, elevate and educate in a practical way the present, and still more, future members of that profession, exactly as if it were the profession of law or medicine."[9]

In his essay in the North American Review, Pulitzer went further and predicted that "before the century closes, schools of journalism will generally be accepted as a feature of specialized higher education," like law school or medical schools. Pulitzer's essay ended with what was to become the foundation statement of the school:

> "Our Republic and its press will rise or fall together. An able, disinterested, public-spirited press, with trained intelligence to know the right and courage to do it, can preserve that public virtue without which popular government is a sham and a mockery. A cynical, mercenary, demagogic press will produce in time a people as base as itself. The power to mold the future of the Republic will be in the hands of the journalists of future generations."

Those four sentences in which he explains why he wanted to fund a journalism school at Columbia are cast on a bronze plaque in the lobby of the school.

When the school opened in 1912, the first-year undergraduate curriculum consisted of general subjects tailored to journalism. A single course in journalism was taught in the second year, with two in the third year and four in the fourth year. Tuition for a term was $85.

A MAGNET FOR CRITICISM

Not until 1935 did the J-School became exclusively a graduate school, elevating it to the administrative status of law and medicine. It became a year-long program and it abandoned for good Pulitzer's wish to accept special students who did not possess any formal credentials. In his understated history of the school, Boylan unearthed an editorial from the *New York Daily News* commenting on the change at the school: "We see by the papers that the Pulitzer School of Journalism at Columbia University is going to curtail its course to one year. We consider that a step in the right direction, but believe that course is still one year too long."[10]

Journalism education in this country—and Columbia in particular as its shining exemplar—have become a magnet for criticism. Perhaps this is because those who succeeded without formal education look down on those who chose such a path. Perhaps this is because many journalists are jealous that they did not receive formal training. Perhaps it derives from a syndrome of killing the messenger, where people transfer their unhappiness with the news to those who train the chroniclers of the news.

At any rate, bashing of journalism education in general and Columbia in particular has spawned its own subgenre, some of it quite witty, much of it off the mark. In an essay "How to Learn Nothing" that appeared in the *Wayward Pressman*, the incomparable press critic A.J. Liebling, a student at the J-School in its early years, wrote that Columbia's Pulitzer School possessed "all the intellectual status of a training school for future employees of the [supermarket] A&P." His J-School instructors, he wrote, were preaching conformity to the writing standards of the "especially tasteless" *New York Times* of 1923, "a political hermaphrodite capable of intercourse with conservatives of both parties at the same time."[11]

Writing with a pen dripping with acid in 1938, the well-regarded and iconoclastic president of the University of Chicago, Robert Maynard Hutchins, called journalism schools, "the shadiest educational ventures under respectable auspices." These schools, he continued, "exist in defiance of the obvious fact that the best preparation for journalism is a good education. Journalism itself can be learned, if at all, only by being a journalist."[12]

The strains of anti-intellectualism introduced by Liebling and Hutchins were evident throughout the rest of the century. The cover of a *New Republic* issue in April 1993 contained a crude replica of the *New York Daily News* with a fake front-page banner headline from the tabloid: "J-School Ate My Brain."[13] The story, by Michael Lewis, at the dawn of his hugely successful career as a satirical best-selling author, made merciless fun of one of the school's larger-than-life instructors at the time, Steve Isaacs.

A one-time editor at the *Washington Post*, Isaacs was an easy mark. Lewis exposed some of his most notable quirks. Early on, Isaacs had banned from student assignments the use of adverbs and adjectives as well as variations of the verb "to be." In conclusion, with tongue firmly in cheek, Lewis wrote, "The essential point here is that the desperate futility of journalism instruction becomes clearer the closer one gets to the deed."

Then toward the end of the last century, the criticism of journalism education took a more serious turn. Vartan Gregorian, a highly regarded intellectual who had been president of Brown University, joined the Carnegie Corporation, which was really a foundation, as president. In an interview in the *New York Times Magazine*, in the midst of a shopping list of thoughts, Gregorian—seemingly from nowhere—offered this opinion:

> "Journalism schools are teaching journalistic techniques rather than subject matter. Journalists should be cultured people who know about history, economics, science. Instead they are learning what is called nuts and bolts. Like schools of education, journalism school should either be reintegrated intellectually into the university or they should be abolished."[14]

In the summer of 2002, Lee Bollinger, a First Amendment scholar who had been president of the University of Michigan, had just assumed the presidency of Columbia University. He was looking to make a splash and had consulted with, among others, a leading public relations specialist. He was seeking advice about what to do with the search for my successor as dean, which had been narrowed to two excellent choices: Alex Jones, author and director of the Shorenstein Center at Harvard, and Jim Fallows, the well-rounded editor and prolific commentator on current affairs.

Rather than choose either of them, Bollinger halted the search and named a task force of more than three-dozen East Coast journalists to consider the future of journalism education at Columbia. "To teach the craft of journalism is a worthy goal, but clearly insufficient in this new world and within the setting of a great university," Bollinger wrote.[15] In the end, Bollinger did not go to the short list of candidates and instead named as dean Nick Lemann, a well-seasoned writer of important social topics who had actually thought deeply about journalism education and who had recently written a flattering profile of Bollinger for the *New Yorker* magazine.[16]

In the 50 years since we graduated, six deans have served the school. (I point out with pride—and humility—that I was the only one who had taught before.) Just about every one of these searches was marked by one glitch or another. This search was no exception. However, in no previous search had the top executive of the university gone out on such a limb to express his interest so publicly in assuring the success of the J-School. Inevitably, that on-the-record declaration would translate to greater resources for the school.

AN EXPENSIVE CREDENTIAL

We went to Columbia in simpler, more affordable times. In 2019, the J-School website tells students that their nine months there will cost them $100,869 for tuition, fees, and living expenses—many times what the Class of 1969 needed to get by on. My parents were dubious when I applied, until I told them it was the equivalent of getting into Harvard Medical School. Like most classmates indicated in the informal survey, I loved the J-School.

Like many of my classmates, I got my first job through the school. Stan Asimov, the hiring editor at *Newsday* and a part-time teacher at the school, hired me to work on the overnight desk at the newspaper based on Long Island. In the fall, I resumed my studies at law school, but working through the night at a distant newsroom while going to school proved too much for me. So, I got my second job through the journalism school. I called up the Associated Press in New York City and, after I recited my situation, the secretary to the bureau chief Doug Lovelace told me that "I was just the type of person AP wanted."

Over my career, I am sure the J-School credential helped me get many other jobs. I know for certain that I got my current job through Columbia. I am now founding dean of the journalism school at a new school, O.P. Jindal University, situated 90 minutes from the center of New Delhi. The vice chancellor of the university, Raj Kumar, a highly credentialed lawyer (Harvard Law School, Oxford, Rhodes Scholar), was looking to start a journalism school. He had heard of only one other: the Columbia School of Journalism. He Googled it and found that at the time three former deans were living. Raj called an American academic friend of his, whom it turns out I also know. The connection was made and I moved to India.

However others view the J-School, I am grateful for what it did for me. I cannot argue one way or another that it is the best journalism school. I find such measures meaningless, even dangerous.

Now, only two other universities—the University of California at Berkeley and the City University of New York—offer journalism exclusively at the graduate level, an insufficient sample to yield meaningful comparisons. Over the years, several attempts have been made to rate journalism schools, but they have failed. The J-School has never done particularly well in those surveys. For instance, the surveys that count the number of citations by faculty members in refereed journals are unfair to Columbia inasmuch as few faculty members choose to publish in such journals.

The number of people pursuing professional master's degrees in journalism has always been quite small. It was always the J-School's philosophy that an intense year of practical instruction should follow a traditional liberal arts education. Columbia was an outlier in that thinking. And even among schools that offer both undergraduate and graduate programs, the graduate degrees constitute a small percent of the total. In recent years, an added factor to the equation is the astronomical cost of even an extra year of school.

Speaking of journalism programs generally, schools are incorporating new technology into their basic curriculum—sometimes at the expense of teaching the basics, which are still essential building blocks for young journalists. Technology also adds an entirely new factor to the budgets of journalism schools.

I do think journalism schools have kept pace with changes in the news industry and in a few instances have been ahead of the curve.

As the job market for journalists has shriveled and the appetite of students has grown for coursework in media studies, public relations, and event planning, the proportion of straight journalism courses has shrunk. In addition, many communication and journalism schools insist on faculty having a doctorate—a credential that most journalists do not possess. And a credential that the J-School (along with Berkeley, Medill School of Journalism at Northwestern and a few other places) has never required.

As students, I can safely postulate, we were not interested in scholarly citations. Perhaps our class can be accused of fuzzy thinking. But what comes through in my 2019 survey of the class is an appreciation for intangibles, for the opportunity the J-School gave us. For us, its strong reputation was deserved. It taught us to think fast, it taught us how to collaborate, it taught us to be resourceful ("Go with what you got" was the watchword of Professor John Hohenberg), and to evaluate evidence. Finally, it opened us up to multiple points of view and to appreciate different ways of seeing a situation. We received top-notch editing and we were encouraged to experiment. Teachers were our coaches who spent endless hours editing our copy. I still keep the edited versions of all my J-School assignments.

Whether deserved or not—and I think it is largely is deserved—the J-School has an outsized reputation. It sits at the epicenter of American journalism. And for all the criticisms, whatever the reasons, it still is viewed by many as the premier journalism school in the world.

Once, when I was dean, I was staring outside my seventh-floor office with David Laventhol, a former top editor and executive at the *Los Angeles Times*, who took a post-retirement assignment to help me oversee the *Columbia Journalism Review*. In June 1999, the heirs of Ruth Whitney, a long-time editor of *Glamour*, had asked to hold her memorial service at school. Dave and I watched as one black Lincoln Town Car after another deposited its occupants on the cross walk near the school, which was closed to traffic except on special occasions as this. "The crossroads of the journalism establishment," Laventhol whispered.

It was a comment brimming with ambiguity. It is hardly clear that this distinction is worth bragging about, given that many of the best journalists possess a strong anti-establishment bent. It is clear that what constitutes the journalism establishment has shifted considerably in the last 20 years, and it is now the J-School's challenge to maintain its special aura—that is, if it wants to.

CLASS OF 1969 SURVEY

In preparing this chapter, I sent out a decidedly unscientific, informal questionnaire to my classmates. Of the 101 people who started in our class, 82 were living in 2019. Of those, class officers could not locate addresses for seven students. That means 75 graduates received the questionnaire. Of those, 51 responded—an unusually high percentage for a questionnaire like this.

I asked six questions:

- Did you apply to any other journalism schools when you applied to Columbia? Which ones?
- Before you applied, had you any journalism experience?
- Before you applied, had you taken any formal journalism courses at colleges?
- Had you worked on your college newspaper or other news outlet?
- After graduation did you pursue a career in journalism or a career related to journalism?
- Whatever your career choice, did you find your journalism education helpful?

Thirty-three of those who responded applied only to the J-School. "The only school I'd ever heard of was Columbia," was the response of Karen Rothmyer, who went on to a career as an editor and teacher.

Thirteen also applied to Northwestern's Medill School of Journalism. Fewer than half had taken a journalism course before, and about half indicated they had some journalism experience, including work at a college news outlet. Most pursued a career in journalism, at least for a while. Almost without exception, graduates unreservedly praised their time at the J-School and the boost it gave them in their careers.

Larry Leamer, who has churned out books at an astonishing rate, said: "It was the most significant part of my education."

Many recalled with fondness the admonition of Professor John Hohenberg: "Go with what you got." That, recalled Susan Anderson, who started working in television, was "a lifelong nudge away from perfectionism toward meeting deadlines!" The Class of 1969 had the slogans printed on sweatshirts. Many still had these mementos half a century later.

NOTES

1. James Boylan, *Pulitzer's School: Columbia University's School of Journalism, 1903–2003* (New York: Columbia University Press, 2003), 217.
2. Boylan, 40.
3. Archives, Graduate School of Journalism, University of California, Berkeley, accessed Spring 2013.
4. Boylan, 173.
5. Ibid.
6. Marty Gottlieb, email message to author, February 13, 2019.
7. Boylan, 2.
8. For an excellent summary of the origins of journalism education, see Everette E. Dennis, "Whatever Happened to Marse Robert's Dream? The Dilemma of American Journalism Education," *Gannett Center Journal*, Spring 1988, 2–22.
9. Joseph Pulitzer, "The School of Journalism at Columbia University," *North American Review*, May 1904, 2.
10. Boylan, 79.
11. A.J. Liebling, "How to Learn Nothing," in *The Wayward Pressmen* (Garden City: Doubleday, 1947), 28.
12. Robert Maynard Hutchins, "Is There a Legitimate Place for Journalistic Instruction? No!" *The Quill* March 1938, 13.
13. Michael Lewis, "J-School Ate My Brain," *The New Republic,* April 17, 1993, 20.
14. Vartan Gregorian interviewed by Claudia Dreifus, "It Is Better to Give than to Receive," *New York Times Magazine,* December 14, 1997, 54.
15. Karen Arenson, "Columbia President, Rethinking Journalism School's Mission, Suspends Search for New Dean," *New York Times,* July 24, 2002, 27.
16. Nicholas Lemann, "The Empathy Defense: Can the University of Michigan Save Affirmative Action?" The *New Yorker,* December 18, 2000, 46.

CRUNCHING THE NUMBERS

Formal journalism education in the U.S. traces its roots to the early twentieth century, but it wasn't until 1971 that, for classification purposes, the U.S. Department of Education created a field of communications that included journalism as a part.[1] Statistics since then show a dramatic growth in the number of bachelor's degrees awarded in the broad field of communications between 1971 and 1991. "No other field of study showed such consistent and dramatic change during this period," said Prof. Lee Becker of the Henry W. Grady College of Journalism and Mass Communication at the University of Georgia and Joseph Graf of American University.

However, communications programs now include a heavy dose of advertising and public relations, and the number of students enrolled in courses and programs specifically designed to prepare them for a career in journalism has been dropping.

Becker counted 480 programs that included at least 10 courses in core communications subjects as of 2013, but the Accrediting Council on Education in Journalism and Mass Communication had accredited only 113 journalism programs in the U.S. as of 2019.[2]

The number of students enrolled in all journalism and communications programs around the U.S. grew sharply from 1976, when the total was a little over 100,000, to more than 213,000 in 2013. The number in the years immediately before 2013 had been dropping slightly.

It is clear, Becker and Tudor Vlad, also of the University of Georgia, wrote in 2018, "that journalism and mass communication enrollments were declining as the media industries in the United States experienced dramatic changes resulting from a variety of forces, including those brought about by the internet and the recession of 2008."[3]

Increasing numbers of women enrolled in journalism courses over the years. Slightly under 40 percent of journalism students were women in 1968. That number grew to about 64 percent in 2013.[4] Much of the growth of the female student population was due to the expansion of public relations and advertising courses in journalism programs.

In 1968, what was classified as "news editorial" courses in communications programs far exceeded courses in public relations and advertising, but both of the latter had become more numerous than news instruction by 2013. The representation of minorities in journalism programs also has risen dramatically, from only 2.8 percent of the student total in 1973 to 34.6 percent in 2013.[5]

Looking specifically at journalism courses, Becker and Vlad said, "The data suggest that the journalism component of journalism and mass communication education or of the larger field of communication is not a growth area in terms of enrollments. This is hardly surprising, given the dramatic changes in the media landscape itself."[6]

Of course, journalism is not a regulated profession and it never has been necessary to earn a journalism degree to enter the field. Still, a growing number of journalists have academic credentials. Roughly 60 percent of journalists had journalism degrees as of 2013, up from only 27 percent in 1976.[7]

Becker completed a quarter-century of annual surveys involving journalism schools in 2013. The Association of Schools of Journalism and Mass Communication took over where he left off but is doing enrollment surveys only every other year. Its 2015 survey noted that over all, "journalism and mass communication education had been in growth mode for a long time." Between 2013 and 2015, of the 182 programs that responded, the number of undergraduates enrolled in news editorial/print journalism decreased by 13.9 percent, and the number in broadcast news/broadcast journalism decreased by 6.7 percent.[8]

NOTES

1. Lee Becker and Tudor Vlad, *The Changing Education for Journalism and the Mass Communications Operations* (New York: Peter Lang, 2018), 110.
2. Accrediting Council on Education in Journalism and Mass Communications, accessed on May 23, 2019, http://www.acejmc.org/accreditation-reviews/accredited-programs/.
3. Becker and Vlad, 116.
4. Ibid., 120.
5. Ibid., 123.
6. Ibid., 132.
7. Ibid., 213–214.
8. R. Glenn Cummins et al., "2015 Survey of Journalism & Mass Communication Enrollments," *Journal & Mass Communication Educator* 72: 2 (June 1, 2017), 139–153.

Postscript: An Informed News Consumer's View

ALLAN MANN

I came a bit late to this book project. As one of the few members the Class of 1969 who did not pursue a career as a journalist or author, I didn't feel I had much to add during its inception. I would stand on the sidelines and cheer.

I was drawn into the fray by our harried editors who needed someone to do basic copy editing, a skill I gained at the J-School and never lost. Soon I was giving every chapter a final polishing, checking for grammar and punctuation, turning passive sentences into active ones, and raising questions when something was unclear.

In the course of checking every leaf of every tree, I also got a chance to see the whole forest described in the book—the world of journalism and how it had changed in the half-century since our graduation. Many of my classmates had been there, experiencing and, in many cases, creating the changes. I had been watching as an interested but not directly involved bystander while pursuing a career in education and corporate communications.

As I read the manuscript, however, I realized that I had honed an additional skill at the J-School—that of a highly informed consumer of news. Each day during my bus and subway commute to the school, I had read at least three New York City newspapers. In class, we read and analyzed papers and magazines all day, and I watched TV news at night. Those habits have persisted. I'm now a certifiable news junkie who can't get through the day without a constant news fix.

It is from this perspective as a consumer of news that I look at how the news media has changed in the 50 years since graduation.

I'm enthralled by much of what I'm seeing. In our lifetimes, we have experienced the introduction of jet travel, wireless phones and microwave ovens that can cook a meal in seconds. But nothing has changed our lives as much as that little machine that Steve Jobs wanted to see on everyone's desk and the World Wide Web that it connects us to. Those inventions changed everything. Suddenly, the knowledge of the world was quite literally at our fingertips.

You've read in this book how the internet disrupted the news business. As more information became available online—and free, to boot—the less we were dependent on the daily newspaper on our doorstep.

But to lament this change is to miss the point. We didn't stop traveling when the car replaced the horse. We didn't stop communicating when the telephone made letter writing obsolete. We didn't stop watching movies at home when Blockbuster folded. In fact, we continued to do all these things, but faster and easier.

I may be a Luddite in other aspects of my life, but I revel in the ability to create a newsfeed in the palm of my hand that delivers to me the best thinking of some of the most insightful people in the country—the men and women who report and comment on the news every day.

Of course, that newsfeed can also reflect the viewpoints of many without formal journalistic training. Yet they may nonetheless have valuable information or opinions to share. We are experiencing a democratization of the news business that puts the power of the pen into the hands of people who never could buy ink by the barrel.

Yes, there are foreign adversaries and home-grown zealots trying to mess with our minds and our opinions. The ability to spread misinformation at lightning speed has given social media in specific and the internet in general a bad rap. The ascendance of the internet may be making the mainstream media less and less viable, but killing the messenger is not the solution.

The news business is not the news*paper* business; it is the news *gathering* and news *disseminating* business. The technology by which news is collected, packaged, and distributed is secondary to the process of deciding what to report and how. With all due respect to Marshall ("The Medium is the Message") McLuhan, the journalist creates the message; the medium simply transmits it.

As I look at today's media landscape, I see great newspapers like the *New York Times* and *Washington Post* shaping public discourse with their ferocious investigative reporting. I see television news magazines and public radio digging deeply into untold stories. I see legacy magazines like *Vanity Fair* and *Newsweek* reinventing themselves to retain their relevance. I see upstarts like *Politico* and *ProPublica* harnessing the power of the internet to deliver news to a broader audience. I see citizen journalists making a difference in their communities. And, yes, I see Fox

News bringing its unique brand of journalism to an audience long neglected by the mainstream media.

If we have to sift through a mountain of manure to get to the great journalism that is still out there, then so be it. We're bound to find a pony or two in there somewhere.

Index

A

ABC News 26–27, 37–38, 40, 51–52, 147
abortion 34, 144
Accidental Anchorwoman (Tolliver) 51
Ackerman, Carl 33, 176–177
Advocate, The 8–9
Africa, coverage of 82–84, 119
African Americans 8, 37, 47–61, 107, 155
AIDS 114–121
Ain, Stewart 147, 149, 170
Altman, Lawrence K. 110–112, 118
Amazon, impact on publishing 153–173
American Journalism Review 81
American Journal of Psychiatry 169
American Legion convention 118
American Society for Newspaper Editors (ASNE) 43
American Values That Divided a Nation (Spruill) 144–145
Anderson, Susan 33, 44, 185
APBNews.com 103
Apple Computer 132–133
Arafat, Yasir 56
Arledge, Roone 26
Arnett, Peter 89
Asian-American journalists 48, 56, 59, 61
Associated Press (AP) 32, 72, 81, 89, 98, 151, 182
Association of Health Care Journalists 113
Association of University Presses 159
Atex system 21, 26. *See also* technology
Attica Prison 53
The Authentic Voice: Best Reporting on Race and Ethnicity (Morgan) 57. *See also* Morgan, Arlene Notaro
Authors Guild 157–167

B

Badhwar, Inderjit 92
Baker, John 23
Baker, Richard 177
Baltimore Sun. 115
Baquet, Dean 60, 151–152

Baron, Marty 129
Barsky, Neil 104
Becker, Lee 186–187
Bell, Alan 19, 26
Bergen Record xx, 9
Berke, Rick 122
Berkeley Barb 8
Berkman, Leslie xxi, 7, 32, 36, 42–45
    on business coverage 128, 130, 135
Bernstein, Carl 6, 69
Beucke, Dan 129, 136
Birand, Mehmet 87–88
Birch, David 133
Bishop, Jerry 111
Blackmun, Harry 100
Black Panther organization 53
Blake, Jeanne 121
Blendon, Robert 120
Block, Lillian R. 141
Blood, Dick 5
Bloomberg, Michael 128, 138
Boardroom Reports 127–128
Bollinger, Lee 181–182
book authors
    income 159
    experiences as writers 154, 156, 158, 160, 162, 164, 166, 168, 170.
    (See also book publishing; Authors Guild)
book publishing 153–173
    Amazon's impact on publishing 153–173
    decline in author income 159, 161, 163, 169
    self-publishing 163, 164–167
Borg, Stephen 9
Boroditsky, Lera 106
Boston Business Journal 133
Boston Globe xx, 109–117, 121–123, 142
Boston Guardian 57
Boston Phoenix 8
Bottom Line 127–128
Bowie, David 19
Boxall, Bettina 42
Boylan, James 33, 177–178, 180
Boys on the Bus, The (Crouse) 72
Bradlee, Ben 19, 51–52
Bradley, Ed 55

Bralove, Mary 12, 32, 38–46
Bremerton (WA) Sun 143
Breslin, Jimmy 6
broadcasting 2, 13, 22, 25, 27, 31, 48–54, 66, 70, 74, 81, 87, 104–106, 112, 136, 187
Broadcast House 24
Brown, Dotty xix, 31–45, 110, 166, 35
Bruck, Connie 44
Bruzelius, Nils 113, 117
Bulletin. See Philadelphia Evening Bulletin
Bumpers, Dale 72
Burnham, Margaret 53
Burton, Phil 68–69
Bush, George H. W. 101–102, 120
business news xx, xxi, 20, 29, 45, 91, 109, 115, 127–139
    newspapers slow to embrace 129
    entrepreneurship as topic 132–135
    financial challenge of internet 135–138
Business of Being a Writer (Friedman) 165–167
BusinessWeek 102, 127, 135
BuzzFeed 81, 104–105

C

Campolo, Tony 145
Carey, Jim 176
Carter, Jimmy 7, 101
Casper (Wyoming) Journal 44
CBS xx, 1, 10–14, 19, 22–24, 38, 119, 147,
    Marquita Pool-Eckert at 44–65
Cheney, Dick 68
Chicago Seed 8
Chicago Sun-Times 109–110
Christgau, Robert 178
citizen journalists 81
civil rights movement 8, 17, 22, 25, 47–51, 57–58, 178
Clinton, Bill 7, 79, 102, 120
Clinton, Hillary 66, 120
CNN 11, 44, 58, 81, 87–88, 114
    Kenneth Tiven at xxi, 19–22, 27–28
    internet and 28
Coffin Jr., William Sloane 145–146
Coll, Steve xv, 176

INDEX | 195

Columbia Journalism Review 103, 121, 175, 177, 184
Columbia University School of Journalism 175–185
    Class of 1969 xiii–xv, 33, 48, 96, 155, 184–185
    Quotas at 33, 48.
    (See also Boylan, James; Friendly, Fred; Kimball, Penn; Robinson, Leonard; Trump, Christopher)
Colvin, Marie 86
computer revolution 17–30
Congressional Black Caucus 59
Congressional Quarterly 67, 69–72
Control Data Corporation 27
Corinthian Broadcasting 25–26
Cowan, Paul 8
Cox Broadcasting 24–26
Cox, Harvey 149–150
Craigslist 21
Crain's Chicago Business 133
Cranston, Alan 69
Crewe, Jennifer 159, 161
Crime Report 104
criminal justice xix, 95–107
    crime rates 95–96, 106
    covering courts 100–101
    crime as politics 101–103, 107, 148, 162
    reporting wrongful convictions 105
    over-reporting of crimes 105–106
Cronkite, Walter 1, 3, 10, 54–55, 65–66, 74–75
    Uncle Walter 13
Cross, John 129–130
Crouse, Timothy 72
C-SPAN 68, 74
Cushman, Lt. Gen John 90

D

Daily Beast 66
Daily Mirror 3
Dallas Times Herald 34
Dana Farber Cancer Institute 116–117
Davis, Angela 52–54

Dawes, Martin 84
Dear Abby 143
Delaney, Paul 57
Des Moines Register 6–7
Detroit News 129
Dickinson, Daniel 84
Digital Equipment Corp. 131
Dirksen, Everett 67
diversity in newsrooms 47–61
    African American media 8, 52, 61
    discrimination complaints 52, 59. (*See also* Kerner Commission; *United Church of Christ vs. WLBT-TV*)
    hiring initiatives 57, 60. (*See also*Journalism Education)
    Divided We Stand: The Battle over Women's Rights (Spruill) 144–145
Dodd, Christopher 73
Dole, Bob 102
Dominique, Jean 44, 80, 86
Doriot, Georges 131
Dossey M.D, Larry 150
Doyle, Pat 5
Duckham, Penny 122–123
Dukakis, Michael 101–102, 120
Duvalier, Jean Claude 78–80

E

East Village Other 8
Eck, Diana L. 147
Edelston, Martin 128
Editor & Publisher 121
Edna McConnell Clark Foundation 103
Ehrenhalt, Alan xix, 65–75, 160
Eisenberg, DD 37, 46
Eisner, Jane 41
Emmy Awards 44–45, **50**, 53, 55, 59
Entrepreneur magazine 128, 133
Equal Employment Opportunity Commission (EEOC) 52
Equal Rights Amendment 35, 58, 144
Erlick, June Carolyn 81
Esper, George 89
Essence Magazine 52

F

Faas, Horst 89
Facebook 6, 29, 81, 82, 137, 163, 165
Fading American Newspaper, The (Lindstrom, Carl E.) 17
fake news xv, 14–15, 80, 88, 181
Fallows, Jim 181
Farmer, Paul 119
Federal Bureau of Investigation (FBI) 95–96, 100–101, 105–106
Federal Communications Commission 22, 49
Fine, Benjamin 157
Fine, Carla xix, 153–173
Fisher, Lewis 21, 158, 165
Foa, Sylvana xix, 44, 84–87, 91–92
Foley, James 86
Forbes 135, 138, 167
Ford, Betty 39–40
Ford, Gerald 40
Ford Foundation 48, 103
Fortune 127, 137
Fortune Small Business 135–136
Fox News xv, 7, 66, 190
Franken, Al 72
Frederick, Pauline 40
Friedman, Jane 167
Friendly, Fred 19, 23, 48–49
Front Page, The 95, 97, 99

G

Gelfand, Lauren 83–84
Gendron, George 134, 136
General Motors 130, 176–177
Gest, Ted xix, 95–107, 97, 162
Gillespie, Marcia Ann 52
Gilliam, Dorothy 51
Gingrich, Newt 68
Gitlin, Todd 176
Glamour 184
GlobalPost 81
Globe-Democrat 96–97, 99
Goldberg, Carey 121–122
Goldhirsh, Bernie 132–133, 136
Goldman, Ari 150–151
Goldstein, Richard 177
Goldstein, Tom xv, xx, 175–186
Goldwater, Barry 95, 99
Google 23, 29
Google Books 161, 163
Gottlieb, Martin xx, 1–10, **4**, 54, 178
Great Emergence, The (Tickle) 149
Gregorian, Vartan 181
Ground Truth Project 10
Gumpert, David E. xv, 127–139, **164**

H

Hall, L. Priscilla 59
Hallberg, Garth 156
Hamill, Pete 6
Hammer, David 153
Hammond, Dorothy 83
Hannah-Jones, Nikole 61
Hare Krishnas 142–143
Hart, Gary 58, 71
Hartford Courant 17, 20
Harvard Business Review (HBR) xx, 131–133
Heald, Don 25–26
Health News Review 115
health reporting. *See* medical reporting
Hearst newspapers 111, 118
Hearst, William Randolph 6
Heckler, Margaret 114
Henry, John (Red Sox owner) 122
Henry, John (book author) 168
Hispanic journalists 44, 56, 60–61
Hohenberg, John vii, 183, 185
Holleman, Edee 33–36
homosexuality 118, 144–145
Hruby, Blahoslav 146
Huet, Henri 89
Huffington Post 66, 81, 104–105, 137
HuffPost xv, 61
human immunodeficiency virus 118. *See also* AIDS
Hutchins, Robert Maynard 181

I

Inc. magazine xx, 128, 132–137
India Legal 92
Ingelfinger, Franz 112, 113
Ingelfinger Rule 112–113
Institute for Journalism Education 54, 61
International Federation of Journalists 88–89
international reporting 77–79 102, 86
internet xv, 2, 6, 17, 19, 21, 43, 44, 60, 70–71, 104, 190
   international reporting and 74, 78, 81, 82, 84, 91
   business reporting and 135, 137
   employment 150, 186
   See also technology
"In the Land of the Sick" (Cowan) 8
investigative journalism 6, 8, 10, 40, 52, 61, 77, 105, 116, 118
Isham, Christopher 60
Israel 147, 150
Ivins, Molly 34

J

Jablow, Alta 83
Jackson, Derrick 57
Jackson, Jesse 57–59
Jackson, Luther P. 48
Jennings, Peter 26
Jobs, Steve 132, 133, 137, 190
John S. Knight Fellowships Program 57
Johnson, Corey 61
Johnson, Lyndon 47–48, 65, 99
Jones, Alex 181
Jones, Topher 61
journalism education 48, 56, 61, 70, 78, 103, 122, 175–185, 186–187. *See also individual journalism schools*

K

Kaiser Family Foundation (KFF) 121–123
Kaiser Health News (KHN) 121–122
Kapor, Mitch 133
Kaufman, Monica 26
Kennedy, Bobby xiii
Kennedy, Jacqueline 51
Kennedy, John F. 3, 17, 48, 71
Kennedy, Ted 7, 12
Kerner Commission 51, 60
   Report 47–48
Kerner Plus 10: Conference on Minorities and the Media 54
Khomeini, Ayatollah 146
Ki-Moon, Ban 44–45, **79**
Kimball, Penn 33, 177
King Broadcasting 31
King Jr., Martin Luther xiii, 48, 49
Knight Ridder newspapers xix, 40, 45, 57
Knox, Richard xx, 109–123, **111**
Koch, Ed 7
Konner, Joan 176–177
Kraft, Scott 136
Krajicek, David J. 95, 102–105
Krugman, Paul 110
Kumar, Raj 182
KYW-Television 19, 26

L

Last Week Tonight (John Oliver) 14
Laventhol, David 184
LA Weekly 8
Law Enforcement Assistance Council 99
Lawrence, John 129
Leamer, Laurence (Larry) 34, 185
Lebanon 55–56
Lehman, Betsy 116–117
Lemann, Nick 181–182
Lewis, Michael 181
Lewis, Ralph 131–132
LGBT (and LGBTQ) issues 142, 147. *See also* homosexuality
Liebling, A.J. 180–181
Like It Is (WABC-TV news) 38, 52–53
Linotype machines 3, 20
Living Memories Project, The (Ain) 149
local journalists 87

Local Media Association 21
Los Angeles Business Journal 133
Los Angeles Herald-Examiner 7, 36
Los Angeles Times 37, 176, 184
    Business reporting at 129, 135–136
    Gender gap at 32, 42, 45, 128
    Internet and 137–138
    Orange County edition xxi, 45, 128, 136
    View section 35–37
Louisville Courier-Journal 7
Lovelace, Doug 182
Lower, Elmer 51
Lynch, Don 70

M

Mahoney, Robert 88
Mann, Allan xx, 189–191
Maria Moors Cabot Prizes 81
Marcuse, Herbert 178
Marshall, Thurgood 49, 104
Marshall Project, The 104
Maryland Public Broadcasting 127–128
Mason, Debra L. 150
Maynard, Robert C. 54. *See also* Robert C. Maynard Institute
Maysles Brothers 178
McCain, John 73
McLuhan, Marshall 178, 190
Mears, Walter 72
Medical reporting xx, 8, 40, 44, 104, 109–123, 143, 150
    emerging scourges 117–120
    health insurance 120
    interest in 110, 121–123
    money and 115–116
    naiveté of early years 111, 114
    pushed by journals 112–114
    uncovering errors 116–117
Medill School of Journalism 105, 183, 185
MedScape.com 113
Mele, Nicco 5
Mercury News 57
#MeToo. See Women, sexual harassment
Miami Herald 41, 57, 71

Michelle Clark Fellowship Program 48. *See also note 4, page 62*
Miller, Susan 43, 45
minority training programs 56 *See also* diversity
Missouri School of Journalism 34, 149–150, 179
Mondale, Walter 58
Money magazine 127–128
Montas, Michèle 86
Montas-Dominique, Michèle xv, xx, 44–45, 77– 82, 86, 92, **79.** *See also* Dominique, Jean ; Radio Haiti
Monteleone, John 154, 167
Monterey County (CA) *Herald* 45, 143
Moore, Acel 52, 56, 58
Morgan, Arlene Notoro 38, 57
Morris, Valerie Dickerson Coleman 49, 58
Morrison, Patt 42
Morton, James Park 148
MSNBC 66
Muhammad Speaks 53
Murdoch, Rupert 7
Murrow, Ed 22
Myers, Michael F. 169, 171

N

Nation, The xx, 44, 83
National Advisory Commission on Civil Disorders 47
National Association for the Advancement of Colored People 49
National Association of Asian Journalists 56
National Association of Black Journalists (NABJ) 52, 56, 60
National Association of Hispanic Journalists 56
National Institute of Medicine 117
National Institutes of Health (NIH) 110, 121
National Lesbian and Gay Journalists Association 56
National Organization for Women 31
National Registry of Exonerations 105
Native American Journalists Association 56
Nevada State Journal 70
New England Journal of Medicine 112–113

INDEX | 199

New Jersey Herald–News 33
New Journalism xv, 6
new morality 142. *See also* LGBT
A New Religious America, How a "Christian Country" has Become the World's Most Religiously Diverse Nation (Eck) 147
Newsday xx, 39, 52 182
Newspaper Association of America 43
newspapers
    job losses 8, 21, 28, 44, 121, 136, 150
    circulation 1, 3, 8, 10, 22, 25–26, 31, 40, 42, 45 , 89, 121, 128
    revenue 2, 3, 6–7, 10, 21, 25, 28–29, 30, 40, 89, 121, 157
    See also specific newspapers
Newsweek 33–34, 44, 66, 85–86, 102, 135, 147, 176–177, 190
New York Herald Tribune 6
New York Post 7–8, 98
New York Times xx, 4, 6–10, 59, 67, 82, 98, 176, 180
    business news 127, 131, 138–139
    digital adoption 10, 137–138
    medical and science news 110, 114, 116
    opinion vs news 6–7, 65–66, 75, 77
    religion coverage 142, 147, 151–152
    sex discrimination 40
    staff diversity 57, 60–61
New York Times Magazine 181
Nieman Foundation 57
NiemanLab.org 8
Nixon, Richard xiv, 35, 100
Nixon, Ron 61
Northam, Ralph 72
No Time to Say Goodbye: Surviving the Suicide of a Loved One (Fine) xix, 155, 157
NTV (Germany) 87–88

O

Oakland Tribune 56
O'Dell, John 137
Oliver, John 14
O'Neill, Tip 67–68
O.P. Jindal University 182

Orange County Newschannel 19
Oransky, Ivan 113, 122, 123

P

Palestine Liberation Organization (PLO) 56
Pauley, Jane 25–26
Paxson, Marj 34, 36
Payne, Les 52, 57
PBS 92, 129, 136
Pearl, Daniel 86
Pennebaker, D.A. 178
Pew Research Center 6, 12, 60, 70, 106, 144, 151
Philadelphia Evening Bulletin 34–41, 35
Philadelphia Inquirer xix, 38–41, 45, 52, 56–57, 110, 166
Pinkham, Larry 177
Pinkston, Randall 48
Platt, David 31
Political reporting xix, 7, 9, 37, 65–75, 78, 102–103, 118, 142
    access to politicians 66–73
    declining respect for 65–66
    impact of internet 74–75
    of presidential elections 73–74
    of statehouses 70–71
    opportunities for minorities 58–60
    religion and 142, 144–145, 147–148
    bargain broken 66
    presidential sweepstakes 71
    TV political reporting, impact of 74
Politico xv, 123, 190
Pool-Eckert, Marquita xx, 37–38, 45, 47– 61, **50**
Prince, Richard 61–63
Princeton (NJ) *Packet* 20–21
Pruitt, John 25–26
Pulitzer, Joseph 6, 96, 179–180
Pulitzer Prize 9, 40, 42, 45, 52, 89, 142, 157, 175
Pulitzer's School: Columbia University's School of Journalism (Boylan) 33, 177
Pyle, Richard 89, 91

R

radio xv, 12, 19, 22, 24, 47, 66, 78, 92, 122, 128, 190
Radio Television Digital News Association xvii
Radio Haiti xx, 78–81
Rather, Dan 55
Reader's Digest 40
Reagan, Ronald 7, 68, 73, 78
Red Herring 135–137
Reinhardt, Burt 19, 87
religion news 141–152
    mental health and 143
    new age religion 148–150
    opportunities for reporters 150–152
    politics and 142–146, 147
Religion News Association 150
Religion News Service (RNS) xx, 59, 141–151
Reporters Without Borders 86
ReVista: Harvard Review of Latin America 81
Reynolds, Frank 26
Riley, Dick 98
Robert C. Maynard Institute for Journalism Education 56. *also* Maynard, Robert
Roberts, Gene 40–41
Robinson, Leonard 171
Robinson, Max 26
Robinson, Roxana 161
Rodgers, Joann 111–112, 118
Romney, Mitt 120
Rosenberg, Steven 114
Rosenstiel, Tom 41
Rothmyer, Karen xx, 32, 39, 44, 82–84, 91–92, 129, 184
Round Earth Media 92
Royko, Mike 6
Russell, Cristine 116, 123
Russo, Richard 163

S

Safer, Morley 55
Salganik, Bill 115
Sandinista National Liberation Front 78
San Francisco Chronicle 40
Schlafly, Phyllis 144
Schmidt, Christine 8
Schork, Kurt 85–86
Schudson, Michael xvii, 176
Schultz, John 23
Schwitzer, Gary 114–115
Science News 112
Scripps Howard 43, 143, 150
Secular City, The 150
Sforza, Dan 9
Shelby, Joyce Young 58–59
Shorenstein Center on Media, Politics and Public Policy 5, 83, 181
Silberner, Joanne 112
Simons, Howard 176
Slate xv, 104–105
Smietana, Bob 149, 151
Snyder, Jim 23
social media 2, 12, 18, 23, 27, 30, 74–77, 137, 153. 166–167, 170, 190. *See also* Facebook, Twitter
Sommers, Zach 105
Somoza, Anastasio 78
Sony 24–25
Spencer, Susan xx, 1–2, 10–15, **11**
Spruill, Marjorie 144–145
STAT 122–123
Steiger, Paul 129
Steinbrenner, George 5
Steinem, Gloria 35
Stone, Amy 31, 147
St. Louis Post-Dispatch xix, 96–98, 101
St. Petersburg Times 35–36
Stucky, Mary 92
Sturm, Paul 135, 138
Suburban Newspapers of America 21
Sunday Morning 38, 50, 59. *See also* Pool-Eckert, Marquita

T

Tanaka, Tammy xx, 59, 141–152
Taylor, Jean 36
technology in journalism 17–30
    traditional media, effect on 1, 13, 14, 137–139

INDEX | 201

digital reporting and delivery 30, 75, 82, 85, 92, 137
video evolves 24–25, 28
television 62
See also individual networks
television news 1–2, 10–15, 17, 22–30, 66, 74, 102, 104–105, 107, 112, 143, 212
    Kennedy funeral 24
    See also Pool-Eckert, Marquita; *individual networks.*
Thibodeau, Paul 106
Tickle, Phyllis 149
Tiffany Network 10–11. *See also* CBS
Time Inc. 48–49, 128, 135
Time-Life photographers 48
Time magazine 6, 33, 52, 59, 66, 81, 102, 142
Times-Picayune 8–9
Tiven, Kenneth xv, xxi, 17–30, **18**, 87–89, 129
To Err Is Human: Building a Safer Health System 117
Toledo Blade 20
Tolliver, Melba 51, 54
Touched by Suicide: Hope and Healing after Loss (Fine) 169
Townsend, Dorothy 32
Trailblazer: A Pioneering Journalist's Fight to Make the Media Look More Like America (Gilliam) 51
Trentonian 20
Trump, Christopher 33
Trump, Donald 7, 10, 71, 75, 77, 81, 142
    denigration of press xv, 77, 80, 88, 91, 66
    religious Right 144–147
Turner, Darrell 145–146
Turner, Ted 19, 28, 87
Twitter 75, 81, 82, 137, 165, 166
Tye, Larry 123
Tyndall, Andrew 105–106
Tyndall Report 105–106

U

Under-Told Stories Project 92
United Church of Christ vs. WLBT-TV 49
U.S. News & World Report xix, 21, 101, 106, 112, 135, 147, 162

Unity: Journalists of Color 56. *See also* Diversity
University of California at Berkeley xx, 56, 177, 183
Ut, Nick 89

V

Van Es, Hugh 89
Van Phuoc, Dang 89
Vice.com 81
Vietnam War xiii, xix, xxi, 6, 22, 24–25, 33, 89, **90**, 92
    Walter Cronkite and 65, 74
Village Voice xx, 4, 8, 178

W

WABC-TV 38, 51–52
Walker, A.J. 51
Walker, Joe 53
Wallis, Jim 145
Wall Street Journal xx, 10, 86, 176
    business reporting at 127, 129–130
    internet and 137–138
    women at 32, 38, 39, 40
Walters, Barbara 40
Washington Post 6–7, 9–10, 19–20, 23, 35, 65–67, 75, 116, 123, 142, 147, 176, 181, 190
    Katherine Graham 33–34
    minorities at 48, 51–52, 57
    sex discrimination 40, 42
Washington Star 67, 74
Watergate scandal xiv, 6, 19, 67, 69, 176, 178
Watkins, Richard 53
WBLT-TV 48
WBZ-TV 121
WCCO 13
Webster, William 100–101
Whitney, Ruth 184
Why Physicians Die by Suicide (Myers) 169
Wickham, DeWayne 57
Wikipedia 28
William Monroe Trotter Group 57

Winfrey, Oprah 26
Wolfe, Tom 6, 178
Wolkerstorfer, Terry 89–92, **90**
women as journalists 31–34, 36–39, 41–43, 44–45
    battling inequality 34, 37, 41–42
    discrimination against 11, 33, 37, 40, 41, 48, 98
    marriage and motherhood 31–32, 38–39, 58
    in journalism schools 186
    successes 43–44, 55, 58, 59
Women, news coverage of 34–36, 39–41, 43–44
    decline in readership 49
    Equal Rights Amendment 144–145
    renaming Women's sections 35–36
    sexual harassment 39, 71, 147
    targeting women readers 43–44, 52, 147
    Women's Liberation 32
Wood, Tracy 37

Woodward, Bob 6, 69
Woodworth, Jim 142–143
Working Woman 133, 136
Wozniak, Steve 132
WPLG television 24
WSB-TV 24–26
WTOP-TV 23
WLAC-TV 25

Y

yellow journalism 6, 96
Young, Andrew 49
Yu, Frederick 175

Z

Zirinsky, Susan 59